CHASING AFTER DANGER

Terence O'Brien was born in Maitland, Australia and was working on a Solomon Islands plantation when war broke out. He paid his own passage to the UK to join the RAF, and completed two tours of operations before Japan entered the war. After leading a bomber flight to Singapore, he escaped finally to India where he later joined the Wingate Force. After the war, he worked as a freelance journalist, built a small hotel in the Canaries, qualified as a school teacher in England at the age of fifty-three, and then became a director of a tile-importing company. He is married with two sons and lives in Sussex.

His two previous volumes of autobiography, *Out of the Blue: a Pilot with the Chindits* and *The Moonlight War*, a first-hand account of clandestine operations in South-East Asia in 1944-5, are also available in Arrow.

G000229568

CHASING AFTER DANGER

A Combat Pilot's War Over
Europe and the Far East,
1939-42

Terence O'Brien

ARROW BOOKS

Arrow Books Limited
20 Vauxhall Bridge Road, London SW1V 2SA

An imprint of the Random Century Group

London Melbourne Sydney Auckland Johannesburg
and agencies throughout the world

First published by William Collins Sons & Co. Ltd
Arrow edition 1991

'High Flight', which appears on page 6, is reprinted by
permission of the Rev. J.G. Magee, and the editor of
the RAF *Journal*

The right of Terence O'Brien to be identified as the
author of this work has been asserted by him in
accordance with the Copyright, Designs and Patents Act,
1988

Printed and bound in Great Britain by
Cox & Wyman Ltd, Reading

ISBN 0 09 987410 5

For Timmie
and Nico and Landy

We enjoy watching the kite hawk's marvellous flying skills, and the sunsets behind the palms at Juhu beach, and our time with the girls on the lake at Kashmir, so why do we keep on chasing after danger? Isn't it time we grew up and began to think about a future?

> Letter from S. D. Mayhew to the author posted four days before his death in 1944 in an attack on an enemy airfield in Indo-China.

Oh! I have slipped the surly bonds of earth
And danced the skies on laughter-silvered wings;
Sunward I've climbed, and joined the tumbling mirth
Of sun-split clouds – and done a hundred things
You have not dreamed of – wheeled and soared and swung
High in the sunlit silence. Hov'ring there
I've chased the shouting wind along, and flung
My eager craft thro' footless halls of air.
Up, up the long, delirious, burning blue
I've topped the wind-swept heights with easy grace
Where never lark, nor even eagle flew –
And while the silent, lifting mind I've trod
The high, untrespassed sanctity of space,
Put out my hand and touched the face of God.

> John Gillespie Magee, born 1922,
> killed in air combat 1941.

PREFACE

I started making my wartime notes in December 1939, encouraged by the 'Diary of Flight' which Imperial Airways issued to its passengers on the flying boat service from Australia to England. Subsequently, until just beyond the end of the war, I went on to fill a series of notebooks which were written up, not in diary discipline but from time to time when the urge became compelling. These were private records of scenes and events and feelings never intended for publication, just for imprint on memory and occasional nostalgic review. At the end of the war I combined what was written in the notebooks and what I remembered into a single story of those wartime years, and then the pencilled sheets of foolscap were put away – unread for nearly forty years until discovered by my son, who persuaded me to edit the account for publication.

The original manuscript completed in 1946 has not been edited for publication in chronological order, because it was so temptingly easy to take first the distinctive period spent behind the enemy lines with the Wingate force which was recounted in *Out of the Blue*. That book when published in 1984 led to a revival of contact with many wartime friends who had operated behind the enemy lines in the various clandestine forces, so it became convenient to follow it in 1987 with *The Moonlight War* which covers that subsequent period when I commanded a Special Duty flight working with those secret and secretive organizations. This book, therefore, although the final work in the trilogy, is historically the first volume of memoirs.

It needs to be stressed yet again that the scenes and incidents recorded here are simply those which I happened to note down at the time; many are mere observations of the natural background, many are not provided with their context within the war and many important contemporary events have not even been noticed. I make no apology for these diversions and omissions. This is a personal memoir, not an historical study. It simply recounts what I as a young man saw, and did, and knew, and felt – and happened to record – during those wartime years.

Chapter 1

—•○•—

The news came to us on Guadalcanal three days late, on 6 September 1939. I was walking back towards the bungalow, and the trade wind was making such a swishing and creaking of palm fronds that I never heard the schooner approach. Then as I passed the copra drier there was a lull, and within it there came suddenly clear the sound of chain clattering through hawse-pipe; looking towards the beach I saw a Chinese trader dropping anchor in the shrill green water inshore of the reef, and within seconds I was down on the black sand shouting for news of the war.

'Him he come now,' Ah Kong called back.

For months I had been dreaming of reaction to the event. There would be an urgent call for volunteer pilots, and, just as happened twenty years earlier, we would be rushed through a few weeks' flying training somewhere near Sydney and then off in a troopship to death or glory over the trenches in France. Leaving the Solomon Islands was no heartache; at twenty-one you know there are far more exciting activities in life than work as a plantation assistant – duel to the death in flashing aerial combat, for fantastic example.

There was a practical difficulty about realizing this Walter Mitty scenario, however, for the steamer called only once every six weeks, so it was mid-October before I managed to reach Australia. I went straight from the wharf in Sydney to the recruiting office, but there to my astonished dismay discovered the Royal Australian Air Force was merely taking the names of volunteer pilots, 'to be contacted in due course'. I actually had my luggage waiting outside in the taxi, confident they would be inducting me into the RAAF that very day.

Weeks of frustration followed as I tried to prise entry into the service, even taking civilian flying lessons then claiming I was a qualified pilot, but all to no avail, until in December I could bear the delay no longer and decided to make my own way to England. I tried to get an advance against future dividends from our family company and my uncle, a solicitor, was called in to lecture me about squandering the security provided by our father – 'rushing off into the blue for no reason at all'; but I insisted and in the end, still refused an advance, I signed away my shares in return for a deferred payment and five hundred pounds cash, which was more than enough to get me to England by flying boat – by then it had to be on the flying boat, for that took only twelve days as against another interminable six weeks by steamer.

The air service between England and Australia had been started more than a year earlier. It was running twice a week, with a total of thirty-nine stops on the lakes and rivers and harbours where the flying boat refuelled during each day's run and halted for night; since the outbreak of war the route was being altered frequently, and in the following year civilian passengers were excluded altogether. The subsidized mail was always given precedence over passengers, seventeen being the maximum that could be carried in the three cabins. There were seven seats available on our trip, as I discovered that morning in early December when we met at the Rose Bay jetty in Sydney, handed in our income tax clearances, filled up the next-of-kin forms, were put on the scales with our luggage, and given the booklet that contained maps of the various stages with a blank inviting page opposite each of them headed 'Diary of Flight'.

It was just after nine when we taxied away from the anchorage at Rose Bay, zigzagging so that the wing-tip floats thumped down alternately into the flat blue surface and roughened it up for take-off. When the captain opened the throttles of the four engines at the starting buoy the thrust set the hull down into the surface, the bow wave climbed to cover the windows in lively green water and for a few seconds we roared through a tumult of foaming brine; then he rocked the hull up on to the step and we were heaved forward in our seats, the water went streaming away from the wing floats, and seconds later the hull lifted clear and we were soaring up into the bright Pacific morning.

The blue water of the great rambling harbour was flecked with dozens of ferries and launches trailing their stubby hamster-tails of wake, and the great dark arch of the bridge was blurred from sight through the whirring propellers. We circled for height, banking over the golf course with its curving fairways and circular emerald greens, over a park where fallen petals gave blue shadow to a huge jacaranda, then across the white-rimmed rocks of Sydney Heads and northwards over golden beaches with their scallops of foam spreading out to the vast cobalt expanse of the Pacific. The moment I finally turned away from the window the steward, in white jacket with black bow tie and peaked cap, was beside me asking if I wanted coffee in my seat or on the promenade deck.

He and the ship secretary were our cabin attendants, and both were cooks – as I discovered when stopping by the galley later. The steward was cutting bread and tomatoes for our morning tea while the secretary was squeezing orange juice for the captain, dropping the peel through a chute into the sea. I learned that we usually landed for lunch but on two days they would be cooking and serving the three-course meal on board. They kept using nautical phraseology – 'amidships . . . the bilge pump . . . our moorings . . . the boat hook' – as they described the journey ahead of us. This was scheduled for twelve days, but with all those refuelling stops, no back-up aircraft anywhere en route, and the wartime disturbances, delays were inevitable, and we were to have our share of them.

The steward, who was in his forties, had been a fitter in the Royal Flying Corps and he talked lovingly of the men and machines he had known those days in France. He impressed on me how lucky I was to have the chance of partaking in the excitement and camaraderie of wartime flying, and told of his own longing to get back on to a fighting squadron again. Enthralled by his stories I became his surrogate volunteer and we spent much time together during that first week when I would help him every morning after breakfast with the washing-up.

On the third day we had a brief, and disturbing, experience of night flying on the take-off from Darwin; this was the longest stage of the whole journey, with two refuelling halts, so take-off had to be exceptionally early to ensure we reached the Java night stop before it grew dark. A launch was dropping off a line of kerosene-lamp buoys as we drew up alongside the hull, and, after the secretary had hauled in the nose mooring, you could see the orange glow of the exhausts as the pilot revved up the outer engines and went zigzagging along the lighted flare path to ripple the calm surface. At the end he turned back into the buoy-lit line, opened the throttles fully for take-off, and we surged forward with the quivering hull thudding into the wavelets.

This time however I was concerned to see through the spray a great sheet of flame flaring out from below the port inner engine just by my window, and it was a relief when I looked across to see the other window was also fitfully aglow; as it seemed unlikely two of our engines had caught fire, and the steward just grinned at me from his seat by the galley, I began to relax, but the little fat man in the seat on the opposite side kept looking anxiously from his fiery glow towards the unsighted steward in obvious alarm. Then the hull tilted up on to the step, the spray cleared from the windows, and the inner engines were suddenly visible in alarming clarity. Great goblets of flame were bursting out from under the trailing edge of the wing as we went skimming across the dark water, and the little fat man toppled into panic.

'Fire in the engine!' he screamed. 'Look! Fire! Fire!'

It was all I could do to stop joining in his panic. The steward saved me, however. He was beside the man in an instant, calling out that it was just the normal exhaust, and making him look out my side to see the other inner engine also shooting out such alarming flame.

We lifted clear of the water during his attentions, sheering up through the low mist into clean dawn sky, banking towards a rose-pink eastern horizon, and in the improved light the flames were suddenly less fearfully lurid. The little man, a shirt manufacturer from South Africa, spent the rest of that day complaining to me that we should have been warned about the frightening sight of the exhaust at night, there was nothing about it in our flight diaries. The steward did apologize to him, and told me later he had been remiss in not mentioning it to all of us, for it was actually part of his drill; night flying was so unusual that very few civilians had ever experienced it.

For day after day we flew at our steady 140 m.p.h. cruising speed through the equatorial lands of the East, low enough at times to see the silvery flying fish skittering across the water, and diverting from track here and there to inspect a ruin or view an active volcano. In the late afternoons we would come dipping over a palm-lined shore towards the setting sun, touch down on the pre-ruffled water and skim on smoothly for a few moments, then the hull would settle down off the step making a great whoosh of a wave that rocked you in your seat and brought the flying boat to a heaving halt. A launch would come streaming out to bob about by the doorway, and you would be borne away to one of the great hotels of the East – the Oranje in Surabaya, Raffles in Singapore, the Eastern and Oriental in Penang. Then in the mornings you would go roaring down the frittered seaway again to climb just a thousand feet or so above the bright blue sea, and presently from the galley would come the smell of fresh coffee, a tinkle of cutlery and crockery, then the steward would bring your breakfast of freshly squeezed juice, pawpaw with a lime, cereal, boiled eggs, toast and marmalade.

We spent an extra day in Batavia when the hatch cover had to be replaced, another in Bangkok when the port wing float was damaged by a teak log – after we had been given a low circling view of the glittering spire of the Temple of Dawn studded with fragments of pottery that flashed like precious stones in the setting sun. At Rangoon we circled the golden pinnacle of the Shwe Dagon twice before landing and at Benares had a low-level aerial inspection of dhoti-clad pilgrims massed writhing on the banks of the Ganges. We made a special detour to see the Taj Mahal resting on the opalescent morning mist like a palace in the clouds, at Udaipur were taken to see the carvings of flute players and willowy dancing girls, and at Gwalior stayed the night in a maharajah's gull-white fairy palace on an island in the lake. Then, eight days after Sydney take-off, I had to leave the flying boat at Karachi.

The problem was a visa. With night stops in so many different countries you needed nine visas, and I had been unable to get the Iraqi one in time. Imperial Airways assumed responsibility for this, installed me in the pukka Killarney Hotel and posted the passport off to Delhi. It came back just the day after a flying boat had left, and that meant waiting a week for the next one; however, Imperial Airways had a landplane Middle East service, its aircraft was due off two days later, so I seized what I thought would be the quicker alternative.

Again it was an early morning take-off. The compacted sand airfield at Karachi was marked from miles away by the tallest building in India, the huge beet-red hangar built for the R101 airship which never arrived, for it crashed with its 500 million cubic feet of hydrogen into flaming destruction at Beauvais on the maiden flight. It was literally in the shadow of the massive building that our Hannibal aircraft was waiting that morning.

There was a picture of this huge contraption in our flight diaries but a Hannibal in reality was still an astonishing sight. It was one of the greatest biplanes ever built and gave the impression of a structure abandoned incomplete, a Gaudi cathedral of the air, deserted by workmen with just the scaffolding holding up the two floors. There was a huge wide upper wing, below which was a maze of girders and struts and wires connecting it to the shorter bottom wing; scattered about between all this scaffolding were four engines, two on the top wing so close their propellers almost touched, and two on the lower wing much wider apart. At the rear of the long fuselage, which was made of corrugated metal like ordinary roofing iron but with narrower ribs, was a large box-like assembly of rudders and elevator. The Hannibal could carry a total of eighteen passengers at a speed of 95 m.p.h. – when in perfect condition and without a breath of contrary wind.

This was the version Imperial Airways used on flights between India and Egypt. Among the five crew on our trip was a fitter who carried out minor engine repairs during our stops, and on learning this I asked the pilot, a gloomy Canadian, how long it would take us to Cairo. He said the schedule was four days but as they stayed on the ground when the wind speed exceeded 30 m.p.h. I should go by boat if I wanted to be sure of my times.

Happily the wind was forecast to be more or less favourable that first day and he grudgingly admitted we might reach the night stop within schedule. There were only six other passengers, all Indians; the two men joined me in the aft saloon and sent their women off to the forward cabin, which also had panelled wood walls, wisteria chiffon curtains, and navy chintz-upholstered cane chairs. The engines coughed and spluttered into life, we went bouncing across the bumpy earth surface to take off with surprisingly easy lift, banked into a ponderous turn around the great airship hangar, and went chugging off westwards over a glinting Arabian Sea towards the Persian Gulf.

Unfortunately the gusting tail wind was not our only contact with the atmosphere. It was a hot cloudless day and we were flying at only a few thousand feet above the crumpled coastline, so the diverse vertical currents from bare brown rocky cliffs, black shadowed valleys and shimmering sea surface were all causing further disturbance within our fluctuating tail wind. As a consequence the Hannibal was soon swaying and bouncing and swerving about in the air like a blowfly caught in a haze of insecticide.

Within ten minutes of take-off the two Indians were nosed into the sick bags; one however had waited too long, failed to open it properly in his frantic haste, and the navy carpet had received the lot. I moved further away to the front of the cabin, trying to avoid sight and sound and smell of their distress, but when the steward did finally arrive after a long delay with basin and mop I decided to move. As he squeezed aside to let me pass he gave a little negative shake of his head that mystified me until I reached the front cabin. Clearly he had ministered to the women first. Two of them were still suffering into bags with the same wretched sounds as the men, another had the top of her silver-edged sapphire sari pulled across her face as she rocked from side to side wailing in misery or terror, the fourth was shut away in one of the toilets and sounded equally distressed.

I stood in the midway passage for a time while the plane went on creaking and bucketing about the sky, with the wing tips flexing more than six feet at times. Then the steward returned and invited me into his pantry. It was true refuge there; you could open a window, gulp in the fresh air, and listen fascinated to his experiences in the three-engined Hercules which opened the Middle East service – they used to follow across the Arabian Desert a 470-mile furrow that the RAF had ploughed as a directional guide, and beside which fuel dumps had been established. Some of these were still in use.

At our refuelling stop that day the pilot had brought a ground engineer aboard, and he was evasive when I asked him about this after dinner that night at Sharjah where we were sheltered within a grey stone fort with armoured gun ports and a huge steel gate; the Hannibal close outside was protected from marauding tribesmen by a barbed-wire enclosure, with a manned cannon and pyramid of cannon balls above it on the parapet. The DC3 of KLM's East Indian service also stopped the night with its twelve passengers; the only scheduled flights to Australia were by the flying boat, but KLM did run a service from Holland to Java, their landplanes taking a day less on that part of the journey.

The pilot's engine consultations were repeated next day when we stopped on the hard sand outside the capital of Bahrein, a town of mud huts surrounded by a wall with strings of camels halted in its shade. Afterwards we continued on to the head of the Gulf, the water so clear that when we passed slowly over the arrowhead shape of a giant ray you could see its shadow on the sea floor. After another refuelling stop at Kuwait we followed the Euphrates westwards over clusters of grey mud houses set in glistening green palm groves along the river bank, and with vultures sliding past our quivering wing tips – I threw out a leg of cold chicken near one but he gave it only a brief contemptuous glance then sailed aloofly on his way.

We were delayed in Baghdad. When we arrived from the hotel for the morning take-off our fitter and another mechanic were clinging to the scaffolding of the Hannibal wing structure as they prodded at the lower port engine, and we had a wait of about two hours while they started and stopped the engine, took the cowlings off and put them on again. There were only four of us in the aircraft when we did finally take off, myself and three Egyptians who happily had stronger stomachs than the Indians. The wind was now blowing directly against us, only a gentle breeze at first but after a fluttery landing and take-off at our first refuelling stop I began to take an interest in our progress and could see the wind had strengthened considerably.

The evidence was below us. We were flying over flat reddish desert, with our shadow flittering continually about an oil pipeline which the occasional vehicle down below seemed also to be following, for there was no delineated road but just straggly track marks at varying sides of the straight black pipeline. An empty utility truck kept in sight for a minute or more, and then, as I pressed against the window looking ahead to see if we were catching up any other vehicle, a plum-coloured sedan car suddenly came forward into view from *behind* us. For a moment I wondered if the pilot had changed course and so brought it into sight, but then it caught up with the Lorraine cross of our shadow on the ground and the truth was manifest. It passed our shadow in only a second or two then continued out of sight ahead; I reckoned, assuming it was doing about seventy, that our ground speed was less than fifty miles an hour.

I knew it was standard procedure for the Hannibal to put down in the desert by one of the prepared fuel dumps, or wait for a truck to come out with petrol, whenever they were caught short by headwinds, and wondered if that was now our prospect. Before I could check with the steward, however, there was a sudden spluttering from the lower port engine outside my window, the yellow wooden propeller faltered and in the resultant vibration the bottom wing particularly began to flutter with the pliancy of a hovering hawk, the mudguard over the wheel wobbled from side to side, and there was a clinking and clattering from the steward's pantry. He appeared a moment later and told me to fasten the seat belt – I was alone in the rear cabin – as we were going to land, and he gave a weary shrug that suggested he was tired of these endless mechanical problems.

The engine had stopped by then, the propeller just wind-wheeling, but although the aircraft was running happily enough on the other three the pilot went ahead with the landing; down below the desert showed faint swirly markings like watered silk, made by camel thorn bushes along the wadis, otherwise the surface was clear. The plane wheeled over the pipeline in a full circuit and alighted gently as a tern among the tyre marks on the gravelly surface, raising a flurry of reddish-brown dust. The steward opened the door and put down the steps, the fitter came hurrying back and went outside, and we waited. Hot dry desert air came gusting into the cabin. No one seemed particularly disturbed, the steward told me it had happened to him dozens of times.

I assumed this an exaggeration but began to wonder presently when a yellow Shell van drove past with the driver merely slowing down in passage, then continuing on his way after a wave from the fitter. It emerged that an oil-feed pipe had ruptured and the pilot had deliberately shut down the engine. The fitter re-entered after about half an hour, having effected some temporary repair, and the pilot started the engine and revved it up to full power for a minute or so, with the aircraft trembling and red dust billowing through the open doorway. Then the steward shut the door, we took off to bank around in a half circuit, and with the wind now in our favour went scooting over our refuelling stop and back all the way to Baghdad at well over a hundred miles an hour, with never a vehicle able to keep pace.

Next morning just three of us arrived for take-off – the other passenger was in a hurry to get to Amman, our next night stop, so had taken a car instead. The pilot met us in the cold black-marbled hall and explained his engine problem. I cannot remember the details but he assured us there had been a thorough overhaul of the engine during the night and that we should have no more trouble with it.

Nor did we – with the engines. We went out down the steps and across the gravelled surface to the Hannibal, the door clanged shut, we strapped ourselves in, and then waited for the engines to start. And waited . . . but there was no whine of starter motor, no whirl of propellers, just a series of heavy thuds from the cockpit. Then silence. The steward, raising his eyes to the heavens as he passed me, opened the door. An engineer entered . . . went forward . . . more heavy thuds from the cockpit . . . then he returned shaking his head and went outside. I followed the steward to the doorway. The engineer disappeared towards the tail, and both of us went after him down the steps to see what was happening.

He had gone back to the tail assembly. This was a complicated structure, rather like a huge three-tiered bookshelf placed across the end of the fuselage, and he was making quite a business of taking a firm grip on one of the three rudder fins. Once in position he bellowed to the pilot, who was leaning out of the cockpit window some thirty yards away and looking back at him, 'Feet off!'

With that the engineer swung himself violently from side to side and, after a barely perceptible pause of resistance, the three fins suddenly began to move under his efforts. The pilot put his head out of the window and shouted for him to stand clear, then as the rudders began to fan from side to side we could hear the clattering of cables along the fuselage and clumping sounds from the pilot on the pedals in the cockpit. The engineer came back past us to the steps, gave a cheerful thumbs-up sign, and we followed inside to discover him and the pilot having a hissing disagreement outside the pantry. It ended abruptly when the pilot turned his back and strode forward to the cockpit. The engineer came back scowling, and disappeared down the steps.

We were told to disembark and on the way across to the terminal the steward told me what had happened. Before starting the engines the pilot had tested the controls as usual, pumping and rotating the truck-sized wheel for ailerons and elevator, then trying to work the huge pedals to get the rudder moving. But somewhere along the ninety feet of rudder cable, with all its pulleys and chains and couplings, something had jammed and, despite the heavy kicks we had heard, neither the pilot nor engineer could move the big pedals. Then, inexplicably, they had unjammed when the engineer went out and swung the big fins by hand. He thought that ended the difficulty. The pilot, however, insisted that the cause for the temporary jamming had to be manifest to him before he would take the aircraft off the ground. Happily he had the final word.

I have no idea what happened to our Hannibal, for Imperial Airways removed us from sight of it. A flying boat was due to land the following day at Lake Habbaniyah, some fifty miles away, so when the car collected us next morning we drove past the airfield and on to the sudden end of the tarred road. The driver just continued on steadily at fifty miles an hour over the vast expanse of rust-brown desert, glancing from time to time at the compass above the dashboard, and after about an hour another tarred road started up almost directly ahead. He swung over to join it and a few moments later we cleared a rise and saw the vast turquoise expanse of Lake Habbaniyah ahead of us. The flying boat had been kept waiting, it took off as soon as we were aboard, we landed on the Sea of Galilee to refuel, then continued on to Alexandria. There I was switched to a Flamingo landplane for the last two days of the journey.

We reached England in the last week of December 1939, flying over a gloomy alien countryside – ashen snow, leafless trees, black hedgerows – and already dark although it was only mid-afternoon. I kept thinking the louring sky would clear presently and the sun come out again but there were no thunder clouds to clear, and the sun was not still high above the horizon. Far beyond the latitudes of my experience I had yet to appreciate that sunrise and sunset are not immutably fixed in time, that it was not always light when you rose in the morning, nor always dark when you went to bed at night.

A passenger on that final stage had recommended the Langham Hotel at the top of Regent Street, and a taxi with tiny slits of lights took me there through the dank blackout that first evening. I was grateful to escape from the chilling blackness into the glowing luxury of the Langham. It was a Victorian hotel – wine-red carpets, gilded mirrors and tinkling chandeliers, centrally heated warmth, muted voices of elderly clientele, uniformed porters and aproned maids, service that bordered on the obsequious. I thought it an appropriate final halt that evening as I strolled about on the thick pile carpet, glanced through *The Times* in the empty writing room, and padded across the foyer to the dining room where evening dress predominated, and where I chose from a massive menu a Lobster Hamburg that was delicious. And that night, after handing over my trousers to be pressed and leaving shoes outside the door to be cleaned, I slept in a bedroom where the crinkling of linen sheets was the loudest noise to be heard.

Two days later I was in coarse serge dungarees, washing dishes in cold greasy water, at the Royal Air Force depot in Uxbridge.

Chapter 2

———◦———

It was the worst winter in living memory. Telephone wires snapped under the weight of ice, diesel oil solidified, birds froze to their perches on the trees – and one of our sentries at the Uxbridge RAF depot lost toes from both feet through frostbite. He was on duty at the radio hut, and the sentry post there remained exposed afterwards until I had a brush with the corporal about it.

When I came off duty from the radio hut one dawn, cheekbones hard and ears burning in frozen pain, I argued with the corporal that we should be allowed shelter from the icy wind inside the sentry box instead of standing outside. He scoffed at such weakness. Demonstrating how to counter the cold he opened out his forage cap to cover his ears, turned up the greatcoat collar to button across his face, then strode out across the snow and back again. But he was wearing glasses; the instant he came through the blackout curtain into the muggy guardroom they frosted over, and he blundered into the fire bell with a thudding clang that broke not only his glasses but also a front tooth. We were allowed to stand guard inside the sentry box after that.

Not a word about the dreadful cold appeared in the newspapers and this made it all the more depressing for those of us who had come from far-off sunny lands, for such lack of notice implied these were normal conditions that could persist forever. Perhaps even worse than the cold was the loss of sunlight. Possibly never before in my life had I passed two days without being touched by the sun, being aware of the chiaroscuro of light and shadow; a sky hidden by storm clouds or mist was only a fleeting diversion from normality. Not so in that first cold dark winter of the war. There was one period of nine full days in January 1940 when the sun was never for an instant visible at Uxbridge.

On the tenth day there was an event. I was washing saucepans behind the airmen's mess, in a partly covered courtyard where black-crusted wedges of snow filled the corners, and the icy water in the galvanized tub was prevented from freezing only by a thick layer of grease. There were thunderous sounds from inside the mess where another of our group, an American we called Tex, was pushing benches and tables about the concrete floor as he swept up after lunch. Suddenly he came bursting out into the courtyard.

'You gotta see this, Pat,' he cried, tugging at my arm.

I followed him inside to look through the blast-strips of the south-facing window. It was, to us, a weird and wondrous sight. A huge orange circle was visible in the murk above the parade ground, a stricken sun you could look at directly without even a blink. It was the sort of sun we tropical aliens associated with some natural disaster, a sun seen through the haze of an approaching hurricane or through smoke from a catastrophic bush fire. The corporal cook, a Manchester native, discovering that our chatter of excitement was all about a common wintry sun, ridiculed our colonial naiveté and ordered us to return to work. I realized that day that in the Turner picture of the *Téméraire* bound for the scrapyard it was not a symbolical dying sun he painted in that misty scene but one of pure photographic realism.

There was such a shortage of training facilities that new English volunteers were being sent home to await call-up; we who came from overseas, however, had somehow to be absorbed at once, so we were enlisted in the lowest rank of AC2 (second class aircrafthand) and utilized for any menial tasks requiring simple manpower – they added 'u't (under-training) pilot' to our classification, but that had no significance until training actually began. Meanwhile the trickle of volunteers from America, Canada, Australia and the colonial enclaves continued and the Uxbridge depot became clogged, so we early arrivals who had passed the pilot's medical and selection tests had to make way for newcomers.

I was posted with five others to a balloon station near Newcastle. It was a bleak snow-covered site ten miles out of town where within an hour of arrival we were given shovels and told to start clearing snow. This was a Sisyphean task, fresh snow kept falling as fast as we cleared, but the work was less depressing than at Uxbridge because at least we were now in contact with the war. Although the Luftwaffe did not begin land attacks until that summer, they were at this time bombing ships and laying mines off the east coast, activities that did occasionally bring them over land in the area, so our balloon barrage was part of the fighting war. The work was not only purposeful but for those who actually handled the balloons highly dangerous, dealing as they were with a potential inferno of twenty thousand cubic feet of hydrogen.

The balloon, made of silver rubberized fabric, was about tennis-court length and much the same width when inflated. It had three tail fins, one a vertical rudder that kept it into wind, and two horizontals that prevented it rocking and so overstraining the cable; these two stayed only partially inflated, always drooling down like the dewlaps of a royal gormandizer in a Gillray cartoon. Spread out at nine to a square mile in planned barrage, the balloons had a one in ten chance of stopping an intruding aircraft – not the balloon itself, that was merely a support for the real killer, the specialized cable.

It had been found in pre-war tests that a tethered cable could not stop modern bombers, they cut through it without any serious damage, so links had been fitted to allow the cable to break away from both balloon and winch when hit. At the same time two small parachutes opened at the severed ends so that the aircraft suddenly had draped over its wing a 5000-foot cable, with each end being restrained by a parachute. Resistance was such that aircraft were stopped almost dead in their tracks – the hull of a Wellington bomber was torn apart in one test. It was a lethal weapon that certainly discouraged low-level attacks, and made the balloons themselves reasonable, if easy, targets for enemy fighters.

Two weather factors put the balloons at risk, lightning being the most dangerous, turning the balloon into a fury of incandescent gas. It took eleven minutes to get a balloon down to insulated anchorage and this was frequently not time enough; lightning conditions could build up undiscerned in cloud, only to be discovered when the balloon was struck, then others in the area would suffer the same fate before they could be brought down to grounded safety. An electrical storm in London that winter destroyed seventy-eight one afternoon, and more than thirty people died in the resultant fires.

'They were coming down like bloody great meteors,' a sergeant told me.

The other hazard was the wind, and this was far more costly in losses. The balloons were designed to operate at winds up to 60 m.p.h., but this was in a steady wind-tunnel test. At operational height in the outside world the wind was rarely steady in speed or direction; you could be standing in calm conditions on the ground but have the balloon yawing and straining so much the cable would be grating in the winch, and the truck heaving about on its springs like a freighter in a heavy sea. To prevent the truck being dragged about, the cable was designed to break away before such a strain was reached.

The penalty for this safeguard was that balloons were constantly being borne away on the wind – coming down to wreak havoc among the stalls of a market day, covering a hearse waiting outside a church, wedging between two gasometers, and finishing in a semi-deflated state draped over a railway viaduct. My favourite escapees were the two that were seven miles apart when they broke away in a high wind one night but were found together half-gassed next morning, nuzzling one another in a remote glade on the Yorkshire moors.

I went one morning with a crew to a terraced house in Wallsend to bring back a stray. As usual most of the gas had escaped by the time we arrived and we found in the back garden something like a huge silver jelly wobbling about on top of the maculated snow. Six of us, including the sergeant, ranged into line at the far end of the garden, and then, in a sideways crab-like movement, advanced across the fabric crackling ice underfoot as we drove the remnants of gas to the vent in the tail. We repeated this carefully choreographed exercise several times until the carcase was evacuated sufficiently for our next move.

This was to get the deflated body to our truck outside the front door. Here again there was an established drill for moving balloons through houses. The flattened carcase was transformed into three dimensions by rolling it up so that we finished with something like a monstrous sausage, some seventy feet long. We spaced ourselves out along its length, then carried it sinuously through the kitchen, up a staircase to the dining room, along the hall, and finally out of the front door. It was like one of those colourful dragons the Chinese set weaving about the streets in holiday processions; when I was moving towards the hall, second in line behind the sergeant, I could see through the window the back end of our silver dragon just leaving the frozen garden, see its middle weaving up the staircase into the dining room, and see its head going out of the front door. Two days later it was back on duty over the slipways on the Tyne.

Balloon Command was organized just like an ordinary aircraft command, with Groups controlling Stations on which were Squadrons divided into Flights. We had two large maintenance hangars, a staff of engineers and mechanics to service the trucks and winches, seamsters and seamstresses to deal with fabric repairs, and gas technicians to handle the dangerous hydrogen. Two balloon squadrons were based on the station, each with twenty balloon-flying crews; they would drive the winch truck and the one with gas cylinders out to their designated site, there fill the bag with hydrogen, then winch it up and down according to telephone instructions from squadron headquarters.

We cadet pilots had no part in these interesting activities, we shovelled snow, pick-axed icy roads, washed dishes and mopped floors. Presently, wondering how to break this dreary round, I decided to write to Marshal of the Royal Air Force Lord Trenchard, the man regarded as founder of the RAF. We were not acquainted, of course, but there was a filigree of connection in that he was a director of the Unilever empire; I had worked with Levers Pacific Plantations, so that was the thread I utilized. I wrote to him saying I had come all this expensive way with the blessing of their Solomons manager – a lie, the manager had become rabid when I gave in my resignation – and now the RAF would not start my flying training. Would he please help? I never received a reply but then relief did come, fortuitously, just a few days later.

I was polishing a brass tea urn in the kitchen that morning when the outer door burst inwards with a flurry of snow through which emerged the duty officer, ushering a wing commander from group headquarters. All the staff officers were veterans of the First World War, this one was wearing wings and two rows of ribbons among which the Distinguished Flying Cross commanded my respect. He looked friendly, so when he gave me perfunctory notice with a comment about the cold I got back at once, saying that as I was deprived of flying anyway the bad weather made no difference. It worked. He was interested. Flying? What did u't pilot mean? Where had I come from? The outcome was that I was posted that same afternoon to the group headquarters in Newcastle.

This was located in a Victorian gothic building, massive, pillared windows with heavy pediments, grimy stone balustrades. It had a long garden to the rear, featureless under dirty snow most of the time we were there except for a wide greenhouse against the far end wall. Through its misted glass you could from the main building see faint separate blurs of crimson and orange and yellow, tantalizing suggestions of summer warmth and light and twittering birds and buzzing insects. The glass in the greenhouse was unprotected but all the windows in our building had been trellised with gummed brown strips against bomb blast, and the main entrance was protected by a sandbagged angle.

The group commander was Air Commodore Sydney Smith who, I knew, had commanded Cattewater RAF station when Lawrence of Arabia was posted there after enlisting under the pseudonym of Shaw, in the same basic AC2 rank as me. Despite their mountainous difference in rank, Shaw had been befriended by Smith and his wife, and I longed to hear him on Lawrence. However, this was not easy to arrange. Although Smith came frequently into the operations room, where my task was to transform the four-hourly reports from balloon stations to pin-readings on the table map, he was always on some specific operational quest. For my purpose we had to be alone, with him idling – so to speak.

The weeks passed without ever a chance of such contact, and then at last an opportunity arose when he came in late one evening to ask the duty officer for a file that necessitated him going downstairs to the registry. When he had gone Smith turned to study my pin-filled map for a moment and was about to return to his office when the lights went out. Smith sighed. From below someone shouted that the basement lights were still on, a fuse must have blown, he would check.

'Then let us both be patient,' Smith said.

He started by asking how long I had been in the service, was also surprised by the 'u't pilot' designation, and wondered what I was doing in his command. He was quick to identify my accent and that led on to a stream of questions about Australia, the Solomon Islands, and my journey to England. When we came to the detail of the arthritic old Hannibal with its locked joints I prised an opening, saying I understood it was there at RAF Habbaniyah that he and Lawrence had become friends. He corrected me at once, of course – to my simulated surprise.

'No, no. Cattewater seaplane base, that was.' He gave a sort of half-chuckle and added, 'I'll tell you one thing about him you won't find in any biography.'

I scarcely dared breathe. Secret Service shenanigans? Weird sexual practices? A brawl with G. B. Shaw?

'We were chatting on the veranda this day. A fly buzzing between us. Then his hand shot out. Quick as a gecko's tongue. Held his closed fist near my face and I could hear the thing buzzing. Couldn't squash it in his hand, of course. You know.' (Did I?) 'Took it over to the corner of the veranda and threw his fist open. Let it go like that.'

There was noise down below, and I heard a shouted response from the duty officer. Anxious to keep him going – that he was good at catching flies was not much to add to the Lawrence legend – I gave a prompt. Keen entomologist?

'No, no. The fly is not the point. When . . .'

At that instant two things happened. The phone rang, and the lights came on. I answered the caller from Porlock, mundane business about repositioning a balloon on the estuary, and whilst I was dealing with this the duty officer came hurrying back with Smith's file. By the time I had finished taking down the particulars about the balloon's new position Smith had retired to his office with the file. He emerged ten minutes later in greatcoat and gilded cap, exchanged goodnights with us both and went on his way. Those were the last words I ever heard from him.

The following morning I was posted to Dishforth in Yorkshire. The sergeant said it was an operational bomber station, and when I set off next day with rail warrant and 'unexpired portion of the day's rations' (two bacon sandwiches and an apple) I had managed to believe flying training could now at last be about to start. And Dishforth airfield, at first sight on a bright cold morning in early March, was not unattractive. The jigsaw camouflage curves of brown-green-black on the big hangar were bright in the country-clear sunlight, and the blinding white snow about the edge of the airfield had drifted into sharp ridged curves as clean as desert dunes. But at the orderly room the corporal clerk dulled the scene immediately with his opening words.

'You're on cookhouse duties,' he said.

I began to wonder if that letter to Lord Trenchard had finished up on the desk of some pompous staff officer who had deemed it such an outrageous impertinence as to call for salutary grinding down to proper AC2 base. There followed days of dreary drudgery in the airmen's mess. I was the only u't pilot on the base, billeted in a Nissen hut where the condensation streamed down inside the roof during the night and froze into icicles during the day, my only companions being four Glaswegians who talked with gurgling-sink sounds I could not interpret. What made resumed cookhouse duty particularly hard to bear was that I was now so tantalizingly close to the heroic scene visualized back in the Solomon Islands. Dishforth was an operational airfield, Whitley bombers of 10 Squadron were taking off most evenings for Germany, and though only carrying leaflets the aircrews were coming under fire, some aircraft returning damaged, a few never getting back at all.

One, returning over France, came down in extraordinary circumstances. In freezing cloud, the ice built up to such an extent the pilot finally could no longer move the controls. With the aircraft slanting inexorably towards the ground, he ordered the crew to jump. The tail gunner, however, had become disconnected on his intercom, heard nothing, and remained huddled in his rear turret when the others flung themselves out into the icy blackness.

He was alone in the aircraft – except perhaps for his fairy godmother in the cockpit, for the aircraft continued on its frozen decline for several minutes with him blissfully unaware of his appalling solitude. The ice-locked Whitley slanted down on a steady even keel towards a huge ploughed field devoid of trees and hollows where it belly-flopped with a heavy but not disastrous impact, and after a single stable bounce slithered through mud and ice to a standstill. The gunner, fearful of fire after the belly landing, swung his turret round at once and blundered over the icy ground to the front of the plane to help his friends get clear. And there he had his surprise.

It was a story that started me out of half-sleep in cold terror the night I first heard it; but when I asked him about it in the cheerless dimly-lit airmen's mess one dawn, just after he had returned from another sortie over Germany, he was stolidly matter-of-fact in his account.

'Frightened afterwards? No, I was down all right, you see.' And then he went up to the serving hatch for another sausage – they were allowed extras after an operational flight.

28

Then suddenly the leaflets were exchanged for bombs. Hitler launched his attack on Denmark and Norway, and on 11 April 1940 I first saw bomb trolleys being towed across the tarmac to a waiting aircraft. I can be precise about the date because a few weeks earlier I had bought in the NAAFI a little brown exercise book, the back of which was covered with tables of various weights and measures, including one for 'apothecaries'. Into this I had transcribed my Imperial Airways 'Diary of the Flight' from Australia, and written about subsequent events since arrival in England. It was filled up to date by then, and after the bomb trolley note is a single line in exultant capitals:

'11 APRIL. 4.30 P.M. SIGNAL SAYING POSTED TO ITW TODAY!'

The Initial Training Wing at Cambridge – which meant the start of flying training. 'To proceed without delay,' the signal said. I would have left within the hour had they let me.

Chapter 3

———◦———

It is difficult for anyone brought up in the warmer latitudes to understand all the fuss in English poetry about daffodils and cuckoos. In Australia when I was awakened on the veranda by the chuckling of kookaburras in the gum trees I never experienced any of that mystical exaltation English poets seemed to feel on hearing the hiccups of a cuckoo. To me it was just the normal mechanical laughter of kookaburras up among the leaves of the gum trees. The morning might be cold or hot, the sky clear or cloudy, the sun behind or just above the top of the pergola – the angle did seem to vary slightly between December and June – but none of these conditions made any difference to the light or the leaves or the kookaburra's laughter; they came and they went among the gum leaves, laughed or were silent, according to mood. Nothing to make a song about there, surely?

So coming down to Cambridge that April in 1940 was a revelation. Suddenly I was in harmony with the English poets, thrilled to hear birds bursting into song, to see on the trees the pale green translucent leaves just crinkly-fresh from opening, and to catch the flashes of golden daffodils in the gardens. What made it all so wonderful, of course, was that it marked the end of the cold dark winter. Browning was deceiving himself when he thought he could share the delight of being 'in England now that April's here'. Having spent his winter in Mediterranean sunlight surrounded by gaudy melon flowers he lacked the essential qualification; to those who have not endured an English winter the call of the cuckoo is merely the sound of a Swiss alarm clock.

Everything was perfect that spring. The sky was blue every day, I was sharing a room with three other cadet pilots in St John's College with its quadrangles and oriel windows and great screen wall giving on to a wide emerald lawn sloping down to the Cam, and the conditions under which we lived were civilized. We ate in the same panelled dining room as the distant dons and friendly undergraduates, walked the age-undulated flagstones across the Bridge of Sighs and through the medieval decorated gateway of the outer court to our lectures. It was a gracious milieu on any count, but to those like myself who had been in dreary servitude for many months it was paradise. We had clean uniforms and clean rooms in a beautiful old building and, this above all, were at last embarked on the adventure that had attracted us into the war.

It was not an easy passage. During that six weeks of ground instruction at Cambridge I worked far longer and harder hours than at any time in my limbo period. The syllabus included navigation, meteorology, signals, gunnery, Air Force law, and military history; we spent four hours a day on lectures, another four on drill and inspections, and at least another four preparing or practising for both. But it was all for a purpose, and that was the difference. I did earn a black mark on my record, however, caught out one night after having dodged back to bed when I should have been down in the dank cellars during an air raid.

We had little social contact with the members of the university. The undergraduates were mostly amiable, some would chat with us as we lined up together in the hall at lunchtime or sat out on the bank of the river afterwards, but the dons were distinctly aloof. There was never an offer to talk to us on any subject, to give us benefit of their knowledge or enthusiasm or expertise. We were intruders. The only words I ever heard any of them address to a cadet was at the gateway of St John's one afternoon when returning from a lecture on Air Force law; we were arguing whether civil law recognized some aspect or other, and an American cadet said we might be able to check it in the college library. A don who was talking to the porter at the gate turned – only briefly – to say, 'You people: are not allowed in the library.' The first two words, which he accentuated, and segregated slightly from the rest of the sentence, made plain his feeling about our intrusion into his academia.

We were inoculated the day after our final exams. All thirty of our group were lined up three abreast in the colonnaded walk that gives on to the riverside lawn, the leading trio some five paces back from the table where the doctor sat with his steely apparatus, so we all had a continuous view of his action as he grabbed the exposed upper arm of each cadet and stabbed in the needle. I was midway in the group, saw the first piercing thrust and shut my eyes, then opened them again when someone just in front of me thumped down on the flagstones. Three others fainted before our trio arrived at the table. It is the cold-bloodedness of the action that makes it so shocking. My first memory of a jab was with my young brother Frank and the family doctor; he told Frank to turn his back and then, with me watching in readiness for my turn, he pinched a chunk of flesh on Frank's back and deliberately plunged the long shining steel needle straight into his body. I was filled with horror. And when he then turned to me and said, 'Now your turn, Terry,' it was all I could do to stop myself running screaming from his surgery. Perhaps that hardening experience saved me from joining so many others on the stone floor at St John's that day.

Immediately before being posted to flying training we had a day pass, and a few of us hitch-hiked to London. I finished on my own, picked up in a two-seater Morris by a man and his wife going down to visit their daughter who was an air-raid warden in Kensington. The civilian scene had changed markedly since the German army moved into action, and though no bombs had yet fallen there was now everywhere in London evidence of a country at war. Auxiliary firemen with pumps and hoses were practising at one of the street water tanks, nearly every window in the shops and houses had blast-strips, there were sandbagged entrances to many of the buildings, and air-raid shelters were visible or indicated in almost every street. We must have passed a dozen mobile canteens run by coffee-uniformed WVS women, and in Hyde Park a line of camouflaged lorries was queuing to enter the sandbagged area around an anti-aircraft battery. It was such a clear morning I could see the actual cable slanting up to one of the silver barrage balloons scattered about the cloud-flecked sky.

The couple dropped me near St James's Park, where colourful carpets of daffodils, narcissi and red tulips were laid out on the green, and pretty girls in gay cotton frocks were hurrying past with their curled hair bouncing up and down, and pleated skirts excitingly aswirl. I walked up Piccadilly past the RAF Club, startling two junior officers with a splendid salute, then along past Fortnum and Mason where people were emerging with neatly wrapped packages – no sign of shortages there or in the other shop windows. There was an immense variety of colourful and exotic uniforms from the overrun countries of Europe. I almost bumped into a man wearing a uniform that seemed to have come from a musical comedy show: cerise cavalry-type trousers, lavender-blue jacket with black braid on the shoulders, and on his head a peaked cerise cap with long black tassel. He looked uncertainly at me, and I at him, and in the end we just grinned at one another and dispensed with the salute.

At Piccadilly Circus the statue of Eros was boarded over and bearing placards: a warning that careless talk cost lives, a call for everyone to buy War Loan, and an appeal for aluminium pots and pans. A few plump flower-girls, scarves on their heads, were selling bunches of daffodils and narcissi and violets. One incident stays clear in mind right down to this day. It happened when I turned to look back after leaving Piccadilly Circus, feeling so excited at the immediate prospect of flying again, so happy in the bright sun with everyone looking so cheerful, that I suddenly laughed aloud. A middle-aged couple just by me were starting to cross Regent Street and they stopped and looked at me. Then they both smiled also and the woman, who was wearing a flower-printed chiffon dress and a huge picture hat, said softly, 'Good luck, love!'

She kept looking back, smiling, as they crossed the street, then were lost in the crowd by Swan and Edgar's. To my mind her wish was granted just two days later when I had my first dual flight at Fair Oaks airfield.

It was a wonderful excitement to strap on a parachute and climb into the cockpit of a Tiger Moth again. No other aircraft has ever commanded such tender affection from its pilots. The little Moth biplanes had been playing a great part in aviation history during the previous fifteen years, many of the firsts to Australia and Africa having been made in them – first solo, and first woman, for example. They were rugged, responsive, forgiving, reliable, simple. Had flying developed a little earlier, the Tiger Moth, and not a motor car, would have been the subject of Toad's ecstatic tribute: 'Glorious, stirring sight! The poetry of motion! . . . Villages skipped, towns and cities jumped – always somebody else's horizon. O bliss! O poop-poop! O my! O my!'

Like all aerodromes in England, Fair Oaks was a grass field – before the war aircraft always landed on a natural surface such as

33

grass or gravel or water, whether in New York or London or Wagga Wagga. I landed on twenty-six grass fields during the first eighteen months of the war before first touching down on concrete. Fair Oaks was absurdly close to Brooklands, which was famous for its high-banked motor-racing track and of great interest to the enemy because of the huge aircraft factory there where the Wellington bombers were built. It had been a civilian flying club and on the outbreak of war the RAF took over the tiny field as a job lot. They made the instructors Pilot Officers, camouflage-painted the little hangar, erected six wooden huts for classes and accommodation, then provided a regular inflow of trainee pilots.

That the instructors were not regular RAF officers, had had no hardening into the exclusive hierarchy of service life, made it easy to establish friendly rapport with them. You could go out and drink at the pub with them on evenings off, go to their houses for dinner, and sit on the grassy slope at the top of the field and chat with them whilst waiting for an aircraft to return. When so idling one afternoon with my instructor, I asked if he ever felt like getting away from such a peaceful role in the war, to which he replied, 'I did, in November. I flew on operations in a Tiger.'

It was in protection of North Sea convoys; such was the shortage of aircraft at the time that after a series of submarine attacks Tiger Moths had been utilized. They were too small to carry a useful bomb and there was no suitable radio, so they went out in pairs, carrying in the back cockpit an extra petrol tank that gave them five hours' endurance. The plan was that on sighting a submarine one of the Moths would dash off at full 90 m.p.h. speed for base where a bombed-up Hudson was on stand-by; the Hudson crew would get rough course and distance from the breathless Moth pilot, then go off to find the other Moth pilot who would point down to the submarine which the Hudson would then bomb and sink. Not a single submarine was even sighted, let alone stayed waiting on the surface to be destroyed, during the month they ran the scheme.

To my surprise I was appointed Senior Pupil of the course. There were many others older than me but I had been longest in the service, so that may have been the reason. It was a worthwhile privilege. I had my own room partitioned off in the hut, took morning inspection so could not myself be faulted, ran the duty roster so could choose my own, and had plenty of excuses to call at headquarters where a pretty WAAF corporal, the desire of us all, was ever happy to stop typing and chat with any pupil who could reach her presence – in an act of strange disloyalty late that summer she married a naval petty officer.

It was glorious flying weather throughout that summer of 1940. We made the best of it, enjoying the crowded hours as we flew in our open cockpits above the green hills of Surrey, over flower-flagged parks and curving swathes of tree-lined fairways at Sunningdale with the little Moth shadow flitting over copses and hedgerows, and the aircraft itself springing lightly up and down in the varying currents as if suspended on elastic from the cloud-dabbed sky.

Before arriving at that carefree stage, however, there were lessons to be learned, skills to be mastered. Our ground training consisted not only of lectures but also practical work with engines and machine guns, and this was a problem for me; I am mechanically illiterate, and would stand by in uneasy silence when fellow students pointed to parts of our training engine as they mentioned gaskets or torque tappets or some such engineering term. And though the dual instruction back in Australia helped me get away first solo among the eighteen on our course, I had more navigation problems than the others. When the instructor in the front cockpit called through the speaking tube to fly to some place like Windsor or Aldershot, they could turn towards it at once, whereas I had first to discover on which fold of the fluttering map the unknown town was located – then identify it when it finally came into sight below.

Failure to identify Guildford led to a forced landing the very day after my first solo. I had been sent up to do half an hour of right-hand turns – all landing circuits are left-handed, so you rarely make steeply banked right-hand turns in normal flight. I flew a few miles west to carry out the practice over the colourful gardens in the Sunningdale golf-course area, worked at it for half an hour, then, belatedly, looked below to check my whereabouts. There was not a single golf course in sight. Even the balloons at Brooklands had disappeared from the horizon. There was, however, a distinctively shaped town which looked like the page from a newspaper: lines of terraced houses arranged in rough columns, sub-headings of larger buildings in spacious grounds, occasional gaps making paragraphs, and a few blocks of advertisements made by parks and large factories. Other pupils would have recognized it at once as Guildford, but I needed the map for this, so I reached into the pocket of the cockpit with my left hand and groped . . . and groped . . . then remembered the map was in the overalls I had left on the fence because it was such a warm day.

A rough square search, fifteen minutes on each of the cardinal compass points, proved unhelpful. I finished over a small church with the usual cluster of houses, thatched roofs golden in the afternoon sunlight, and beyond them a long straw-coloured field devoid of obstacles. I decided to land and make enquiries. Paying close attention to the wind as disclosed by blue smoke trailing from one of the houses, I came in with sweat-damp hands to put the Moth down in a solid three-point clump that stopped it in less than a hundred yards. I then taxied across the stubble to halt near a roadside gate and just as I cut the engine a red MG tourer pulled up and a naval lieutenant scrambled out. From him I learned I was just a few miles from Petworth.

The correct procedure now was to ring Fair Oaks, then wait for an instructor to fly down and make decisions; on no account were you to take off again after a forced landing. But this correct procedure would disclose my crime in taking off without a map, so instead I checked the naval officer's road map, asked him to swing the propeller, then took off without difficulty and followed the London road north until the Brooklands balloons came into sight and I was home. There I apologized for the delayed return, saying my watch had stopped.

It would have served me better had I told the truth, but unfortunately I did not then know the staff were tolerant of such a common failing as getting lost, even with a map in hand. They were never tolerant, however, about any infringement of safety regulations, and you could be hauled up before the Chief Flying Instructor if you had not followed exactly the engine-starting drill, taxied across the landing line, or failed to look behind before making a turn.

The gravest offence, and also the most tempting, was low flying. All instructors were ruthless in reporting anyone found down below five hundred feet skittering over housetops or banking around isolated trees. You would be out with your instructor on some exercise, such as blind flying, when abruptly the stick would be wrenched from your control, the plane would bank steeply and roar down on full throttle towards another Tiger Moth below – far too far below.

In a moment, bouncing over the trees, you would be beside the culprit, he would glimpse you or your shadow, turn his head and you would see his eyes suddenly widen and his mouth open. Then, after a wave from the instructor, he would follow you up in a sedate climb to a thousand feet and you would start off in loose formation on the solemn return to the airfield. There was a real threat of being thrown off the course for this crime: one pupil on the previous course was so despatched after having had a warning, and even a single first-time offence meant a thunderous interview with the Commanding Officer and confinement to station for a fortnight on the dreariest duties his anger could conceive.

Apart from the lush green of the fields there was another difference between the Surrey countryside and the one seen from the Moth the previous year. In Australia there had been little evidence of boundary lines down below; either none existed or they were marked by grey ironbark fences that merged into the sunburnt landscape when seen from height. The English countryside, however, was a netting of hedgerow divisions, with the black-shadowed lines as sharply defined as the grid of a crossword puzzle, though not so precisely regular, of course.

Not all these hedgerows were genuine, for false ones had been created early in the war to camouflage airfields. An oil-tar mixture was used to spray dark lines across the field to abut neighbouring hedgerows, and wider lines to abut approach roads. Many times in those early days I missed seeing an aerodrome until sighting an aircraft taxiing straight through an apparent hedgerow. Then, when invasion threatened after Dunkirk, orders went out that all possible landing areas for gliders had to be similarly treated, and it was this that made the whole landscape in south-east England so heavily patterned, covered as it was by these deceitful tar-oil hedgerows and roads.

There were alternatives to this anti-invasion camouflage. Some farmers scattered carts, tractors, bailers and other agricultural machinery all about potentially risky fields; in the large parks about south-west London such as Richmond they dug wide trenches, on Sunningdale and other golf courses they created wartime bunkers or set out logs on the long fairways. One afternoon I flew down low for a closer look at a lovely eighteenth-century house with curved gables and small pediments, brick stuccoed a warm apricot colour, and there they had obstructed the great swathe of clear pasture fronting the house with a scattering of short lengths of huge concrete sewage pipes, the napkin rings of a giant. Along the roads from the coast at this time, white concrete pillboxes were sprouting up at many of the junctions, and stretching away from them into the nearby fields were concrete anti-tank bollards that looked like great white centipedes feeding on the tender green wheat.

Our airfield at Fair Oaks was protected by old cars. We had twenty-eight in all, a motley collection of tourers, sedans, two-seaters, and a lorry that had been a troop carrier in the First World War. Most were about fifteen years old, early 1920s models, some with trunks at the back, batteries under the running board, and, as in an early Bentley, handbrake outside the driver's door. There was a solid-wheeled Trojan with a high driving seat like a horse-drawn carriage, and a 1919 Overland on which some of the wooden wheel spokes had been repaired with iron splints. One or two had been luxury vehicles in their prime, a Hispano-Suiza tourer that had been so stripped we had to attach the tow to its dashboard, a Hotchkiss with only three wheels so that it had to be towed in a slow short straight line, and a 1920 Moon with a bonnet the exact copy of a Rolls-Royce. Only a few had any air left in their tyres, many were fitted with solid rubber, and all had been sloppily overpainted with the standard camouflage green through which the original colour was patchily visible. When lined along by the fence during the day they looked from the air like a hedgerow that had been damaged by careless weed-spraying.

Every afternoon when flying finished we pupils had to disperse the battered veterans about the field, like taking cattle out to pasture. You connected the tractor cable to a bumper, front axle, or anywhere else possible – the steering shaft on a Pierce-Arrow two-seater – then you sat on the seat if there was one, or steered from the running board, until you decided upon its strategic stop for the night. My favourite was a Buick tourer that was about fifteen years old, like one we had back home in the twenties. My older sisters, Jule and Mary, would sometimes drive me out in the evenings to Compton's ice-cream parlour, thereby legitimizing the sortie in the eyes of my father who never discovered that they left me with money to stuff myself with luscious sundaes like the Knickerbocker Surprise, while they sat around the corner in the Buick, the side curtains up, with their non-Catholic boy friends. In the Buick at Fair Oaks the top section of the split window was missing, and a spring was thrusting through the seat, but nostalgia rectified these faults whenever I sat in it that summer, stroking the wooden steering wheel and swivelling the spark retard in memory of those pleasant evenings at the ice-cream parlour back at Maitland.

The war came closer as summer advanced. One bright sunny afternoon in mid-July I was flying over St George's Hill on the far side of Brooklands; the attraction there was the colourful display of crimson and purple rhododendrons about the roads and golf course, and the many spacious private gardens flecked like a painter's palette with dabs of brilliant colour. I used to do a lot of my flying exercises over there, on the eastern side so as to keep well clear of Brooklands, and on this sunny afternoon I was doing slow rolls, making blue sky and green earth go whirling about me, when a columnar cloud suddenly started up beyond the hill. When I straightened out into a climb so as to check the source of the phenomenon two more grey clouds rose just as swiftly, then I realized Brooklands was being bombed. A moment later a German aircraft crossed directly ahead of me about half a mile away.

The recognition, and its identification as a Ju 88, came only from visual memory because the instant it came into sight I flung the Tiger Moth into a convulsive turn and went diving down into the cover of the green wooded slopes and valleys of purple rhododendron. I stayed low about the hills for ten minutes or so, making the most of this legitimate low-flying opportunity, then poked my nose up to check all was clear before flying back to Fair Oaks.

A few days after this first sighting I was marching the others off to lunch when a Heinkel 117 came low over the field with guns blazing. Fortunately he ignored us and concentrated fire on three unserviceable Moths on the far side of the field. The same afternoon a Ju 88 crossed the field at only a few hundred feet in slow level flight as if out on a leisurely sightseeing tour over England. We had a Bofors emplacement at the bottom of the field but the army must have been having tea because he passed directly over it without a shot being fired. A few minutes later, however, a short-nosed Blenheim came bustling on to the scene and circled around as if trying to pick up the scent, whereupon the Bofors fired a series of throbbing rounds, pom-pom-pom-pom. Whether the Blenheim was hit or not was a matter of argument between us, but what certainly did happen is that he shot off a red-green identification cartridge and banked steeply to disappear behind the trees in a dive towards Brooklands.

The anti-invasion measures made road travel a trial, for all the road signs were removed and even the milestones, some of which had been in place for centuries, were uprooted and taken into storage. At the same time the ringing of church bells was banned so that they could be reserved to warn of parachute landings. I discovered a further extension of these anti-invasion measures the day I made my cross-country flying test, when I had to make my first change of course at the village of Wylie on the edge of Salisbury Plain.

At ETA (Estimated Time of Arrival) I found myself midway between two Wylie-like villages, both on the river, both at a cross-roads, both with a railway station. So down I went to determine the genuine one. On the opposite side to the station platform was a field where the wind was stroking and ruffling the tender green corn, and I flew low across the lively field to look under the platform roof, only to discover that both the name boards and the brown seats against the wall had been over-painted – the stationmaster behind a line of milk churns waving at me (or shaking his fist?). Then as I pulled up to avoid some trees I saw a large notice on the roof of a tin shed across the road. It read: 'THE   TIMBER CO. LTD'. The blank area had been covered in red paint. It was a Wylie-like space, however, and my guess turned out to be correct.

We were due to finish the course on the last day of July, and to be posted on to FTS (Flying Training School) immediately afterwards. There was a basic alternative here: you either went to a single-engine FTS for fighter training, or to one of the twin-engine schools where pilots for Bomber, Coastal or Transport command were trained. All of us, as usual I was told, wanted to go on to fighters but our postings were determined externally by service requirements at the time, and internally by the instructors' opinion of personality and flying ability. Fifteen of our course were posted to fighter training, I was among only the three posted to twin-engines.

The five pupils who were caught low flying were all posted to fighters, so too the three who force-landed when lost and dutifully rang up to be collected. Had I only known those were the local rules I would have played the course differently.

Chapter 4

At Brize Norton we were upgraded to the sergeants' mess, though promotion itself did not come until we had passed our final tests. The output was sixty pilots every three months, thirty each on single- and dual-engine courses; the fighter trainees had Harvards, we on the duals flew Oxfords, and I had a chilling introduction to the aircraft the morning after arrival.

We had been told the new course was to parade at midday, so after breakfast that morning the others in my hut began preparing themselves for an inspection, polishing buttons and boots, sprucing up their uniforms. I felt sure it would only be an informative session, but no one was prepared to risk this view so I went off alone to explore. Just outside the doorway I was stopped by the antics of a song thrush. He had hold of a snail by its lip, was raising his head slowly to stand on tiptoe then slam the shell down on the cornerstone of the path; two or three times he did this before smashing the shell and getting his meal. I looked up to see another pupil had come out of the next hut and stopped to watch me watching the thrush.

He was about three inches shorter than me, a podgy figure with a bald patch on the crown of his head I just had time to notice before he plopped his cap down on it carelessly at a non-regulation angle. He was Peter Lander, an Oxford graduate in his mid-twenties who had spent some time in Hong Kong where his father had been the bishop. Swopping backgrounds between us we walked down to the end hangar and watched the accident happen. The Oxford pilot misjudged his height, instead of levelling out he slanted straight into the ground then ballooned up to teeter in the air, and Peter uttered a cry as he grabbed my arm.

In such a situation, watching from the sidelines, you react as if at the controls; your hand gives either a quick jab of the throttles to try and ease her down, or it jerks forward for full power in an attempt to flatten out for speed enough to climb away for another circuit. He

41

did neither. I think he simply pulled back the stick and hoped to stall-settle heavily on the ground. The consequence was that the port wing rose against the sky in a stall turn, then the nose dropped to angle down and smash into the ground. By the time we heard the thump some three hundred yards away we had seen the front of the aircraft crumple like a matchbox crushed under a boot.

I had begun to run even before he hit and Peter came trundling after me. The crash-tender was first there, however, thundering past me across the grass before I had gone a hundred yards. The ambulance followed and when I arrived the sergeant had already got into the shattered cockpit. He screamed at me to stand clear, the stink of petrol was overpowering and the threat of an explosive fire must have been in his mind, but they did not use the extinguishers.

Peter joined me in silent survey of the wreck. What shocked us was the fragility of the Oxford. It seemed to have given the pilot no protection at all, certainly far less than from the body of a car. The nose and port wing were a tangle of splintered wood, instruments dangling from their leads, white fractured timber piercing through camouflaged fabric like skeletal remains. The pilot did survive, but he lost the sight of one eye and that finished his flying. My most vivid memory of the incident was the picture of that shattered bone-protruding woodwork. This was the type of aircraft we were about to fly.

These misgivings about the Oxford were not allayed when flying training began. Peter and I had the same flight-sergeant instructor, who, we discovered presently, was aptly nicknamed 'Frighty' – an adaptation of 'Flight', the normal address to a flight sergeant. On my introductory flight he warned about the dangerous stall character-istics of the Oxford, the need for vigilant attention to engine sound because of failures he had known, and stressed the necessity of constant practice in abandoning aircraft. He did not allow me even to touch the controls in our first flight, and when he did ostensibly hand over to me on the second lesson he kept his hands on the stick and feet on the rudders, and I could feel his dabs of interference at every manoeuvre.

The five of us condemned to his tutelage all had the same experience and I felt we should go as a group and discuss the problem with the Chief Flying Instructor, but Peter was happy to dawdle along and the others were unwilling to risk making complaint. Midway through the three-month course five pupils were to be selected as officers, and this inhibited any criticism of the system. As an unsupported complaint would be unlikely to get sympathy, I decided to wangle a private lesson, so that night in the mess joined two sergeant instructors who looked friendly. We talked a lot and drank a lot, and the result was an extra-curricular half hour of dual instruction, including two landings, from one of them next afternoon. He was then confident I was ready for solo, and so was I.

Only Frighty could authorize that, however, and next day he refused at first to let me go. But when I wondered about discussing incompatibility with the Chief Flying Instructor he agreed, and after a final babble of warnings which I resolutely did not hear I was up and away on my own. For the first time I flew the machine. He told me to do half an hour of circuits and bumps, but for an hour I stayed in the sky practising turns, diving and climbing, and even deliberately precipitating a stall. It was a sunny morning with little streaks of flimsy stratus scattered about at a convenient height to utilize as practice landing fields, and I must have done a dozen approaches and wheel-down landings on them, plunging through fleeting whiteness to burst clear over a brighter greener land, before finally having a break to look at the countryside.

It was a much more agricultural scene than in Surrey. There were big fields of barley not yet fully ripe, still a sheen on the stalks, so that the wind was creating green waves across the slopes, and fields where the bean crop had been harvested and the black stalks made them look as if swept by bushfire. There was a wedding scene at Little Barrington, a group of people clustered outside the soft warm-hued stone church, and bride streaming white as she entered a car. On the brow of the hill beyond there was a single tree, probably a white poplar, and with its felted under-leaves fluttering on show in the wind it looked as if overwhelmed by a mass of white butterflies.

Frighty was in a dither, as expected, when I finally landed but I told him I had seen what looked like a stick of bombs exploding on the railway line, so had flown west to wait a while. There was a particularly successful German attack the very next day. The bomber came unwarned low over the lecture room, the sound so unmistakably foreign it stopped the armament officer in mid-sentence and stilled us all in tension. But the pilot bombed the hangar, not the instruction block. And he struck gold. Incredibly, twelve Harvards were inside

43

and all were destroyed in the fire that followed the hit. To have allowed that number of aircraft inside one hangar together in August 1940 – the field had been bombed several times by then – was an act of monumental stupidity for which no one seemed to suffer blame, for the station commander and staff were all still in the same posts when we departed six weeks later.

Again the perimeter guns had not opened fire, this time because the AA army captain had not rung through to the three gun-sites with permission to shoot. This was late August, weeks after the Germans had launched their assault on the RAF, flying up to 1500 sorties a day with the sole objective of obtaining mastery in the air. Invasion was expected at any time, the whole country was apprehensive – you could be fined £100 for 'spreading alarm and despondency' – and nowhere was the reality of the threat more apparent than on the airfields in the southern half of England. In those dire circumstances you would have thought that airfield gunners could have been given freedom to open fire at all aircraft with black crosses, not to have to wait for telephoned permission.

Peter finally managed to go solo, then at last we were free to fly together. The general standard of his flying remained low right to the end, simply because he had no interest in improvement; he would drop a hundred feet in a turn or do a four-bounce landing without ever thinking about a repeat so as to get a better performance. Day after day that August and September as the Battle of Britain was fought over the southern skies we would be off together on blind flying exercises, cross-country flights, taking drifts, dropping smoke bombs on the range. These set exercises bored Peter – he always wanted us to go off flying over houses and sites he had known as an undergraduate – but my rule was that we did the set exercise before any such memory visits.

He was just as casual about our classroom subjects but his experience and intellectual standard was such that this mattered little, he could stay near the top of the class with minimum study effort. The subjects were mostly as before, taken to an advanced level, but bomb instruction was new and thorough. We learned about the types of bombs then in use, armour-piercing, anti-personnel, fragmentation, general purpose, anti-submarine and so on, about their fuses and release mechanisms and safety margins when dropping them, and we practised taking a bomb apart and reassembling it. Surprisingly,

Peter was good at things mechanical. He knew all the terminology and could use the tools. One afternoon he made me help him strip down a motorcycle engine and put it together again so as to give me a basic understanding of the internal combustion engine.

We were both among the first dozen in the mid-term exams, and the next day they posted the names of the ten selected as officer cadets. Both of us were among them. Peter's inclusion did not surprise me, but I had decided my letter to Lord Trenchard and the offence at Cambridge had put me out of the running. I could only think that the records of those black marks had been lost in the RAF archives. The following day we received the officer cadet's white band to wear on our airmen's uniforms.

Oh blessed white band! That mark of distinction that lifted us away from the wooden huts the same afternoon into the Officers' Mess, a gracious red-brick building with Georgian portico and tall arched windows, where ministering batmen performed all those tiresome tasks that had occupied so much of our time since entering the RAF. Thenceforth we could wear shoes instead of boots, and our trousers would no longer have to be put under the mattress to guard the creases but would be ironed for us when we wished. And the mess itself! What a ridiculous name for a beautifully ordered palace where we were each given a private room, a proper bed with complete mattress rather than three hard 'biscuits', crisp cotton sheets and soft white blankets, where clothing could be hung in a cupboard, and tea was brought to your bedside in the morning. We dined in a spacious hall at two huge polished tables with individual chairs, silver cutlery and sparkling cut glass, and a particularly welcome change in food was the cold buffet available every lunchtime, for I could happily live on salads. The three public rooms were furnished with soft leather chairs, the functional blackout curtains concealed by powder-blue ones, and on the floor was a thick carpet deeply blue as the Pacific on a bright sunny day. It was all so wondrously luxurious after those months in the underworld.

The same day I received £8 back pay due on six-month service promotion to Leading Aircrafthand, and Peter and I celebrated the double occasion by taking the bus into Oxford, treating ourselves to dinner at The Mitre and then onwards to a pub he used to frequent as an undergraduate. There we met some of his acquaintances, including an attractive girl with green eyes and a handshake as velvety soft to touch as the petals of a flannel flower. She was wearing a navy linen dress with flared skirt that allowed a good view of her attractive legs clad in substitute stockings – suntan cream, with a seam pencilled neatly down to the heels of her white shoes. Such was her seductive presence that we missed the last bus back to the aerodrome. Deciding it would be unwise to report back late the very day we had been selected for commission, we set off to hitch-hike but on the way passed a garage still open at nine-thirty, and there all alone in the showroom was a red Baby Austin seven, single-seater, strapped-down bonnet, hood lowered, running board re-blackened, and on it a placard: GOOD RUNNER £8.

It reminded me of one of those puppies you sometimes see in a pet shop window, all alone in the big space. We both fell for it, counted our money and found we just had enough. So in we went, bought it between us, and Peter drove us back in style to our luxurious new home in the mess.

The little Austin never gave us a single tremor of concern in the remaining weeks at Brize Norton. Our petrol ration was four gallons a month, a total cost of six shillings, and far more than we needed for the local trips we made in the little free time we had on the course. We drove often out to Burford in the evenings to enjoy sight of the lovely girls who worked in The Lamb, had nine holes on the golf course at Chipping Norton one night at nine o'clock, and spent one full free sunny afternoon following the trail of Matthew Arnold's Scholar Gypsy – starting from his stripling Thames at Bablock Hythe where a painted-lady butterfly was dithering about the sweet-scented thyme on the bank, pausing at Cumnor to climb his green-muffled hill where grasshoppers were screeching amid the ripened corn, and finally stopping by his bridge at Godstow where we watched a kingfisher preening its brilliance while all about and above the green willows the swifts were screaming in swirling flight.

The last hurdle of our course was night flying. For this we used a special field about five miles from base where the only building on site was a bomb-replaceable Nissen hut; most RAF stations had such satellite fields for night flying, thereby saving the blacked-out aerodrome from attention by German raiders who by this time in September had switched their major effort into night attack. Frighty had been posted to Canada – most aircrew training was carried out safely there or in Rhodesia from that summer onwards – so we were fortunate to have a new instructor for our night flying. He had me off solo after just a single circuit together when he did not touch the controls once, and he even had Peter off solo before we finished the night.

Enemy aircraft were an obvious menace in daylight – one Oxford was shot down – but the night raiders caused far more disruption to our flying programme. Peter and I were caught in the air one night when doing a joint exercise flying a triangular course between three beacons. I was flying, and Peter's courses were scarcely necessary as there was a gibbous moon, high in a sky scattered with luminous star-dust, so it was light enough to map-read most of the time. You could distinguish railway line from road by glints of steely reflection, woods were patently darker than open fields, and even in the fields themselves crops like ripened corn or the stubble were discernibly paler than pure pasture.

Yet, on return, we failed to sight our flare path ahead. The mystery lasted only a few seconds, however, then there were four stabbing bursts of brilliant light off to our port, each one giving a subliminal glimpse of a small white building set against a rectangular copse. It was a raider. The flare path had been doused. I cut our navigation lights and flew back to our last beacon. The drill was to wait there till the flare path was re-lit, but when there was still no sign of it after half an hour we flew a few miles south to check on a flare path seen on our exercise which we reckoned to be Abingdon's satellite. It was still alight, orange flares streaming wisps of smoke, so we decided to put down and check if our field had been bombed out of commission.

The approach was good, wheels and flaps down, throttles back to idling, but then, at about two hundred feet, I saw the dark mass of a tree directly ahead by the first flare. With throttles slammed wide open, wheels retracting, we just managed to clear it, at the same time glimpsing the black bulge of a hedgerow directly across between two flares. This was no airfield, it was just a patch of ordinary Oxfordshire countryside. Peter thought the lights might be incendiaries dropped by the raider, but the colour and power were wrong, nothing at all like bright spluttering flashes from incendiaries. It was definitely a flare path, and yet not a landing strip – as incongruous a duality as a wharf in a desert.

So mystified were we that when our own flare path presently dotted into life my main interest was to get down for an explanation of the wrecker's lights. But the Night Flying Officer was not at all mystified, the raider was still around and he had one more Oxford to get down before he could douse the lights. It was a bloody decoy site, of course. Didn't we know that? Apparently there were quite a few about the countryside, and when raiders were plotted in the vicinity they were lit to attract bombs. Some of the other pupils admitted having heard of them but I thought this was too important a matter to be left to chance discovery. I said all pupils should be briefed about them. The NFO said, 'No need to warn you. You're already genned up now, aren't you?'

We thought this an asinine reaction, and at lunch next day I told the CFI how we had nearly crashed. He recognized the need at once; a notice about the decoy site was immediately posted in the night-flying hut, and the warning about it was added to the pilots' notes issued to all incoming pupils.

There were a lot of wasps abroad that summer and one pupil made a belly landing when distracted by one darting about wildly in the cockpit. One nest had a regular route across the end of our dispersal. Peter and I tracked it down by following their line of flight. I was fascinated by a height adjustment they made across the entrance to our dispersal. The nest was in the embankment around the fuel dump, their target was a pear tree half a mile away, and they flew between at about two feet above the ground. Across their flight path was a wall, a wire fence and two hedgerows, and in all but one case they curved up over the obstacle and down to two feet again the other side.

The exception was the thirty-yard gap between the two hedgerows where we entered our dispersal area. On that stretch alone they stayed up at about fifteen feet, clear above the whirling propeller height of any Oxford which might be entering or leaving the dispersal when they were crossing the entrance, and once beyond the danger zone they dipped down again to normal flying height of two feet. We wondered how on earth they came to devise this safety measure. And how did they pass it on to new recruits?

We had a fatal raid the day of our final examination. This was in armaments, a practical test taken in the garage attached to our main instruction block. For an instant, when we heard the roar of the low-flying aircraft, we were stilled, but the crescendo left no doubt and we had hurled ourselves to the floor before hearing the faint whistling sound of the actual bombs.

A string of four . . . thunder of explosions . . . juddering of the floor . . . clenched rigidity of your own body (you only track down these details later). All glass in the building was shattered and went on tinkling long afterwards . . . combination of thick dust and smell of cordite . . . people pouring into the corridor and out of the front door . . . everyone shouting. All four craters were outside, two each straddling the corner of the block, their edges decorated by curlicues of upturned tar.

It was the second bomb that had been the killer. It had landed just outside the examination room. The instructor and one of the pupils had been killed, the second pupil badly injured – he lost a leg, but did survive. The door from the corridor into the garage, beside which we had been standing, was still in place afterwards. In it was a sliver of glass about eight inches long that had penetrated like a dagger right through the solid wood to leave a triangular point two inches long jutting out of the far side.

Our course ended two days later. By this time we white-banders had all bought our new uniforms; representatives of the military tailors in London had come to the mess by appointment to measure us. As we had to have two uniforms I was left with very little money, certainly not enough to pay for accommodation on the ten days' leave we had been granted, and fortunately Peter had insisted I join him and his mother down in Bournemouth. His argument was that since I owned half of the little Austin he could not take it all for himself on leave. So on the last day at Brize Norton we dressed ourselves in airmen's jackets and caps as usual, but with the trousers of our officers' uniforms; the new tunics with their thin Pilot Officer's stripe and the Wings brevet were behind the seats, for we were told to assume our new ranks only when clear of the station.

At the main gates we waved to the corporal on duty and then drove on till out of his sight. Then we stopped, changed into our officers' tunics, put on our new caps, and drove back to get out just short of the guardroom. The corporal, still standing below the steps, cocked his head to one side like a bird, wary.

'What do you want?'

'We wanted our first salute,' Peter said.

'Bugger off,' he said.

We got back into the car, reversed it, then as we began to move he gave us a sort of salute; the bent arm started from the salute point by his forehead but then he stretched it into a friendly wave high above his head. And I stood up to grip the windscreen and gave him a splendid drill version in reply, holding it till we took the turning, and so we started off on the road to Bournemouth singing 'The Donkey Serenade' and envying no one in the world.

Chapter 5

Leave ended in late October, then we had to part. Peter had been posted with several others to a bomber Operational Training Unit (OTU) up north and I, alone, to the Army Cooperation OTU at Andover. He took me to the station at Bournemouth, gave me four pounds for my share of the Austin, and drove away alternately squeezing the horn bulb and waving till out of sight. It was the last time I ever saw him. Five months later he was shot down on a shipping attack off the Dutch coast.

Andover was one of the oldest stations in the RAF, built twenty-five years earlier when aeroplanes were first used in war and the Royal Flying Corps was formed to fly them – five of those first-war pilots were still on the station staff in 1940. The mess had sepia photographs of those wonderful men and their flying machines, most of the pilots in cavalry twill breeches, and mounted above the fireplace was a polished wooden propeller of a Sopwith Pup aeroplane surrounded by silver trophies for flying competitions dating back to 1919. The dark polished-wood floor was covered by a maroon carpet bearing the Flying Corps emblem, there was a series of Edwardian hunting prints on the panelled walls, and in the dining room was a huge oak sideboard with silver covers and dishes for the self-service type of breakfast associated with stately English homes.

Andover had retained its links with the army after 1918 when the Flying Corps was transformed into the Royal Air Force, the field being used to train both army and RAF officers for the two army cooperation squadrons, Nos 53 and 59. After Dunkirk, however, as the squadrons had no active army in England to cooperate with, they were loaned to Coastal Command, which meant army officers were being trained by the RAF to attack enemy naval forces. Someone presently discovered this ridiculous set-up, and from my course onwards no more army officers were accepted. Those already on a course or on the squadrons went on to finish a tour of operations, after which they had to transfer to the RAF if they wished to continue flying. Andover turned out about eight crews a month, which was roughly the loss rate on the two squadrons at that time.

The oldest of the flying staff, the CFI, was around thirty years of age but among the administrative staff were many who had been there during the First World War. They adhered to peacetime tradition, with a Mess Night once a week at which some of them actually wore dress uniform. We were all expected to attend, but few did; after a year of war, these traditional practices were crumbling, instructors who had flown on operations in France earlier that year, and pupil army officers who had been on the beach at Dunkirk, resented being treated like cadets and were unwilling to accept the finer distinctions between officer ranks that had obtained in the starchy pre-war days. So there was a division between the pilots and the non-flying permanent staff on the station, between the impudent young officers with their metal monoplanes and casual standards of dress and discipline, and the elders of biplane days who adhered to the traditional practices of one of the oldest stations in the Royal Air Force.

The station commander, Group Captain Hubbard, had been with the original Royal Flying Corps and could become quite hysterical about the actions and attitudes of this new breed of officer. I saw him one day on the path, literally speechless, just standing there as he pointed with shaking hand at one of the army officers walking down to the hangar wearing an Irvine jacket, flying boots, and a Seaforth Highlanders kilt in full swish. He used to hide behind the sentry box at the entrance and pounce on us for not carrying gas masks, and one morning in the mess he went quite berserk about this. He passed me as I was walking into the breakfast room, muttering to himself, and a moment later I heard a shriek that made me turn around sharply. Hubbard had stopped just by the doorway, was waving a hand wildly and perhaps even frothing at the mouth as he screamed at a pilot officer who had sauntered past him – without his gas mask.

'Jesus wept! Am I never to be obeyed? . . . disgrace to the service . . . time and time again . . . respect . . . discipline.' And then he glared across the room at the rest of us standing shock-stilled: 'Riffraff! All of you.'

He turned and almost ran through the doorway, still railing at us for debasing the standards that had ruled his life. I felt sad, would have liked to chase after the old man, pat him on the shoulder and say we genuinely admired the Flying Corps people. But he would never have allowed such contact.

There were five of us on my course. We started our training on the short-nosed Blenheim, the type that had been in use as a fighter plane over France earlier that year, and the instructor who took me up the first time threw it about the skies as if he were back again in aerial combat over the Maginot Line. The first operational sortie of the war, just one minute after the declaration of hostilities, was a reconnaissance of the German naval base at Wilhelmshaven by a Blenheim, and Blenheims had comprised our main bombing force in France as well as operating there as fighters. Though its cockpit layout was probably the worst ever mangled together, it was a lovely machine to fly, quick as a Moth in response to the controls and yet you could trim it to fly hands-off almost as precisely as would an automatic pilot – a new gadget we had read about in the copies of *Flight* and the *Aeroplane* magazines found in every RAF mess. With a good turn of speed, around 300 m.p.h. with the 9-boost, almost as manoeuvrable as a fighter, two Bristol engines which had been battle-tested for more than a year, it was an aeroplane I came to know well, to trust, and to love.

Our flying training, under the guidance of pilots who had been on operations in France, had a strong practical bias that bore little resemblance to the official syllabus signed by Hubbard and posted in the flight hut – radio exercises, for example, were ignored as it was impossible for the pilot to get at the radio in a Blenheim. Instead we learned about the landmarks and naval ports in France where our targets would be located, about the work then being carried out by 53 and 59 Squadrons, methods used to counter enemy fighters, bombing tactics, different types of AA fire and how to cope with searchlights. It was all good meaty stuff given by people who had completed an operational tour themselves, and not just in formal lectures but during convivial sessions in the mess and in the local pubs where we would drink together in the evenings. In the air too they would encourage us to fling the aircraft about in the dive-bombing and low-flying exercises, the better to learn the limits to which we could go on operations. Flying the fast manoeuvrable Blenheim after those weeks on the frail Oxford was like a joyful release from bondage, and every time I climbed up on to the wing to pull back the hatch and clamber down into the cockpit it would be in almost trembling anticipation of the delight to come.

We could legitimately fly low on the bombing range. There you could swoop down to grasstop level for the fleeting run over the whitewashed target circle in the middle of the field, continue on to dip over a hedgerow which the feathery seeds of old-man's-beard had turned into a line of cloud, and then up a wooded valley where the trees were rich in colour, greens and yellows and reds and browns fleeting past the cockpit window in a merging harmony of autumnal tones. The valley was the limit of the low-flying area, so you would finish zooming up into the sky, banking through a gap in the wavy strato-cumulus to straighten out just high enough above cloud to go flitting along through the wispy curves atop the layer.

However, for all the thrill of carefree flight about the skies of Hampshire I did work hard to perfect handling the controls. You needed such dedication to fly the Blenheim with confidence, for it had an appalling cockpit layout. Down by the seat on the right were the flaps and wheel selector, ahead of them the trim, the 9-boost lever in front above the panel; then for the left hand the throttles low down at hip level and therefore difficult to apply leverage, and behind them, out of sight, the pitch, the mixture, and the gill controls in ascending order, so that you had to make a contortionate arm-shoulder twist to reach the last one up behind your left shoulder blade. To compound the problem, you could not rely on sensitive finger touch but had to wear gloves; with so much sharp metal, cutting edges and skin-pinching movements in the controls your hands finished streaked with blood any time you flew without gloves.

I would spend hours at a time in a grounded machine creating emergency situations – throttles slipping, selector missed, wrong pitch, incorrect mixture control, sudden enforced overshot – and to react speedily to the hypothetical danger my hands would be fluttering about like a mute in excited conversation. The driving force for all this concentrated practice was not fear, but response to the challenge of such a baffling layout. It irritated me if in a sudden blind snatch my hand failed to hit its target precisely, I felt any idiot should be able to perform such a simple action faultlessly, so kept punishing myself with practice until the hands got it touch-perfect every time.

From that expertise, saving precious fractions of a second in taking a decision, confidence flowed.

Some pilots did have difficulty flying the Blenheim, and some had bad luck with enemy raiders, but there were also many accidents on landing for it was a disastrous site. There was a valley slanting across the field at right angles to the prevailing wind, and it was never easy even in daylight to get your attitude adjusted exactly to the ground slope at point of touchdown. If you missed the stall on the down-slope, you floated across the little valley to thump heavily into the far side, and if you wheeled down too fast on it you shot into the air from the up-slope. In autumn there was a natural phenomenon that complicated this delicate judgement of height.

This was the webbing created by myriads of money spiders. These tiny creatures seemed to have had a thriving environment on the field at Andover that autumn, and the mower level was well above their flat webs which were not neat orbs but untidy little meshes. There were many species present, the largest I found was about half an inch long and orange brown in colour, but many were so small you could distinguish nothing with the naked eye. The surface on the middle slope was covered with the fine webs, literally covered as I proved to the sceptical gunnery officer one foggy day by checking our footprints in a walk across the slope – every print was on web strands. On dewy mornings they flashed like countless mirrors, but even when dry they provided a reflective glistening surface which, in the afternoons particularly, made it painfully difficult to assess height above ground at touchdown. Even the rugged Blenheim under-carriage collapsed when one pilot flew straight into the slope.

We were given five days' leave at Christmas but I stayed in camp. The salary of a pilot officer was £16 a month; I had made no attempt to save any of it, certainly not enough for a stay in a hotel, which even out in the country could cost nearly £3 a day with meals. With all the pilots gone home to family or friends the mess was a gloomy place over Christmas, just a few elderly staff sunk into the big leather chairs and rustling the newspaper, mumbling to one another, or dozing. By Boxing Day the atmosphere had become so depressing that I went out of camp and caught the first bus that came, its direction unimportant.

After about twenty minutes, then a few miles beyond Andover, I got off by a large wood. It was then mid-afternoon, the sun already low in the west, but the sky was clear and the air crisply cold and invigorating. I set off on a leafy footpath, heading back home towards the setting sun, stopping now and then to inspect a badger set about which drifted a smell of overripe apples, watching a thrush pick at mistletoe berries in a poplar tree, and stooping to stroke the brown velvety cap of a fungus on a fallen trunk. There were few evergreens to block out the tangled vista of deciduous branches; many of the trees I could now identify, spiralling bark of a sweet chestnut, delicate tracery of birch branches, the massive contorted limbs of an oak. The previous winter the woods of England had seemed to me lifeless and gloomy places, but now that I had seen how they were transformed in spring they had become attractively mysterious in their winter disguise, life force concealed under show of death. It was growing dark when I reached the end of the wood and came out on to the black asphalt road with miles to go to the airfield, and at that thought the Robert Frost poem came to mind and I kept repeating the words aloud as I walked:

> The woods are lovely, dark and deep,
> But I have promises to keep,
> And miles to go before I sleep.
> And miles to go before I sleep.

Shortly after Christmas the five of us finished our introductory course and moved on to the operational training flight, where we switched to the long-nose Blenheim as used on the squadrons, and were crewed up with wop'ags (wireless operator air gunners) and navigators. Among the latter were two officers of the Royal Canadian Air Force, one of whom, John Gilmore, was assigned to me. John had been in the Royal Canadian Mounted Police, was ten years older than me, in his early thirties, unusually old for trainee aircrew. A tall thin figure, slow and deliberate in speech and manner, he was reluctant to question even the most pointless orders issued by authority. The other Canadian, Tiny Acland, was a huge jovial character, chubby cheeks and boisterous manner. The Canadians were paid much more highly than us but Acland had private money that swamped his pay, frequently taking a taxi sixty miles up to London to have dinner or see a show.

To complete the three-man crew we had a gunner who operated the radio as well as the gun turret. The gunners were sergeants, so they lived separately from the rest of us. I thought this a stupid system. You learn team work off duty as well as on it. But we were officers, they were sergeants, and though this class difference was of far less significance in the RAF than in the other services, it was still too ingrained in national character to ignore – or be ignored.

It is almost impossible for an officer in the British services to establish a normal human relationship with a man in the ranks, even though the officer may have come from a country and culture where such contact is common, for in England all parties seem to support the class system, quite happy to accord or accept the distinctions it imposes, reverencing title and rank far above achievement and intellect. That I was an Australian, and John a Canadian, was irrelevant to Davy, our gunner; we were primarily officers, therefore in a different class. It would have been difficult to overcome that English characteristic even in favourable circumstances, impossible to do so in a physical lay-out designed to reinforce it; and in the Blenheim we could not even share flight together, for the cockpit was blocked off from the rear, so the gunner was always literally out of touch with us officers up front.

It was a mild January in 1941, snowdrops littered the sheltered area between our two living quarters and were knocked about by hedge sparrows in frequent scuttling wing-fluttery chases about the grass. One morning, after a night raider had bombed a crater in the area and smashed all our windows, but harmed no one, dozens of starlings arrived and began strutting and poking busily about the crater as if it were a favoured food source; word must have got around the starling world about the food available in fresh bomb craters – I saw a huge flock of them jabbing away at one in Cornwall later that year.

Andover did not have a satellite field, yet there were few aerodromes more in need of one. The station was established in the First World War, had actually been visited by a German military mission in the mid-1930s, must have been on the very first of their aeronautical intelligence maps. It had been one of the hardest hit on Eagle Day when they began their assault against the airfields of England, twelve bombers taking part in one attack, and during the four months of our particular course we had sixteen separate raids. There were many more alarms when no attack developed, of course, but on sixteen occasions we were bombed, machine-gunned, or had one of our aircraft shot down by the raider.

Acland's death was associated with enemy action. There were just the two of us up on exercises that black night and a raider joined us in the circuit – a regular ploy by the Luftwaffe. No one was aware of his presence at first and the flare path stayed alight. I was trying to manoeuvre our aircraft to touch down on to the ridge of the treacherous dip when there was an explosive flash away beyond the northern perimeter, and as we taxied towards the perimeter a quivering orange glow lit up the skyline over there. We guessed a crash, and then the raid warning double-red Very Light shot up from the control light to suggest the reason for it. Later on after the raid was over we learned that Acland's aircraft had indeed been shot down by the intruder.

There was a bizarre little sequel to his death. Earlier that week I had been out with John at the nearby Black Swan when Acland came in accompanied by a strikingly attractive girl; with a mantilla over glistening black hair curled about a full-lipped sensual face, and wearing a low-necked burgundy satin dress, she looked like a Goya contessa. She was English, plummily accented, and spoke with apparent intimacy about leading people in the theatre world. We had a pleasant evening together during which Acland arranged to go up to London with her on the Friday evening to see *Gone with the Wind*, so after he was killed on the Thursday I went down to the Black Swan next night to break the news to her. I was waiting just inside the blackout curtain when she arrived, wearing under her fur coat a damson velvet frock with a narrow stand-up collar around which was a double circuit of pearls. As soon as she saw me she said, 'Something's happened to Ian, hasn't it?'

I told her about the crash. She took it calmly, her pale face devoid of expression. But when I tried to go on to explain how quick and painless their deaths must have been she suddenly cut in on me with a smile.

'Well, are *you* doing anything tonight?' she asked. 'I have my car.'

It took me a moment to recover. I told her I was on flying duty, she patted me on the cheek, murmured 'another time', and went on into the bar. I don't know if she had any better luck there, for although I saw her the only other time I went back to the Black Swan we never spoke together again.

We lost a second pilot of our course when after starting his engines one night he put out his hand to clear mist from the window. The propeller of the Blenheim is dangerously close to the cockpit window, he reached too far and the lapse cost him his left hand. So then three of us remained out of the original five. One was John Humphries. He had gone off to get married when our posting came through so we arranged to meet him and his wife for a celebration dinner in London during our pre-operational leave. Our gunner went home for the three days, John and I went to stay at the Regent Palace near Piccadilly – I could afford the one pound a night service rate because we had done a lot of night flying that last month, so I had rarely been out of the camp.

The morning after we arrived I left John at Canada House and set off for the city, hoping to find out if the shipping company had any news of a suitcase sent after me by sea. But the cumulative effect of the air raids had left such large gaps in the building line that even Londoners were having trouble with addresses, and I could not find the right street let alone the building. In the narrow streets of the city the damage was catastrophic. I saw gutless buildings that looked like charred viaducts, others that had collapsed were draped with a cumbrous shawl of netted concrete lumps held together by the webbing of iron reinforcements, tubing and piping lay on one heap like a tangle of intestines. Whole streets had disappeared – a paper seller pointed to a mountain of rubble and told me it was such and such street. Many of the buildings had forwarding addresses somewhere outside, printed on placards or even painted on the remnant of a wall: MARTIN & THROSTLEWAITE LTD. RING WEL 1234 FOR INFORMATION. I saw a white-painted appeal on a smashed door, 'FSW? Where are U??'; it seemed to have been answered, there was writing on a sheet of headed notepaper nailed underneath it. In one place a huge pile of rubble had clearly been there some time, people had made a weaving track up over it like a footpath in the countryside. On the return by bus we had to take a number of diversions, with the conductor calling out when we were closest to normal stopping points. I got off finally near Regent's Park where a great magnolia tree was in white waxen flower, and the bank across the lake was carpeted with crocuses, purple and white and gold.

That evening we had drinks at the Kensington flat of an official from Canada House whom John had contacted that day, and it was from there that we set off late for our appointment with Humphries and his new wife at the Café de Paris. We had not realized the raid was so heavy until we came out into the street; there we could see in the darkness without any difficulty because of the searchlights and gun flashes reflected from the smoke, could hear the throbbing and surging of aircraft engines overhead, and the sounds of shrapnel pinging down on the roadway. Mixed up in the smoke was an element of gas, so strong that John decided to throw away his cigarette. We had to walk some way before we found a taxi, the driver himself was wearing a tin helmet and told us he had been diverted twice by bomb damage near Baker Street.

Clearly the raid had intensified while we had been at our party. There was a difference between an attack on a big city and one on an airfield; you could remain unconcerned during a London raid, you had the security of millions of other likely victims about you so felt statistically safe enough not to worry. But on an airfield the target was pretty much you yourself, the attack was far too personal, and you far too conspicuous, to give the event anything but urgent attention. On the airfield you went for deep cover and tried not to exist during a raid, in London you could stroll about and look at the action with almost academic interest – and a touch of excitement.

So it never occurred to us that the Café de Paris would be hit. Nearing the site the driver had to stop just after our wheels thumped over a sprawl of hoses. Police and wardens and firemen everywhere . . . stretcher being lifted into an ambulance, another reversing on to pavement . . . oxy-acetylene flashings from within the shattered building . . . rescue team with a winch still at work . . . atmosphere peppery with smoke. Only then did we realize that this particular 'incident' – the word used to describe an event that might kill a thousand people – would concern us personally. A warden told us what had happened. The bomb had cut straight through the upper part of the Café de Paris and exploded on the dance floor an hour or so earlier. About fifty people had been killed, double that number injured. Luckily there had only been a minor fire, quickly doused by the firemen who had been first on the scene, or fatalities would have been far worse. Survivors had been taken to various hospitals, he could not help us with names but gave a phone number to call in the morning.

Next day we discovered Humphries and his wife still alive. They were in Charing Cross Hospital – grey stone floors, yellowing chipped ceramic tiles on the walls of echoing corridors. She had not suffered too badly but Humphries was severely injured. He had lost an arm, his sight was in danger and he would never fly again. The Women's Voluntary Service unit at the hospital had their personal details and was already in touch with their families. We undertook to set off the RAF procedure and make arrangements for his belongings at Andover, told her to tell him we had called, and then left the sombre building.

Late next evening we reported back to Andover, and the following morning flew off to St Eval to join No. 53 Squadron.

Chapter 6

────◦────

The crackling opening stanza to Banjo Paterson's ballad of 'The Man from Snowy River' goes:

> There was movement at the station, for the word had passed
> around
> That the colt from old Regret had got away,
> And had joined the wild bush horses – he was worth a thousand
> pound,
> So all the cracks had gathered to the fray.

From early childhood I have had a clear picture of that scene, derived from an illustration perhaps, but coloured and enlarged by imagination: weatherboard house with wide veranda, white paint flaking, red corrugated-iron roof blotched with rust, circular galvanized water tank at one corner, beside it a pepper tree with glistening green drooping branches, and nearby, two great gums with mottled brown-cream trunks, an ironbark fence dwindles away to disappearance beyond the gaunt frame of a metal windmill which I could *hear* clanking and clattering as it turned; in foreground riders packing saddle bags, tightening girths, checking shoes . . . one mounted man with arm outflung towards the distant blue range as if urging haste . . . another group looking dubiously at the eponymous rider on his 'small and weedy beast' slightly apart from all the rest . . . a woman in blue and white gingham dress with white pinafore coming from the house with packages of food . . . two packhorses being hurried forward by small boy clearly thrilled by the quivering atmosphere generated by all this exciting activity.

That was how it was when we arrived in Cornwall to join 53 Squadron, for in that spring of 1941 St Eval aerodrome had suddenly become the focal point of action in the war. Churchill had just issued his directive on the Battle of the Atlantic; the artery of our American supply line, already weakened by submarine attacks, was under dire threat with four German battleships preparing to enter the battle. The *Bismarck* and the *Prinz Eugen* were carrying out their final trials; the *Scharnhorst* and *Gneisenau*, which in a preliminary sortie had already sunk over a hundred thousand tons of shipping, were now thought to be back in port preparing for a joint operation with them that might well swing the Battle of the Atlantic – and so end resistance in the British Isles.

The very day in March 1941 that we arrived at St Eval, a PRU (Photographic Reconnaissance Unit) Spitfire flew over Brest to take a series of routine photographs. Within an hour of its return, when the film had been processed, we knew where the *Scharnhorst* and *Gneisenau* had lodged. The battle against the ships was set to begin, and it was at St Eval that all the cracks had gathered to the fray.

There were the two Beaufort squadrons, No. 22 with its torpedoes and 217 with bombs, our 53 Squadron with Blenheims, and a Fleet Air Arm detachment of torpedo Swordfish biplanes; a flight of Hudsons carried out night patrols outside the harbour to monitor nocturnal movement, and for regular daily checks we had the PRU Spitfires, beautifully smooth unarmed machines, some painted a clear azure blue for high-altitude observation, others dove grey for cloud-base flights. Bomber Command did prepare a hurried raid of a hundred aircraft on the ships, and sent out occasional mass raids in the ensuing months – incidental to their main effort against Germany – but the day-to-day fight against the menace was carried out by the forces at St Eval.

The Germans knew we were the focal point of action, and so St Eval was subjected to strong attacks – up to thirty bombers on some nights. The two big hangars were now only skeletons, their brick crew rooms still in use but the roofless hangars used only for daylight repairs. Normal maintenance was carried out in the dispersal fields, some aircraft having to taxi along a public road to reach the airfield and its concrete all-weather strip – a novelty to me and many others at the time. The most solid building on the aerodrome was the operations room, a low red-brick block surrounded by an earth mound and further protected by blast walls and thick reinforced roof; most of the other buildings were of wooden construction, many of them replacements for bomb losses. General living quarters were off the station. We aircrew in 53 Squadron lived in the Watergate

Hotel, a sombre multi-gabled Victorian structure set in a valley by the beach; there we slept in peace when over the hill behind us the night sky would be flickering with flashes of guns and bombs as the airfield was attacked again.

Two days after arrival we started our operational tour on an easy convoy escort job. Blenheims were often used for this. We had far greater endurance than the single-engined fighters, and, though our speed was about the same as our potential opponents, their Heinkels or Ju 88s, it was presence rather than performance that was effective in discouraging approach; we jettisoned our anti-submarine bombs at sight of an enemy aircraft. The convoy had to be covered for eight hours, which meant two aircraft at four hours each. The other pilot was Nicholson, one of the army officers I had known at Andover the previous year. He was nearing the end of his operational tour and generously offered us newcomers choice of session. Arbitrarily, I took the first – and so perhaps survived.

We took off about midday in cold misty rain. I was wearing the standard wool-lined Irvine jacket and two pairs of gloves, silk inside leather. There was no heating in the Blenheim cockpit, you could get temperatures so low in winter that ice formed on the instruments, and chunks of ice would be flung off the propellers to bang against the fuselage. We flew north over the Cornish countryside where a few slivers of old snow lay in crevices on Bodmin Moor, and passing over a train emitting a stream of white smoke that wavered above the carriages like a woman's hair under water. Cloud base was 1200 feet without a break, and we stayed just below it as we turned out to sea at Bude where on the golf course a gang-mower was churning up green foam as it sped along a fairway.

Normally on leaving the country you switched off the IFF (identification friend'foe), an automatic radio signal identifying you as friendly to our own defences. However, I decided to leave it on as we set off over the grey Atlantic, because convoy escorts were notoriously trigger-happy and anything that might reassure them seemed worth using. The thin spray of rain was making shivery lines across the front perspex, visibility was under two miles and we kept peering anxiously through the murk, not wishing to discover our charge by their flashes of gunfire aimed at us. Just as I had sighted the convoy – one ship, another, then a whole series of them as you discerned the line – there came a crackling on the intercom followed by the gunner's voice: 'Aircraft at five o'clock low. Coming up at us.'

I flung the aircraft around and saw them. Two dark objectiles hurtling towards us. Hurricane fighters. John had come back from the nose to his seat and was already fumbling with the Very pistol as I called for the colour cartridge. He shot off that day's combination and I banked to see the red and green flares arching down towards the grey sea, but the fighters were nowhere in sight. I tightened the turn in anxious search and then suddenly, just as the gunner called about it, a Hurricane appeared off our port wing tip. The pilot stuck up a thumb in greeting. John prodded me in the shoulder and pointed out of his window where the other Hurricane was bouncing gently in formation on us.

The speed at which they had come into position, particularly as we had been banking steeply at the time, was terrifying. We would never have a hope against such an attacker in the open, and, ominously, one had what looked like a line of cuneiform characters on his fuselage, the record of his kills. They had the same camouflage as us, jigsaw curves of brown and green, but completely so whereas we as night bombers were matt black underneath. The gunner identified them from their side letters as from a Polish squadron – all RAF aircraft bore three letters on the side, the first two for the squadron, the third special to the aircraft. The fighters departed presently, to my relief, for like a car that is following you too closely a formating aircraft nags at you with its dangerous proximity.

We began circling the convoy at about a thousand feet, giving the destroyer with its distinctive white wake a specially wide berth. Wraiths of grey cloud kept drifting down from the main mass to envelop us in clammy touches, and thin curtains of rain manifested themselves in the silent sudden appearance of watery streaks on the front perspex. With such limited visibility it was impossible to see all the convoy at any one time; there must have been about twenty ships in the two parallel lines, but they stretched for several miles, and so we flew a long oval course about them. Only the destroyer, trailing white as it fussed about, was obviously moving. The cargo ships were going so slowly they left no visible wake, they were like models set out in line on a grey stone floor.

Nicholson arrived in the late afternoon, already flashing his recognition letter as he came out of the murk, and keeping wide of the destroyer in his approach to us on the far side of the convoy. To make sure we recognized him as the genuine relief, he sidled up beside our starboard wing and waved from the cockpit, a goodbye-and-go-home wave, followed by raising an imaginary tankard to his mouth. We waved back and set course for home in the gathering gloom. By the time we arrived back at the coast the sun must have set behind the cloud mass, and when I dipped the nose at sight of the airfield we slid down into a purple haze, with the mist already beginning to cuddle into the valleys.

The commanding officer of the squadron, Wing Commander 'Tubby' Grant, was waiting in the operations room. He was short and plump, a jovial character with little tufts of down on his cheekbones like the Phiz version of Mr Pickwick. He stayed with us at debriefing, professing interest in our uninteresting sortie, and when we finished he led us out into the main room and introduced us to the Controller whose desk was on a dais overlooking the big map of action in the centre of the room. We spoke about another soft job allotted to us next day, escorting a bomb-damaged ship being towed into Plymouth, decided on a take-off time to get us there at first light, and as we started towards the door Tubby asked the Controller to call him in the mess when Nicholson landed.

Some nine hours later when we arrived back at the operations room to be briefed about our bombed ship, the duty officer's first words were about the previous sortie. Had I actually seen Nicholson's aircraft when handing over the escort task? I told him about the farewell wave, and wondered at his question. He pointed to the operations board. This, typically, carried details of each sortie: pilot's name, target, time of take-off, estimated time of landing and finally the actual landing time. There were about half a dozen entries on the board that night – we had a strike group returning from Lorient – and a WAAF with curly blonde hair was writing up our sortie at that moment.

Nicholson's entry was incomplete, the final column still empty. The navy had been contacted, as had the Observer Corps, but neither had anything to report. I told him about the two Hurricanes that had approached us so rapidly but he merely acknowledged that he had seen that in my report – I had a feeling he had already pursued that line, and did not wish to discuss what he had heard from the Polish squadron. But there was another possibility. Nicholson could have been picked off by a Messerschmitt 110 out of sight of the convoy; there were plenty of these fighter bombers operating about the coast at this time, and a Blenheim would be a fairly easy target for them. The missing Blenheim was never found. John, laconic as ever when I told him the news, said, 'Lucky you picked the first duty.'

But then it always had to be someone else who was dead.

We ourselves met up with an enemy aircraft later that day. It was well after dawn when we found our bombed ship, directed to it finally by a great column of smoke the little tug was pushing up in straining effort. The ship could not have been an easy tow, the bow had taken a direct hit and was just a tangled framework within which you could see lively white water crashing about like surf in a rocky inlet. We had let off the recognition colour cartridge on our approach, for they had a manned gun at the stern, and afterwards we circled them peacefully for a couple of hours. Then, just after Plymouth breakwater became visible and we were trying to work out the distance of the ship from harbour, the gunner suddenly called, 'Aircraft. Four o'clock high. It's a Jerry.'

I swung the wheel and saw him at once. It was a Ju 88, heading south, about a thousand feet above us. I switched the gun-catch to 'Fire' and jettisoned our bombs – they drop unfused, lifeless metal with the safety links still in place. The Ju 88 discarded his bombs at about the same moment, far away from the ship, but his were impact-fused and exploded as a unit directly beneath us as we roared after him on 9-boost. The flash was subliminal, followed by a wide shivering ring on the sea surface. We had to climb slightly to reach his height, and although I pulled the 9-boost there was never a chance of catching him as he continued at full speed on his southerly course. We followed for a hopeful few minutes but by the time we reached the Eddystone lighthouse he was out of sight and we already too far away from our charge.

When we returned two MTBs (motor torpedo boats) were coming out from Plymouth Sound. They were a fine sight, streaming long white wakes in the flat blue sea, but they suddenly heeled over to change direction from the bombed ship and towards us. I guessed the reason at once and had begun to bank away steeply as they opened fire, at the same time shooting off a recognition cartridge. The two streams of tracer came hosing up to cross one another and go fleeting away behind as we continued the turn and straightened out to finish beyond range. From a safe distance we banked about to study the situation and saw they had stopped firing and were heading back towards the bombed ship. Nonetheless, I returned in a cautious weaving approach, wary as the little male spider edging towards a voracious sexy female. One of the MTBs flashed a slow-speed apology: 'SORRY. ANY DAMAGE?'

By Aldis Lamp we reported all well and remained friends thereafter. Presently, when within range of the Plymouth guns, they gave us the all-clear and we were free then to fly on over Penlee Point where escaped daffodils splashed yellow streaks away from a thatched roof cottage, and from there we swung westwards over the sunlit fields and valleys of Cornwall to land back in time to join the throng in the pre-lunch session at St Eval mess. It was unusually crowded that day, about seventy people perhaps, as a major strike on Brest had been planned that night with all squadrons and the navy torpedo Swordfish being involved.

The mess was sparsely furnished; there were a dozen or so leather-covered easy chairs and three sofas scattered about the cornflower-blue carpet, basic blackout curtains, portrait of George V over the fireplace, a narrow table with a shove-ha'penny at one end and at the other a walnut gramophone with its needle always ringed in fluff. Standing about in groups were air force officers up to the rank of air commodore, one or two Australian Air Force officers in their darker blue uniform, a group of Fleet Air Arm in navy, some pilots from our squadron in their alternative army khaki, an American naval lieutenant, and several WAAF officers.

The larger groups were specific to squadrons, and on entry we saw ours at the far end. Tubby Grant, with tankard in hand, was rocking back and forth on his heels as the flight commander gave last-minute instructions to a pilot in flying boots. Just as we joined them the news spread through the room that the PRU Spitfire had reported Brest blanketed in fog, so the raid was cancelled, and the feeling among our designated crews seemed to be one of angry disappointment. I would have felt the same. When you have prepared yourself fully for a test it is exasperating to be deprived of the confident moment. A little later, walking into the dining room, Tubby came up beside me.

'You feel ready for a night strike tomorrow, Pat?'

I nodded, asking the target, but he said that would not come through till next morning. Apart from Brest, our usual targets for night strikes were the submarine pens at Lorient or the naval dock-yards at St Nazaire or La Pallice, and with fog apparently settled on the northern peninsula the consensus was that the following night we would go to the naval base at La Pallice, our most southern target. When I told John this after lunch he replied, 'In that case I'd like to write some letters this afternoon.'

I knew this was not a presage of doom. Most people did keep 'goodbye' letters prominent among their effects, to be posted in the event of death – I had one I kept altering from time to time according to mood and the latest poet I had been reading – but John had two pinned to the inside lid of his suitcase which he never touched all our time at St Eval. That particular task had been completed. John planned his activities. He never became suddenly engrossed in a book or wandered out to watch the waves, he had lists of things to be done. He would clean his shoes, sew on a shirt button, file his nails, in accordance with his list. I was an erratic note-taker, some-times writing nothing for days, sometimes filling pages of the exercise book about a sortie or scenes or feelings, most of it embarrassing rubbish; but John set aside times for writing his correspondence, always with the recipient's letter beside his pad and ticking it off where he had dealt with an item.

This care for order, and the planning that went into it, may have been the result of his service in the Mounties. He volunteered so little information about himself, always braking when you tried to push him into disclosure, that I never did discover much about his work with the RCMP. He would answer specific questions but tended merely to nod at those little urges of agreement – 'Did you?' 'No!' – intended to encourage the flow. If you disagreed with him he often gave no reply whatsoever, and with authority he was particularly subdued, probably the result of service with a stratified police force.

The letters he had to write that day before our first strike were part of his normal correspondence duty, and he said it would take him an hour. I decided to go ahead rather than wait in the depressing lounge of the Watergate Hotel, with its dark red decor, heavy mahogany furniture, and fusty still atmosphere. It was about two miles to Newquay along the cliff path and there were always interest-ing distractions on the way. That afternoon I stopped after about ten minutes, so fascinated by the gulls hovering near the edge of the cliff I had to sit down and watch. They were floating lightly on the upcurrent, bouncing gently up and down as if sitting on an invisible sea-swell, giving their plaintive kittiwake calls. It was a beautiful afternoon with the sun shining spring-warm from a nearly clear sky, the gorse in bright yellow flower, linnets and stonechats twittering and flitting about the dark green clumps, and bumble bees thrumming about the clover growing by the path.

I was still there idly happy when John finally came striding up the path intent on posting his letters in town, but I made him stop to watch the gulls. I pointed out how they were walking to the edge of the cliff and just spreading their wings to be wafted away in effortless flight, a deliberate act of obvious enjoyment – you could pick out individuals doing it again and again. Just for fun. This interpretation did arouse him.

'It's not enjoyment, Pat,' he declared. 'They're working at something.'

He said he had read an article by some scientist who declared that apparent play in animals was in fact purposeful exercise. This struck me as a blinkered specialist view. I argued that to a bird, or child, activity can be spontaneous fun however a biologist might categorize it. John shook his head. I told him about times as a boy when I would suddenly feel impelled to the joy of movement, would strip off sandshoes and go racing around the lawn as fast as I could. Not unusual for a child surely? But John said he had never experienced any such moment of childish joie de vivre, moments when you felt compelled to run, sing, wave your arms about, or fling yourself on to the ground to go flailing and whirling down a grassy slope. He looked at me with a slight smile, disbelieving I had ever indulged in such antics. It was another one of my stories.

The following morning those of us on duty left the hotel in the van as usual after breakfast, up the narrow winding Cornish lane hemmed in by the rough stone walls, and were dropped off at the crew room. This was a concrete abutment to the blitzed hangar, its brown-green camouflaged surface splattered with white rosettes left by a raider who had used machine guns in his attack. Inside the stone-floored room were our green steel lockers, metal-legged collapsible table, two wooden seating forms, and on the end wall posters showing silhouettes of the battleships and enemy aircraft. Just inside the entrance was an easel and blackboard on which were chalked basic operation notices. This particular morning the list read:

Stand-by	–	F'Lt Cundy
		P'O Buck
Strike	–	P'O Francis
		P'O Thomas
		F'Lt Bannister
		P'O O'Brien

(The ex-army officers all had flight lieutenant rank.)

It was a cool morning with grey clouds streaming in from the Atlantic and mostly trailing showers. I changed into flying boots, left John checking Biscay charts and walked along the perimeter track to our dispersal which was about a quarter of a mile west of the hangar. Carrying a ground sheet, which presently was needed when a shower curtain came sweeping across the airfield, I was passed by a tractor towing six of the little trolleys used for bringing bombs from the dump. It weaved in passage like a snake, and on the last trolley an airman was astride the bomb with one hand gripping the fin and the other up to protect his eyes from the slush thrown up by the little wheels.

From the entrance to dispersal a duckboard track crossed to the tent where the flight sergeant had the Daily Inspection forms laid out for signature. Our favoured aircraft was H-Harry, he said it had had a carburettor change in the port engine and that he had done a *ground* test, looking at me as he accentuated the word. I had not planned to do our flight test till after briefing, but after that hint said I would give him the quick engine check he wanted. I signed the Form 600, picked up a parachute and set off through the slush to PZ-H.

The hedgerows had been left intact as camouflage when the Air Ministry took over the nearby fields for flight dispersals; in ours at this time there were honeysuckle and hawthorn in flower on separate sides, the honeysuckle being particularly fragrant at night, but that morning I followed my nose towards the hawthorn side where H-Harry was parked. A corporal was just fitting the control locks, I asked him to take them off again, threw the parachute up on the wing, then climbed up after it.

The windsock was almost horizontal, fluttering from the north, so I taxied around the perimeter track past our crew room and the control tower to the southern end of the runway. There I carried out the cockpit check and did my personal addition to it, then took off across the valley towards the Fleet Air Arm base at St Merryn. Out over the sea in Watergate Bay I did a few turns, climbed and dived and swayed about for a little in seagull fun, tested the trim controls, the boost and the flaps, then took her back to the airfield. There, after reporting all well to the flight sergeant I strolled back in the washed sunlight towards the bombed hangar, swinging the rain cape to flick at the shallow puddles in the perimeter track. Two of the other pilots were playing cribbage on the stonework entrance to the bomb shelter near the crew room; one of them had plucked the flower head of a ragged robin and with it was simulating the action of a shaving brush on his chin as he considered his cards. He looked up as I approached, then flicked the flower at me and said, 'Fog's cleared. We're on Brest tonight.'

Chapter 7

———o———

Inserted into the old notebook which covers this period at St Eval was a slip of paper containing, in my handwriting, a piece about Brest defences. It must have been copied from somewhere later on – it is not my language and the writer knew far more about the subject than I did at that time. This is the piece, complete with its enigmatic heading:

He should know!: Apart from the guns of the battleships themselves there were over 300 anti-aircraft positions (each with a number of guns) in the Brest area, and there were flak ships covering the harbour approaches, and light flak positions were established on most of the exposed buildings about the harbour area. There was probably no other target throughout the whole of the world that was so heavily defended as Brest – and that includes London, of course, whose anti-aircraft defences were puny compared to those of even an ordinary city in the Ruhr.

The briefing hut at St Eval was a green wooden hut about fifty yards from the operations room. Many of our sorties were solo efforts, reconnaissances or offensive patrols, and on these the crew were briefed in the operations room. The hut was only used when a large number were going out to the same target. It was a flimsy structure which, like most buildings on the station, had been bomb-damaged, but being sectional its repair was simply a matter of replacement. The windows were permanently blacked out, there was a thick blanket over the door, and the only ventilation came from a window behind the stage so there was always a dense blue haze of tobacco smoke at briefing time. A single light bulb, unshaded, hung above the stage.

Its light was already blurred with cigarette smoke when John and I entered. There were about fifty people there – crews from 22, 53 and 217 Squadrons – but we found Davy and managed to squeeze two places on the form behind him. On the stage the Intelligence Officer, F'Lt Eddie Shackleton, son of the Antarctic explorer, was talking to the group captain in front of the silvered screen, beside them a map of north-west France hung over the blackboard. There was much noise in the body of the room, exchanges between separated crews, newcomers being called over to reserved places – 'Lofty!' 'Over here, Steve!' – chairs and forms being pushed around, shuffling of feet, rustling of maps. A few sat still and silent.

The action started with a gesture from the group captain. He came to the front of the stage, raised his hand, and the noise faded as if a rheostat had been turned down. He spoke only a few sentences, stressing the importance of the strike, then left the stage to Shackleton. The light was extinguished and an aerial photograph of Brest harbour appeared on the screen. It had been taken that morning, hence our afternoon briefing.

'Notice the *Gneisenau* is still back in dry dock,' Shackleton said.

He pointed to a fuzzy spot on the north side of the harbour. He seemed to assume we were all cognoscenti, and indeed the picture created little interest among the crews. Almost everyone in the room must have been familiar with the scene, even newcomers such as myself having seen pictures of the harbour in the operations room, including a coloured one of the dock headquarters building fronted by a huge rectangular floral display of the French flag, planted – so a gardening enthusiast assured me – with geraniums, alyssum, and lobelia for the three colours. Everyone knew the battleships' silhouettes, we had several pictures of them in the crew room; they were widely known in the RAF as Salmon and Gluckstein, after a chain of well-known tobacconists.

The *Gneisenau* had been moved out of dry dock earlier that week, and that same night Ken Campbell of 22 Squadron, flying just a few feet above the water, had launched a torpedo that hit the stern and caused enormous damage. Campbell's aircraft, the only one that found the target, had no chance of getting through the massive AA barrage and he was killed with all his crew – they were buried with full military honours by the Germans. The *Gneisenau*, so badly damaged she was in danger of sinking, had been towed back to dry dock that same night.

Shackleton gave latest news of the defences. The Resistance had reported huge increase in the number of smoke pots in position about the town, including some in boats anchored in the harbour. Both the battleships, and the dry dock itself, were now draped with camouflaged netting, and there were new anti-torpedo screens off the docks – because of this the torpedo carriers of 22 Squadron were presently withdrawn from that night's operation. He also pointed to two new flak ships on the south side of the anchorage. The next picture on the screen extended into the countryside well beyond the town limits and appeared to have been badly scorched, it seemed a mass of blackened dots and holes. He explained to the uninitiated like me that the dots were gun positions, the rings searchlights. You only had to glance at the picture to realize there was no easy way into and out of the target area. You had to go through the guns.

The navigators were then given the day's letter and position of beacons in Cornwall, and our own recognition letter; this you flashed to stop our own guns and night fighters opening fire, but a colour cartridge also special for the night did the job more spectacularly – and securely. He told us the colours of the German recognition signal cartridge we would carry, information supplied daily by the Resistance. These enemy signal cartridges were of no use over a heavily defended target such as a port or airfield, but it was thought they might stop fire from isolated guns, or bemuse an enemy night fighter on your tail. I never heard of anyone having success with them. The only time I ever tested them was over the French countryside one night to a single bellicose gun-site and the result was that three others immediately opened fire on us. Shackleton offered the silk escape maps, for use if you were shot down, to any of us who still did not have them, then finished his briefing with a map showing the balloon positions about the dock area and giving their latest height.

The Met Officer followed, said the target area should be clear, and gave the navigators wind speeds and directions at various situations. He was confident St Eval would be open on return but offered two good diversions just in case. The squadron commanders then took the stage in turns, Tubby being the last. He said we could take off up to fifteen minutes early if we wished, 'but not one second later'. Time over the target was not so precisely ordered, this was left to your discretion, as was the height from which we chose to attack – the balloons discouraged any low-level gamble, and most of us dropped from between eight and ten thousand feet. Our bomb load was to be two 500-pound SAP (semi-armour-piercing) bombs, and flight tests were to be done immediately after briefing. He left to last his obsession about 'W'T go'.

'If you fail to get W'T go, you land. No question about that. Clear?'

It was not a popular embargo, nor was it of much practical use. That the radio was working when you left was no guarantee it would do so on return, for the wop'gunner had an impossible task in the Blenheim. Once he managed to squeeze his heavily coated figure into the turret he could see the gun controls just a few inches away from his chest, but the radio was down below at knee level and this had to be played blindfold. It might be set up perfectly on the ground but then at night we went bouncing across dispersal to the runway, the whole fuselage shivered and trembled in boosted take-off, the wheels clonked solidly in their bays, the throttles were pulled back with inevitable vibration until both engines were roughly synchronized, then the gunner went groping about his knees to test the delicately pre-set radio.

Even if he did manage to get the sacred clearance, so what? The chances of it working on return depended on careful handling thereafter, and instead we battered it. Shortly after leaving the coast the gunner would shake it violently and whip ammunition belts around it in testing his two Browning guns, afterwards he would be continuously swinging his turret in watch for night fighters, and over the target I would be hurling the aircraft about in a tumult of thudding explosions. After all this, his hands numb with cold, the gunner would start groping blindly down about his legs for the radio so exquisitely set up in contact with base some hours previously. It was cause for astonishment that he ever once in our tour of operations managed to contact base on return, not a surprise that he normally failed to do so.

Down at dispersal for the flight radio test that afternoon we had to wait for the ground crew to remove the bomb doors. The 500-pound bombs were too fat for the Blenheim bomb bay, so you had to fly with the two curved casings protruding like bosoms from the exposed bay; this meant you landed on the actual bombs if the wheels were retracted – I saw a bomb-damaged Blenheim do it at St Eval one afternoon. Once the doors were off we took to the air and within seconds Davy reported radio contact. To make sure it was not a fluke

I asked him to twiddle the knobs about a bit and then see if he could repeat the performance.

To make it more of a test I flew some distance south and circled low over a wooded valley. Some of the trees were ruddy in the sunlight, not yet in full leaf, while others were lightly coated in tender green, and in the open field above on the slope you could pick out clearly among the scatter of sheep the one-and-a-halves that were ewes with lamb. When Davy repeated his success we landed and tucked the Blenheim into the first bay just inside dispersal; this was a prime site, for when a number of aircraft were lumbering about the muddy area in darkness a pilot could have some worrying moments. The bomb trailer was being manoeuvred into position under the belly of H-Harry as we left dispersal.

John and I stayed in the crew room to work out our flight plan and method of attack. In many crews the pilot and navigator made a joint decision about line and height of the bombing run, in our case John insisted I make the decision. So I told him we would come in from the sea, using the offshore island of Ushant as a pointer to the harbour headland twelve miles away, thence the same distance to the docks. He worked out times for three runs: from base to Ushant, seventy minutes, Ushant across to St Matthew point on the mainland, four minutes, and another four from there to the docks. He gave the total but I was calculating a different sum. I reckoned to myself his figures meant we would be under fire for only about three minutes. That did not sound much – at the time.

We were back in the mess at about five o'clock where we joined the other three crews of our squadron on the Brest strike, one commenting on my wily grab of the first dispersal bay. We chatted about visibility over the docks at Brest, whether eggs would be available for our dinner, and the whereabouts of the two WREN girls who had lunched at the mess that day. A group moved over to the shove-ha'penny board, John and another navigator discussed beacons, I worked with two others on *The Times* crossword. No one did nothing, no one had a drink. The dining room was already well filled when we entered, there to discover that not only were eggs available for strike crews that night but also bacon – and on the table was a dish of raw carrots, supposed to help night vision. The tables were a little more crowded than usual, the room a little more noisy because of that, otherwise it appeared like any other night. But I was talking a lot, made a few strained puns, and smoked two cigarettes with the strong tea.

Take-off was set for nine o'clock so we were down at the hangar an hour before that. In the crew room there hung a single naked bulb, almost completely surrounded by a cylinder of black card, so the light was just a dim orange glow outside the spotlit centre. The twelve of us filled the room with flailing preparations, climbing into Irvine suits, swinging radio leads, stretching legs into flying boots, and all the time a clatter of gear about the lockers, metal clanging of parachute harness, and chatter associated with all this activity, some in quickened temper. 'Where's my bloody Mae West?' . . . 'Sure that's your parachute, Mike?' . . . 'For Christ's sake! Don't pull the cupboard down' . . . 'Some goddamn son of a bitch has got my mask' . . . 'Well, have your pee now, then.' With the smashed windows boarded over and blackout blanket over the doorway there was little ventilation, and the air was heavy with the smell of sweat. Or fear.

We were first out into the fresh clean night. The frontal system that had been swiping rain across the field from time to time during the day had cleared and the moonless sky glittered bright with stars, like a great blackout curtain damaged by shrapnel and now letting through countless sparkles of the brilliant light from outside our universe. Another crew joined us at the van. It had room for five only, we gave the place and our parachutes to Davy who had more to carry and started to walk. I asked John if he were excited about the operation.

'We have to get there first,' he said.

He sounded as if he had reduced the experience to one of his lists, each item to be dealt with in recorded turn. I began to query the decision not to go to the toilet before leaving the crew room and once the question arose it was impossible to repress, so I had to go on to the grass and urge out what little I could. Despite the clear starlit sky it was black night on the ground and we had difficulty picking out the duckboard path at dispersal, but then someone started an engine and exhaust flames showed us the way. The scent from the hawthorn was suddenly swamped by mechanical smells of petrol, oil and exhaust gases.

Davy, standing head and shoulders out of his hatch as we came alongside, said our parachutes were in the cockpit. John climbed on to the wing, I went to check that engine and aileron locks had been removed, the pitot head uncovered; there was a drill for the ground crew to raise these on show to me when I was in the cockpit but I liked to check actual removal. The corporal shone his torch for me when I crouched down to ensure the two 500-pound bombs were bulging in place below the fuselage. We were within twenty minutes of earliest permissible take-off time by then, so I gave Davy the all-clear, climbed up on to the wing and dropped through the hatch on to my parachute in the bucket seat.

The parachute was strapped on first, three clips into the central release, then the four seat belts slotted over the pin and locked with the triangular clasp. My hands moved automatically to tap each control for which it was responsible – just a positioning touch at this stage, part of the shuffling and stretching movements you did to assume command. I moved the stick backwards and forwards, swung the wheel, cycled the rudder pedals, toed the brakes, flicked on the navigation lights. John, having by then settled his equipment in the nose compartment, crawled back to buckle up beside me, and outside an airman raised the beribboned locks and cover high above his head. We were ready to start.

The engines coughed into life at once, and after a few moments warming up I opened the port throttle about midway for the magneto tests. The engine paused, backfired, then spluttered and surged in an uneven beat. I swore. The bottom plugs in the Blenheim radial engines tended to oil up, but they could usually be cleared by a burst of full power so I rammed the throttle hard against the stop and punished the engine for a few seconds before easing back to test the magneto again. Bingo! All clear. Breath released in a gust of relief. No problem with the starboard engine. A flash of lights to the ground crew, two airmen cleared away the chocks then one waved the wheel locks in front of his blue torch. I signalled back, he guided us out of dispersal and gave a final good-luck wave of both arms and we trundled past him on to the perimeter track.

Other aircraft were on the move, monstrous locusts lumbering about in the darkness, red and green wing-tip lights wavering and wandering against the black outline of the hangar. We joined the queue for take-off, I ran through the standard cockpit check then repeated most of it with my private mnemonic: 'How To Make The Flight Perfect' gave HTMTFP, for hydraulics, trim, mixture, throttle, flaps and pitch. These were the vital checks, a mistake in any of them could kill. The aircraft ahead of us roared up the runway with flaring exhausts to disappear over the ridge. I taxied towards the Chance Light and swirled to a stop, 'glim' lamps of the runway now a distinct line up the slope.

'Okay, Davy?' I called, and had his reply. John, beside me, raised a thumb.

The throttles were stiff to move once the nut was tightened, you had to squash down in the seat to get leverage with the left hand. The engines gave a roar of response and I released the brakes. We surged into movement, the control column began to shiver, the whole aircraft to vibrate under power. With the tail still on the runway the lights moved past slowly, but when I pulled the 9-boost switch the back of the seat thrust against my spine and the tail lifted quickly afterwards. I saw the runway lights begin to flow rapidly past the port wing then cut them out of sight, concentrating all visual sense on the airspeed indicator, watching it flicker around until at last it reached 90 m.p.h. Then slight relaxation of forward pressure on the stick – gently, sensitively, feeling for lift. Success. She came unstuck, smoothed herself into the air. Right hand slapped down sure on undercarriage grip, stick pressure eased in response to airspeed increase. The ASI, airspeed indicator, is the command centre when too dark to use any external visual aids. I did not see the end of the runway lights nor the black curve of the bomb dump, even the stars were not in conscious vision until we were at three or four hundred feet and doing 150 m.p.h. Only then, safe with speed and height, did I take my eyes off the ASI and orientate visually by the night sky rather than intellectually by the instrument panel. The emergency boost pushed back to 'off', a deep relaxed breath, lips moistened, and a call to the gunner:

'Okay, Davy. It's all up to you now.'

We levelled out at about a thousand feet, and prayed for the essential 'W'T go'. This was the worst time in starting out on a night strike. Nothing to do but wait on the gunner for decision – either clear you to go ahead, or force you back to land. In search of diversion that first night I wondered about the navigation lights; you were advised to keep them on while over England, showing yourself clearly to our night fighters, but you showed yourself equally clearly to enemy night intruders. I looked about the night sky and saw away in the distance three bright jewels on display, an emerald and ruby and diamond on the black cloth of the horizon, and that made up my mind. Our lights went out. A habit was born.

John had given me the course for Lizard Point. I leaned forward and in the luminous glow of the compass twisted the ring to lock on to his figure. Still no word from Davy. The only help I could give was to keep the aircraft steady, so I continued level flight westwards across the pallid strip of beach and out over the sea, setting the trim so perfectly she was flying almost hands off despite the bulging bombs. It was a task of distraction. After less than five minutes in the air I was having to restrain myself from calling Davy to ask if he was having a problem. Abruptly there came the moment of suspense when the headphone crackled to transmit.

'Clear to go, sir.'

'You're worth a medal.'

We set course for Lizard, John went forward to check the flashing beacons. I was flying visually, aligned on brilliant Altair at the edge of the Milky Way, just an occasional glance down to ensure the compass needle was parallel to the ring setting – the gyro compass deviated steadily so the only time we used it was on short-timed runs. By this time night-sight was fully adjusted; I could discern different shades of black in the ground below, pick out the blocks of forest, china-clay workings, starlit glint of a huge reservoir. Then a beacon shattered the darkness to our right, quick bright flashes like a low sun seen behind a passing train. Utilizing its position John brought us to the coast directly over Lizard Point, and there gave me the new heading for Ushant. Once on course I switched off the IFF, then told Davy to make his gun test.

The two Brownings sound like a lorry-load of gravel being tipped on to concrete, and we shivered off course in the recoil. I cleared the safety catch, let off our wing gun and watched the flaming tracer stream away in a lonely parabola across the starlit horizon. Afterwards there was little talk, the gunner had nothing to do but keep lookout, John nothing to do but wait, only I was lucky with plenty of tasks in hand – throttles to adjust, compass to check, height to hold steady, trim to fiddle with, engines to listen to, and constant glances to be given to the instrument panel in checking the pattern remained static. It is activity on a dial that stops a heartbeat.

We had no problem finding Ushant. Other aircraft had already arrived over Brest, from nearly thirty miles away its position was indicated by lightning-like flashes on the horizon. I could not pick out Ushant itself, merely notice the uniform blackness was disturbed in that area, but John now in prone position over the bombsight in front directed me to it. Then, when we must have been immediately above the island, he called out the new course. The faint flashing in the sky had been directly off our port wing, his new course was towards it and I kept glancing from that menacing activity on the horizon to the twirling numbers on the gyro compass, fascinated by what seemed the inevitability of the two coinciding. But we stopped short. The sky flashes were still slightly to our left when we settled on to our new course, but I knew the reprieve was only for four minutes, the time to reach St Matthew point on the mainland outside Brest. At this stage I flipped the bomb-fuse switch.

Slowly, the flashes on our left became more clearly defined. You could see centres of explosive activity within the turmoil, faint lines of searchlights swaying across it. Coming nearer our turning point we began to see individual shell bursts from heavy AA, stabs of orange light high in the scene, and the longer you looked the more frequent these appeared, until finally there were no black gaps in the top layer of stabbing lights. This tumult of flashes and explosions created an arc which blotted out the stars on the eastern horizon, and you could see the shimmer of the port propeller against the flickering background. Directly ahead of us, however, was pure blackness all the way to the stars – then John's voice came through to change that peaceful prospect.

'Alter course o-seven-five.'

There was no need to look at the re-set gyro to watch the numbers roll past. You knew his figure would come up when we were pointing directly into the middle of all that venomous activity. Sure enough, we were exactly on his course when the chaos of splintering, streaking, exploding light was centred in the front perspex. As we approached it the light flak became visible below the heavy AA explosions, first as thin pale lines, then developing colour as we drew nearer, flame-red, orange, and a silvery white. And then John switched to bombsight to ensure there was no averting the maelstrom:

'Left, left. Steady. Steady. Hold it there.'

Perhaps I had edged away subconsciously, slight pressure on the right rudder to divert from the centre of the fury. It was too much, just a flit through the edge was all I wanted, just a spice of danger, not a plunge into the middle. Inexorably, however, he forced me with deadly precision back into line for the centre. It was like a hellish forest, a tangle of fiery trunks below a canopy of stabbing explosions, with great shafts of searchlights swaying about in the turmoil. The heavy AA explosions formed a rough rectangle from about eight to twelve thousand feet, we were heading towards the base where it merged into the top curves of varicoloured light flak.

The altimeter showed we were above our planned height of eight thousand feet, so I was happy to drop down to the figure set on the bombsight. The streaks of light flak were slightly less frightening than the fiery explosions of heavy AA shells. As we drew nearer the barrage I loosened the throttle nut and began a slight wriggling movement of the two levers. The Germans were known to use sonar for gun control, and it was said this could be upset by desynchronizing the engines, and although dubious about the theory I kept twisting my hand nevertheless in urgent desire to do something. The noise was a petty distraction, too, like Gregorian chant heard in the distance, deep murmuring background with a frequent thudding accent . . . wah-oooo . . . wah-oooo . . . wah-wah-waaaah . . . wah . . . wah . . . wah-oooo . . . wah-oooo.

I could still glimpse stars above; below us, however, there was so much smoke that the firing guns made not distinct explosions but continuous widely diffused flashes that created a barrier to sight. I was trying to pick out the harbour entrance when suddenly we seemed to be caught up in a current that swirled us swiftly into the maelstrom. A shell burst close to our left, the flash so savagely bright I was blinded for a moment, the aircraft juddered from the explosion, and as vision returned I glimpsed the small black cloud fleeting past the port wing.

What surprised me was that I had *heard* the explosion. I thought at first we must have been hit; it never occurred to me – nor had anyone ever told me – that you could actually hear above the roar of your engines the sound of an AA shell exploding nearby. In the next minute or so I had learned that lesson for ever. Also that there was a smell to an AA barrage – the smell you associate with a smoking gun barrel, acrid cordite.

The density of tracer and explosions and searchlights all about us was such that I tried to limit view of it, concentrating sight on one particular line of flame-coloured light flak just to the left of our line.

But it was impossible to ignore the streaks and flashes that kept obliterating it. Crowding and cramming and engulfing us. Surely the three minutes must now be up? Had we been hit? John killed? Or me? Three searchlights were groping about near us like tentacles of a monstrous squid, I tried to focus on them alone, to ignore all other threats, but then a stream of the red light flak came shooting up like hosed fire directly in front of us and instinctively I swung away to avoid it. John commanded me back instantly into line:

'Right. Right. Steady.'

The flaming stream came straight up at us, lazily down below but then speeding up rapidly to zip past like a flash – in front, across, from behind. The coloured light flak seemed to be closing in on us, like a crowd converging on a gateway, some of the lines with a swerve in the middle when the gunner must have been swinging the barrel. Suddenly the aircraft shook, just a quick sharp shiver that caused me to grip the wheel more tightly, and again John called me back into steady line. This time I came back at him:

'Can't you see the bloody docks?'

'Difficult to pick them out.'

I would have thought impossible. Down below I could see nothing but streams of coloured lines shooting up out of a flickering cloud of smoke. The searchlights could penetrate it, one swung across the cockpit in a painful blinding flash, and I ducked below the perspex with eyes clenched tight to reclaim night-sight. When I dared look up again another searchlight came slanted up to stand still directly in front of us, one with a markedly different bluish light, looking so sinister that impulsively I banked away to the right to pass clear of it. The awful result was that John lost whatever sight he had glimpsed of the target area, and called out, 'No good. We'll have to try again.'

'For Christ sake!'

But the release from his terrible discipline was something of a relief. I opened the throttles wide, pulled the 9-boost and put the nose down in a dive that sent us searing through the coloured streaks, both hands pumping the stick ever forward until sudden concern about balloons made me jerk it back to level flight. By then we were through, ahead was only safe blackness.

Once in the clear I continued at the same height for a minute or more, then began to circle as we considered the return run. The cockpit stank of cordite and I slammed back the window to clean the air. We were then about five miles east of the docks and down below I could see within the vague pattern of black woodland and ghostly pasture the long glimmering finger of an estuary. I kept this as a guide while we circled in a steady climb, and told John we would make the run in the reverse direction, across the docks and then straight on out to sea, adding ungraciously – and to a sense of subsequent shame: 'And let's make bloody sure of it this time.'

'Hard to see, Pat,' he said. 'They've sure got some guns down there.'

They also had smoke. This may have been partly the artificial stuff from the smoke pots, but the mass of exploding shells in the barrage created varying levels of smoke that did not dissipate because it was continuously renewed. The upstreaming coloured flak seemed to shoot out of haloes of their own separate colours, but it was difficult to see even the vague location of any heavy guns because the whole smoke mass was pulsating with their explosions. I gave John a new speed of 300 for the second run, and to achieve this I used the boost and slanted down from twelve thousand feet in a shallow dive that would put us back at eight thousand feet as we entered the barrage again.

Even in this attitude, when I could see the target area for most of our approach, I still found it impossible to pick out any natural detail such as a distinct shoreline or a promontory. The whole town-harbour area was obliterated by the dense tangle and turmoil of exploding lights. When we plunged into the mass I tried to note details of colour and height to report, another attempt at distractive concentration, but this lasted only seconds before I was impelled to blink and hunch head against shoulder when a stream of whitish stuff came up at us with a hissing wail to explode close above in four thunderous blows: bok-bok-bok-bok. I narrowed vision right down to just a slit, a venetian blind to cut out as much of the fierce light as possible, then had to open up when an entirely different type of light flak went flashing past. It was like the stuff they called 'flaming onions' in the trenches, a string of about half a dozen balls of fire that came up in clusters and seemed to be associated with a green-tinted flak, because both followed the same sweeping line. I could feel my hands shaking in the urge to push the aircraft forwards, to ram a way through the barrage regardless of purpose, let the bombs go down anywhere into the inferno and get ourselves out of it.

This time John did drop them, and the jump the aircraft gave when they were released was echoed in my heart. We dived on down for escape to the sea.

Afterwards, well clear of the harbour entrance, I turned to have a look. Now that it was over you could thrill to the risk taken, delight in the escape, enjoy the wonder of being alive. But that night the mood of relaxation allowed to surface guilt about the way I had snapped at John. He came back to sit beside me presently, apparently unperturbed, made himself a cigarette and lit one of his Sweet Caporals for me, and then I gave my apology:

'Sorry I blew up about that first run.'

'You were right. I should have let them go. The second run was just the same. You can't see anything through all that firepower.'

We four in 53 Squadron all got back without a scratch, but one of the Beauforts failed to return. We were the last to report to operations, to tell the simple tale of bombs dropped 'in the target area' and attempt to answer the questions put by the patient I.O. He wanted you to live again every instant of the experience, recall every detail in the hope you could add to the store of information available for future briefings. You rubbed your stubbly chin as you tried to answer accurately, gulped the hot sweet tea, and pointlessly lit another cigarette.

Afterwards, exhausted after only a five-hour flight, we slumped into the back of the van, and said not a word as we were driven back down the narrow winding road to our hotel on the foreshore. There to sleep – in joy of life, and secret pleasure at having cheated death.

We were not alone in our blindness over the target area of Brest. One of the most experienced and successful bomber pilots of the war was Wing Commander Gibson; he had completed three tours of bomber operations before he earned his Victoria Cross for that attack on the dams, and he continued afterwards on operations until being finally shot down to his death over Germany. (I suspect he was the author of the quote at the beginning of this chapter.) He told how he always watched for his bomb bursts so as to be able to record exactly how successful the attack had been, but he had bombed Brest and there, he said, this was not possible; there the amount of anti-aircraft fire was such that individual bomb bursts could never be identified within the turmoil. He wrote:

The ships were not sunk in Brest because the bomb crews could rarely see them; in fact, the glare of hundreds of searchlights, many decoys, thousands of flak shells filling the sky over the small target area made it impossible to hit even the docks, let alone the ships. The only way to be sure to get even near the dock area was to do a timed five-minute run from a nearby island.

So, many years afterwards, reading the expert's opinion, I realized that it had not been such a bad first effort on our part, after all.

Chapter 8

From the bungalow veranda one afternoon in the Solomon Islands I saw a sudden flash on the calm blue surface behind an outrigger canoe beyond the offshore reef. Squinting to focus on it, I could at first see nothing but a man in a canoe, then I noticed movement above and saw sharply clear against the horizon a kite of some sort in the sky behind him. It was such an incongruous mixture, canoe and kite, that I went down to the beach where a Melanesian, red hibiscus in his bleached curly hair, was wading ashore with a gaudy orange-striped lilac bêche-de-mer impaled on his spear – the Chinese bought them for soup. As I stopped there was again that flash behind the canoe and this time I glimpsed something below the kite, an object bobbing about the surface and giving that occasional flash of reflection that had first attracted me.

'Savvy this one?' I asked the Melanesian, pointing to the canoe.

He did, and was delighted to explain. The man in the canoe was fishing. He had fashioned a bamboo kite, from the tail of which a line hung down to the water; attached to its end was a wodge of a local cobweb that was particularly viscous and tough – it could even trap small birds. There was a type of garfish which launched itself into the air to land amid a school of small fish near the surface, stunning some and so grabbing a meal, and as the canoeist paddled into wind the trailing kite kept the sticky ball of web flittering about the surface and giving silver flashes like the undersides of turning fish. A garfish must have so struck as he was explaining the technique to me, for suddenly the kite was pulled wriggling down to the water. The canoeist backpaddled to pluck it dripping clear, then dragged in the tail line and the ball of web with (so the Melanesian declared) a garfish clogged into it by its teeth.

It was an exhibition of the sort of magical expertise that makes you laugh aloud. It was particularly delightful that day because a friend then taking a siesta had been out all morning with his expensive gear and had caught nothing. He had a library of fishing books, always went off in the launch with a clutter of hooks and spinners and rods, but for all his equipment and theories he was still no match for the man with practical experience in those waters. Instead of relying on advice from armchair experts, he should have gone to local people on the job and asked how to catch garfish.

We pilots at St Eval were locals on a job. One afternoon that May five of us at briefing discovered we had between us done thirty-two night strikes on Brest. Though Bomber Command occasionally diverted a few squadrons from their war against Germany to attack the harbour, the vast majority of their pilots never knew Brest, whereas we had aircraft over the harbour nearly every night that spring. The numbers were trivial, often just a single aircraft, but it meant we did have a rare fund of experience about Brest. Yet no one ever came to St Eval to ask if any of us had any ideas how to hit the battleships. We were required only to carry out the order to bomb the docks, to answer questions on return, then sit quiet to await more orders. It is possible – I put it no higher – that staff officers read the reports we made on return, but none ever came to ask what method we, in practice, found most effective, or whether we had any ideas that might help prevent the ships leaving harbour again to savage our convoys.

Yet we were not just bee-brained workers flying mindlessly backwards and forwards on a prescribed line. We were capable of creative thought, and though only junior officers we did have more practical experience than anyone else in the world in the particular task of attacking those battleships in the harbour at Brest. So naturally we had ideas on the subject.

What about using the Resistance to report results of a series of timed-run attacks from different directions, so determining the most effective? Bomb the dock area in formation in moonlight? Put a Brest harbour layout of tarred lines on Dartmoor, or on floats at sea, and practise different methods on that? Have seminars when all the crews could discuss methods and ideas with the scientists, specialist officers, and senior staff at Command? There may have been difficulties with these schemes but we would have been eager to respond to them in discussion. And would have become *involved*. But no one wanted to hear, so the flow of ideas would usually degenerate into absurdities – such as having the Resistance put huge magnets on the docks to attract our bombs. If no one is interested in your studied efforts then you may as well go on an imaginative spree with the problem, and to hell with the staff.

It is curious that the government did ask civilians for ideas to deal with German night bombers. Over a million sent suggestions – only two were thought worth testing, none ever used – but the appeal did make people feel personally involved in the problem, and more sympathetic about it. Yet we who were going out night after night to attack the battleships were never encouraged towards such intimate cooperation. Had we been invited into such an alliance with authority we would have had a different level of interest – even of commitment.

We did carry out a private test to compare John's bombsighted drops against my dives. We flew at eight thousand feet over the range with eight smoke bombs, dropping two on four different courses, one under John's direction, the second by me in a dive that released at the same height. Though none fell within the bulls-eye, every one of mine was closer, not significantly but without argument. John made his judgement at once. I should do the bombing in future.

The difference did not seem to me to call for such a rigid decision, nor did I so react. Thereafter we varied our method of attack according to target and my mood at the time. Except for low-level attacks, when I always did the bombing, John would usually set up the bombsight and stay forrard on it, but the final decision dwelt with me, and if inclined I would interrupt his patient, 'Left . . . left . . . steady,' with an impatient, 'I'll take it,' then ram the stick forward and go plunging into the dive attack.

This was sometimes a genuine tactical decision. On non-Brest targets, for example, you would often see a clear height-line for all the heavy AA shell bursts, suggesting that their sonar readings were concentrated on another aircraft, so it made practical sense then to dive under the barrage or climb above it to drop the bombs before they switched attention to you. And I did try a glide attack one night, as it was said to confuse their sonar – we received such concentrated fire that I never tried the stunt again.

However, the truth is that whenever I took over in the block-barrage of a well-defended target the decision was almost invariably selfish. I could not bear to sit there passive, keeping on steadily under his instructions with AA and flak exploding and streaming all about us. I felt impelled to take counter action. To hurl something back at them. So I would abruptly seize command, ram down the nose in a screaming dive, start swearing at the opposition and even opening fire with the puny wing gun, then at bomb-release point would jerk back the control column as if physically hurling the bombs against the target. The result may not have been that much better than under John's control, but the psychological benefit to me was immeasurable. He never criticized such takeovers, and I squashed any nonsense from my own conscience about it.

For it knew well enough the motive for taking over. Fear can get a grip on you when sitting passive, but a fury of action blasts away the insidious growth. From talk in the crew room it was clear I was not unique in my self-centred seizure of control. You were always hearing pilots tell of their reactions in moments of fearful stress: 'I decided I'd have a crack at *them* for a change' . . . 'So I dived straight at them' . . . 'I thought, I'll show the bastards.' No one ever mentioned discussing these impulses with the crew. But although such impulsive action by the pilot could kill them all, I never heard any crew member complain. Indeed, when they spoke together about a reckless action by their pilots it was with affectionate pride, like a parent telling of a child's daring impertinence. I marvel now at the forbearance shown by our navigators and gunners.

After two more trips when it was not possible to test the dive technique, we were on Brest again the following week. It was not a successful night. There was such a mass of cloud over the whole peninsula that on arrival we must have flown in blackness directly over the harbour without a glimpse of it; nor any acknowledgement either, for the guns always wisely held fire on cloudy nights, waiting to make sure we did know they were below before assuring us of this. I decided to go above the cloud to see if I could gauge its nature and extent.

It is always a surprise emerging from a long stint in cloud, you become adjusted to the apparent lack of movement, of sitting in something like a boiler room with the furnace roaring away and you just watching the dials, then abruptly you and the room are ejected into the clear with cloud tops wisping past as you hurtle upwards catapulted into space. That night I climbed to some fifteen thousand feet for a clearer picture of the cloud mass; the silvered crescent moon and a million stars then showed up a white chaos of cloudscape down below us, peaks and bulges and canyons and chasms, with here and there a ragged black hole down into the nether region of earth. There was no hope of discovering our target from up there, so we plunged down again through a gigantic crevice into the darkness and there flew about for half an hour without being able to sight anything identifiable. I headed south where better weather had been predicted. Eventually John called from the front, 'Coastline below. See it?'

The cloud had begun to break up, wraiths of it whipping past our wing tips, and within a clear area the crescent moon gave enough light for me to discern smudges below that were just the faintest shade lighter than the wide black surround. By keeping them constantly in sight I was able to descend safely to within a few hundred feet of the sea when John identified them as the Glénans islets north of Lorient. He then tried to map-read us up the coast, as I stayed beneath the cloud which was based at about a thousand feet, but again it became more and more solid the further north we returned.

We finally came to a strip of white beach that was afterwards to become our regular guide line in strikes against the Brest dockyards. It is near the centre of Douarnenez Bay and the line points directly to the dock area of Brest. We might have done better had I changed the flight plan and made a straight run across the harbour at once, for the guns were not firing and we might have been able to see the actual docks by light filtering through the cloud gaps. But I flew straight on to the eastern flank to make the attack, as we had originally planned – and meanwhile the rain clouds also moved steadily over the town.

The searchlights were already groping about as we moved into position and the barrage finally exploded into action just after we turned to make our bombing run, and it was that which showed clearly the rapid deterioration of visibility. At first when I put the nose down to start the approach I was able to see the river east of the town, and that at least gave me the line to the dock area, but when we plunged into the barrage, into the centre of an immense machine that had suddenly seized and was disintegrating in explosion, it was impossible to discern anything outside. The explosive flashes and the coloured flak transformed the thinner low clouds into sheets of dazzling opacity, and about us as we continued the dive the high cloud came whipping past, all mixed up with shell smoke and blinding lights, so that the only guide left to me in the end was the compass heading on which we had started the dive – and that was only a rough guide, being jabbed and jerked about as we were by the ferocity of the barrage.

The bombs went down when I reckoned we were in the centre of the turmoil, and still vaguely on line. A moment afterwards we were in dense active cloud which seemed to whiten all the flak, or perhaps simply blotted out the coloured stuff. It gave the impression we were totally engulfed in enormous white seas. Our last contact with the defences was a spectacular curving trail first of green-tinted and then orange shells, lighting up vividly the edge of the writhing mass of cloud we had just escaped. John had a rare comment: 'Kinda pretty, those two colours all alone.'

As a comparison of bombing methods the sortie merely confirmed what the old hands had told us – you could never check results over Brest. On inspection at dispersal next day they discovered we had been hit. In the port wing was a hole about the size of my fist where a piece of shrapnel had cut straight through without touching the ribs. The flight sergeant photographed it.

One pilot who never handed over bombing to his navigator was the fair-haired Thomas whose gay recklessness I so admired. His solution to the Brest problem was to go up to an immense height, about twenty thousand feet, so he could gauge with some accuracy the centre of the barrage, then he would spiral down into it and bomb at balloon height – even below it on one occasion. He was nearly through his operational tour when I joined the squadron, but despite his experience under fire still treated the war as an exciting game. After he had bombed at night he would usually stay around to pick off searchlights on the perimeter with his guns while the others were bombing, and he was always making darts inland when he had nothing to show for an anti-shipping patrol. He would tell these stories of extracurricular activity not to boast but so that we could share his fun, rather like a schoolboy telling of a stunt that had discomfited the masters.

He was always trying to persuade us to tune our radio for R'T over the target area. We were not supposed to do this, they said it gave away your position, but if guns were already blazing away at you this struck me as a ludicrous argument. In fact, as the R'T was of no use in contacting base, and you were reasonably forbidden to transmit when on anti-shipping or convoy patrols, we rarely tried to set it up. But Thomas and I did make contact one night on a Lorient raid.

Our target was the submarine depot and I thought we were the first to arrive because the area was in calm darkness. It was a clear night, the moon was full, and we stayed inland from the target area at about twelve thousand feet as I considered the approach. We were too far to discern the actual submarine pens beyond the town, but the town itself was clearly visible; lines of streets and blocks of open areas on the edge of the glinting estuary, a place of blue and silver mystery. I decided to attack from inland, pass north of the town on to the submarine pens, then continue out into the Atlantic. When to start?

This question about timing had no simple answer. Tactical considerations such as visibility, orientation, state of readiness, type of bomb carried, and so on, might justifiably determine whether you went ahead on arrival or delayed; but there was also a less scrupulous consideration that was pertinent over non-Brest targets where the defence, unable to put up such massive gunfire, tried to concentrate on individual aircraft. There you could wait until someone else was getting all the attention, then dash in quickly and out again before they had finished with him. That night on Lorient I was undecided whether to start the ball rolling or wait for someone else to do it. As we loitered on the outskirts waiting for decision to come, the gunner did try to set up the R'T as promised to Thomas. To my surprise we found him, calling the world for an answer.

'X X-ray here. X X-ray. Anyone around? Over?'

He sounded as if he had been appealing for hours. I called him back and he pounced on the contact with delight. He was out over the sea, he told me – and any German listener – had not yet bombed but had made a run across 'just to see what they had for us tonight; it's not much'. After this exchange, with still no sign of the other two Blenheims on the raid, and our droning presence having put the defences at the ready, he made a most acceptable offer.

'I'll go in first. And slow,' he called. 'Then you go across when they open up, and you can see where ours fall. A lesson for you colonial types.'

So that was the way we did it, on our different lines of attack from our immediate positions, John on the bombsight doing our drop. The flak, although below the effusive display at Brest, was still disturbing enough and it was clear Thomas must have dived to a much lower level than us. The Germans were good at height detection, you could see the defence make use of that expertise, putting up a box barrage of heavy AA about Thomas's height then lowering it as he approached the submarine pens, the intention being to force him down into the light flak zone. You could pick out the concentrated area of light flak by the crossing lines, it was too thin to discern colour from a distance but once within range the whole looked like a hellish garden spray down below us, none of the greenish stuff, just orange and flame, presently interspersed with the bright stabbing explosions of heavy shells that must have been fused at an unusually low level.

This smaller, precise type of barrage, could be like the view of an orchestra in full play – the bows of the violins were the light flak streaking up and down and across, slightly above was the confused movements of brass and wind instruments, and at the top was the great thunder and clashing of cymbals and drums. Thomas was at the right level for that picture, ours that night was a more vertical and chaotic view. We bombed from seven thousand feet, flashing through a searchlight but otherwise no contact at all, no juddering of aircraft, no smoke, no smell of cordite.

We failed to pick out Thomas's bombs, however; there was a concentration of guns about the submarine pens, their explosive flashes were not all the same, so it was difficult to distinguish bombs from gun flashes. John, lying down in front at the bombsight, had the target area in sight even when we had finished our run and saw ours overshoot, but failed to sight Thomas's. Once safely out over the starlit sea we switched on the R'T to find Thomas waiting.

'We saw ours ourselves,' he told us. 'Bang on. Yours overshot. You colonial types can't compete with the English gentry.'

The following night, the last time I saw Thomas, was in the Club at Newquay. He was sitting on the stairs swopping stories with three torpedo boys from 22 Squadron, and I arrived as he was telling a story I already knew. He had bombed a ship near La Rochelle and instead of returning to base decided to have a look at Belle Île because, he explained, 'I'd never called there before.' The island is about ten miles long, and Thomas was flying low along the main road, a sunny afternoon with not a care in the world, when suddenly he 'almost ran into a gendarme on a bicycle'. The gendarme was travelling in the same direction, must have heard the Blenheim, turned when it was almost on him and hurled himself aside into the ditch.

'I felt sorry for the poor sod,' Thomas said. 'We're not fighting French gendarmes after all.'

So he went back, circled the gendarme who had picked himself up apparently unharmed, and flew in low to drop a packet of cigarettes stuffed into a silk inner glove – sending the gendarme into the ditch again. This was about midday, on an island with at least one AA battery to my knowledge, and midway between St Nazaire and Lorient which both had enemy fighter airfields. Whenever I think of Thomas it is that night in Newquay that comes to mind, sitting on the stairs, a glass of beer in his hand, flipping back his blond hair after the laughter. At that time he had three more trips to finish his tour of operations, and was hoping to persuade Tubby to allow him to do a second tour. But the following night he went missing for ever when out with me in a strike on Brest.

Those offshore islands in the Bay of Biscay were never official targets but illicit calls were often made, and a few pilots dropped unofficial bombs on the German radio station at Ushant when returning from a fruitless anti-shipping patrol – the explanation for missing bombs was that you had jettisoned them at sight of a German fighter. We ourselves paid a visit to Ushant in late April on return from one of these anti-shipping patrols, but not to get rid of bombs – I had already blundered them away.

We had taken off in darkness and run into a frontal system off the Brest peninsula just after dawn. The cloud bank continued all the way down to our turning point off the Île d'Yeu, but base was two thousand feet and little rain associated with it, so we had a wide area of visibility. But no sightings. It was on the return, when we moved in closer to the south coast of Lorient where cloud was patchy, that I bungled it.

Coming out of a squall at about a thousand feet into a brilliantly clear area, blue sky and sea, flashing sunlight on blinding white cloud, we saw the ship. It was a naval supply vessel – about two thousand tons, long forward cargo section with a gun seemingly unmanned, on the rear deck a Bofors-type gun with active figures about it. I slammed the stick forward to attack at once, otherwise we had to circle in that cloud-free area without knowing where the customary fighter escort was positioned. They opened fire with the stern gun as we screamed down in the dive, and the tracer came streaking up at us and seemed to disappear right between my eyes – some sort of optical illusion, I think the shells passed above. Figures were moving towards the other gun when I let the bombs go. We were then at about three hundred feet and I had to stand stiff on the rudder pedals for leverage to pull back the stick, helping it with two quick flips of the trim.

Shooting back up again towards the cloud in a climbing turn we were able to see the ship clearly again, still with only the stern gun jetting up a stream of shells at us. We flew out of range. There was an eleven-second delay on the bombs so we stayed out of cloud, watching for fighters, waiting for the explosions. The other gun opened fire but it too fell away short. Eleven seconds or more passed. Nothing happened. The little white streak astern showed she was still moving, but nothing else. No eruption aboard, no great spouts of water from nearby, no mark of our attack anywhere in the scene. There had been four 250-pound bombs, all four of them must have been duds or . . . or . . .

'Oh, no!' I cried.

John turned sharply. I said nothing, just banged at the bomb switch. The safety link in the nose of a bomb must be withdrawn before detonation can take place, when you press the arming switch a clip in the bomb bay closes over this link and retains it as the bomb drops away, now able to detonate on its set timing. Rushing so urgently into attack I had forgotten to press the switch. Our bombs had gone down with safety links still in place, rendering them mere lumps of inert metal. I was furious at the wasted opportunity and at myself for the blunder. And it was not something you could hide. On return the armourer would see the links were gone from the bomb bay, it was his job to check for them after an attack. To claim an electrical fault would brand me even more ridiculous, for that excuse had long since passed beyond belief.

That was probably the main reason why we went to Ushant that particular day, as petty compensation for the blunder, but the temptation to savour the excitement of a daylight visit had made such a call more or less inevitable. John simply nodded when told, then ducked down into his forward compartment to work out a course.

He stayed beside me on return, as we headed for the island underneath cloud that was now solid, and leaden, and low. We flew about twenty feet above a dark grey sea flecked with white and lined with wind-streaks, window open and the smell of the sea coming in with a roar. It took only about ten minutes to get there, directed finally by haloes of foam about the offshore rocks, and given an aiming point by the wireless masts that soon emerged dark against the horizon. I kept watching them as we sped towards the rocky foreshore, so low we seemed to be skittering across the broken water, bouncing on the white crests of successive waves.

As we crossed the coast I swung to port, away from the direct line of the masts so as to make sure of missing their widespread triangle of stays. We were still banking in turn as we passed, I opened fire on the guardhouse at the site entry, Davy blasted off at the camouflaged blockhouse between the masts. The gun position near the guardhouse had no chance to open fire, I saw no movement, except on the tarred road leading to the site a man was driving a horse and cart loaded with something lumpy green like cabbages. Then we were streaking up a slope of pasture, so low we had to pull up slightly to cross over the brown rock wall at the top of the slope. And it was then, as we curved over the wall, I caught a snapshot.

On my left, about fifteen yards away, was a brown and white cow. It was facing away from our track, we flew along its flanks so to speak, its head was down in a wicker basket. On our side of it a woman was squatting, or sitting on a low stool, covered by her full cherry-red skirt, grey scarf on her head. Her hands were extended to the cow's udder, shocked still as we exploded into sight over the wall. She was already looking in our direction, mouth and eyes all circles – then the tableau was out of actual sight, just the clear imprint left. I don't know the effect of our passage on the woman and cow, both John and the gunner were looking out the other side and saw nothing. Beyond the field was a stone cottage with a column of blue smoke streaming up from a squat chimney, we flew straight through it then shot up to a thousand feet over the sea and I slid the window shut to trap the homely scent of wood fire. It had taken about forty seconds to cross the island, and although I had seen the woman so clearly just a few yards away, her hands stilled and looking straight at us, I could not tell if she was twenty or eighty years old; all I could see in my mind were her circles of petrified astonishment as we flashed past.

I cut out John from the debriefing, said he had diarrhoea and was still down in the hangar, for he would have no part in deceit; in the embarrassing session with the Intelligence Officer I told him we had come back wide of Ushant as usual after the blunder. Only if you noticed some sign of enemy activity on these unofficial calls did you report it, and then somehow solve the problem of justifying your presence there. We saw a truck towing a gun across a field on an islet off St Nazaire one dawn, the information had to be passed on, and our excuse was that we happened to finish there after the futile chase of a German four-engined Condor plane. The debriefing officer on this occasion was Shackleton and he accepted the story without comment, but I doubt he believed it. They were not unintelligent, the intelligence officers at St Eval in 1941.

Often at debriefing you would be surprised yourself at what they uncovered in questioning. I would sometimes look at a scene for private record, colours and patterns of flak seen from the periphery, the white walls of a French village in moonlight, faint tonal differences in a landscape at night, all deliberately noted in mind with the intention of recording it afterwards. You memorized items in the scene. But Shackleton at debriefing could make you recall details you thought you had not even seen, let alone marked in mind for record. He did it by studied questions and prompts, taking you over the sortie right from the beginning, with the result that a crew member would sometimes see the unfiled picture and cry, 'Yes, that's right. There *was* a gun-site the other side of the river.'

In Bomber Command the tired crews went to bed on return, were debriefed next day. Most of us preferred our system; not only were you more likely to remember details if drawn at once, but you could relax completely afterwards. All that most crews wanted to do after a rough sortie was put it out of mind, go back to the hotel, and sleep.

There were times, however, when I would have been happy to stay out all night on the sortie. This was after the attack, after the emotional turmoil of fear and excitement and rage and God knows what other passions that possessed you as you plunged through the barrage. It was when all that was over, out in the soft safe darkness of the Atlantic, there were times when the flight home was the indelible memory of the sortie, the bombing run nothing but a mere prelude to the ecstasy of the return. On each of those nights a near-full moon was sharply bright in a star-filled sky. That was the crucial factor.

I have a vivid memory of the spell cast by the full moon when I was a child. I was about seven at the time, boarding at a Dominican convent twenty miles from home, a day school for girls with the couple of dozen of us small boys as boarders. There were two dormitories, mine for the younger children had a partitioned section in one corner where Sister Francesca slept. One night I was awakened by the moon shining across the balcony directly on my face. The effect was bewitching. I felt compelled to go out into the magical light. It must have been very late, no sound nor light anywhere as I stole out to the washroom, took off my pyjamas and put them under the end basin, unbolted the door and stepped out on to the landing at the top of the covered staircase. Moving quietly down the stairs I kept looking through the lattice towards the nuns' quarters where all was in darkness. At the bottom before stepping out into the glorious moonlight, I paused to have a last look around to ensure no one was about – an extraordinary precaution when you consider how irrational the whole action was.

I launched myself naked out into the enchanting light of the moon, running across the patio to the playground on the far side of the classroom. It was used by the older girls, the ten- and eleven-year-olds, for netball, and when I ran to the far end I swung myself around the post and leapt to touch the base of the net. Then back to the centre of the field where I flung my arms high and danced about in wild abandon for perhaps a minute or more. Beyond the low wall of the playground was a road, and on the far side a row of houses all with verandas, from any of which a roused sleeper could have witnessed this small boy's extraordinary antics. I didn't care. The ground itself was hard and stony, could have cut my feet badly. I didn't care. Nothing mattered against the thrill of dancing under the silver moon with the night air soft against the naked body. After that whirling fling in the middle of the playground I ran lightly to the netball post at the lower end of the field, again leapt to stroke the net, then went dancing back over the bricked area to the foot of the stairs.

What on earth would I have said had I found Sister Francesca waiting at the washroom door? The naked body would have made it not just an act of inexplicable madness but a mortal sin, possibly even a case of possession by the devil. I was regarded as an inventive story-teller but would have been hard pushed to provide an explanation to the Mother Superior had I been caught. Strange also is that I have no great passion for dancing, no dream of performing immortal interpretation by Nijinsky, or flailing about the stage in a brilliant Astaire routine. It was just an active child's response to the spell of the moon.

It was the same moon delight that made some of those return flights so special. The first was at the end of April, when out on a Brest raid again. Under such conditions, full moon and cloudless sky, the defence opened up with everything the instant we came within range, because there was obviously no chance of us failing to find the harbour. We ran straight across the docks from the south with John directing on this occasion, and though the barrage was as tumultuous as ever nothing came close enough to move us off line. But a moment after John gave the call of 'Bombs gone!' we were caught in searchlights.

I had banked steeply towards the harbour exit when the bombs thumped clear, so the brilliant light hit me full in the face like an explosion. I ducked down, but even when sight began to return the light in the cockpit was diamond hard as the searchlight held us, and I had to keep my head bowed near the blind-flying panel, hand over my eyes, to see anything at all. I knew when caught in a cone that your height could be calculated instantly, the guns then ranged to perfection. The recommended drill was to undulate in straight flight, but I went for speed as we were already headed for the harbour entrance. In my hunched position the forward pressure for the dive came more from shoulders than hands and the speed built up rapidly to well over 350 m.p.h. It was impossible to see if the guns were concentrating on us but I could hear them, and one blast of exploded air that thudded against us was like the ground impact in a heavy landing. There was a series of those bok-bok-bok explosions and then, just as I began to haul back on the stick, a crackling thunder-like sound. I thought for a moment there had been some catastrophic airframe failure, for the Blenheim was shivering in stressful speed and I was plunged into the seat by the centrifugal force of the pull-out. But we were intact. And out of the searchlights.

There is no sudden sweet blackness after you escape searchlights, the glare lingers in your eyes after it has left your face, and I kept my head down near the panel for a few moments afterwards. We were by this time well below balloon height so the instant sight did return I looked up and to my relief saw a dark slab of forest on a hillside and not a single streak of flak ahead – I must have turned right during the dive. We flashed over a crossroad with a scatter of white houses nearby, grey smoke was spread like gauze over a dark tree-lined stream, then a ragged edge of cliffs, broken water, and we were away into the wide expanse of the moonlit Atlantic.

At that stage the feeling was simply of relief. We were through, another operational sortie in the bag. I climbed to two thousand feet where attentive flying was no longer necessary, opened the window for crisp clean air, and set course for home. It was then, slowly and gently, that the spell of the full moon shining above the blur of the port propeller began to take effect. John stayed forward, I was alone in the cockpit, all instruments were settled steady, the engines perfectly synchronized for once and giving off that metallic ringing sound they did when running sweetest, my hands resting only lightly on the wheel for the plane was almost flying itself in the calm, cool night. The silver light in the cockpit was so bright that the phosphorescent dials were only dully visible, just the compass low in the shadows by my knee showed the needle aligned and brightly steady in jet-black liquid. I could feel the moonlight on my face, as sensitively aware of its light as one is to the warmth of the sun when you first stretch out on the beach.

That was what made the night so special – all care gone, smoothed away by the spell of the moon. I don't know if the other two that night felt any such mystical bliss as we went ringing our way across the moonlit sea towards England, I dared not ask such a question – no more than I would have dared ask any other small boy back at the convent if they too had ever felt compelled to run naked in the open under the bright silver moon. The feeling that night over the Atlantic was much the same as that earlier time, not of peace but delight, not quiet relaxation but enchantment with life.

I sang aloud in the cockpit that night, the sound covered by the noise of the engines. It was a song I came to sing on other nights afterwards when coming back from a raid. The words were the well-known Longfellow lines, the tune I made up myself that night over the deep moonlit blue of the Atlantic.

> And the nights shall be filled with music
> And the cares that infest the day

> Shall fold their tents like the Arabs
> And as silently steal away.

Back in the operations room we reported that we had bombed from seven thousand feet, results not observed. Little more than that, for this was Brest. The best of the night's events was of no interest to the Air Ministry. I kept that to myself.

Chapter 9

During that spring of 1941 there must have been well over a hundred aircrew officers at any one time on the five operational units at St Eval, and the faces were constantly changing, so the station commander could not be expected to know them all. Group Captain Revington, who had commanded a reconnaissance squadron earlier in the war, did come to know me, however, particularly after a meeting one night towards the end of April.

We were out that night on a strike against the naval base at La Pallice. On return I had dumped my parachute and was waiting outside the crew room for the others, listening to a nightjar whirring away like an electric pump in the hedgerow behind the hangar – I heard him sometimes in the day, too. It was a clear moonless night and high overhead between Orion and the Pole Star the brilliant Capella seemed to be vibrating in flashing light, and as I was looking at it there came the sound of an aircraft approaching low over the skeleton roof of the bombed hangar. The siren had not wailed but the deep throbbing sound was unmistakable. I yelled a warning to the others and dived down to flatten myself on the dew-sodden grass.

The bombs fell on the far side of the field – and then the siren sounded. As John and Davy came out we heard that deep Germanic engine sound again, and we all raced over to the control tower shelter. There I paused at the top of the steps to try and pick out the line of attack, and was startled to hear someone speaking in a perfectly normal voice above me in the dark tower. Our guns had not opened fire, and he could be heard clearly above the throb of the approaching aircraft.

'Coming from St Merryn direction. He's going to pass over this near side of the runway. Can I go down now, sir?'

I scrambled down inside the shelter. The bombs dropped in salvo, exploding close outside like a crackle of nearby thunder, and you felt a shuddering such as you get when driving over an iron ramp. I came up the steps again just in time to see a few rounds of red tracer from our only active gun streaming away after the raider in a gentle arc, like the slow-motion sequence of a ball in flight. But already the airman was back on the balcony, reporting in that same calm tone that the tender had gone to check if the runway had been affected.

The group captain was in the operations room, he called in sometimes to chat with crews being debriefed, but this night I got in first with my tribute to the unknown airman in the tower. Revington diluted special credit by extending it to all who served on airfield defence, but I insisted this was exceptional and deserved his notice. He promised then that he would go down and see the man presently – and he grinned at me as he added, 'You're the first pilot officer who's ever ordered me about my job.'

A few days after that he made some amicable comment about the incident when he joined me in the mess at dinner, clearly ignorant of a crime I had committed the previous night. I suspect that Tubby had deliberately withheld from him any information about this, having decided, quite rightly, I was unlikely ever to commit the offence again after feeling his own reaction to it.

It had occurred on a night strike against Lanveoc. The night before we had been forced to abort again because of failure to obtain 'W'T go', the third time that had occurred, so in preparation for the Lanveoc raid we did two successful radio tests during the afternoon. Yet after take-off that night we spent half an hour roaming about Cornwall without being able to make contact. When the gunner finally called through to admit failure, John, sitting beside me, banged the map-board on his knees in a unique display of impatience. Something had to be done, he urged. I told him we would go on; I had already made up my mind on this, confident I could spin some story on return that the Controller would accept – a misunderstanding on the intercom, something like that.

The strike itself was not an easy one. Three of us were on it but because we had been so delayed the other two had bombed and left for home by the time we arrived on the quiet scene. We came in from the south over the pallid sands of Douarnenez, then suddenly the blackness exploded as if on a prearranged signal; there was no build-up of a searchlight or two and a few hosings of coloured flak, the whole lot opened up against us in a shattering fanfare. We had planned that John would do a bombsight run on this, and he called from his prone position up front that the heavy AA across the bay was also firing at us.

Below us was a thin layer of alto-stratus at about eight thousand feet, with plenty of gaps to see the airfield, and above us as we approached was a ceiling of continuous stabbing explosions from the heavy AA. This began to lower as we drew near the target, and I kept easing the stick forward to stay under the explosions, calling out the height changes to John as I followed his calm instructions, 'Right . . . right . . . steady.'

Such was the height accuracy of the barrage, however, that I felt forced down gradually through the layer of alto-stratus, and in the last half minute or so we were flying close below a ceiling that was in eruption; orange and flame and sunflash-bright explosions seemed to be bursting out of the actual cloud layer which itself was lit up by the sweeping searchlights and coloured streaks of light flak. Although we passed through wisps of ashen smoke, nothing came close enough to blast us off course, but the smothering intensity of the explosions steadily closing down on us was unnerving. John too must have felt hemmed in by it all, for on dropping the bombs he called, 'Bombs away! Let's get the hell out of here.'

I put the nose down and swung violently to starboard, heading inland, for by then we had the harbour and full Brest barrage just ahead of us. In half a minute we were in the clear, then a wide turn brought us back well south of trouble and out over the starlit Atlantic. Only then did I realize my left hand was covered in blood, not from enemy action but as a result of the little finger being caught between the throttles when I was desynchronizing engines over the target area. The sharp edge of one throttle lever had cut through the glove. You really needed mailed fists to come away unbloodied from a Blenheim.

There remained the matter of preparing a story to explain why we had left the vicinity of St Eval without having obtained the obligatory blessing of 'W'T go'. A complication arose. I told John I proposed to say that I thought Davy had called through on the intercom the words 'Go, go', and only on return when he reported the radio *still* dead did I discover his original words had been 'No go'. But John, as I should have known, refused to support me in such a story; he said we had to tell the truth, and give our reason for deliberately disobeying the strict 'W'T go' order. So I decided to rely on a plea of special circumstances, of W'T failure for a second night running despite all our efforts to ensure it was working; I would express sincere regret, assure the Controller it would never happen again, and hope that would get us through without too much fuss.

However, it was Tubby who got to us first, not the Controller. When I climbed down the wing in the grey dawn that morning he was waiting, called me alone over to his car, and there blasted me. I did try to tell him how frustrated we felt at having to abort again despite such careful preparation, but this intensified his fury. Did I think his rule about W'T go was bullshit? Suppose it had been necessary to recall us? . . . target had been changed after take-off? . . . weather had deteriorated at base and we had to be diverted? . . . had a damaged aircraft that necessitated a belly landing? . . . were forced to ditch? Didn't I have any idea of my responsibilities in command of an aircraft? He finished up by ordering me out of his car, then slammed the door and spurted away, leaving us to search for the van to get us to the hangar and thence the operations room. There too I had a frosty reception.

That single sharp disagreement with Tubby did not mar our relationship. I liked him, and I think the feeling was reciprocated – twice he arranged to take a few days' leave with me. And he did fix us up with a number of different gunners after this episode. He was a considerate commanding officer and made positive efforts to establish close contact with us. You could chat freely with him in the mess where he would be drinking with us nearly every day, and from time to time he and his wife would have individuals or groups of us for an evening at his house.

However, despite his friendly nature and the calculated efforts he made to overcome the division, he did belong definitely to one of the distinct halves of the squadron. He was one of those who lived in rented accommodation with their wives; we others lived a bachelor existence at the Watergate Hotel. The married pilots came to the airfield only for duty, whereas we Watergate group would come up to the crew room and mess every day. We had our group habits and codes and talk, and when you met the married men with their wives at Tubby's house, and heard them chat about incidents and meetings and mutual acquaintances, you realized they too had a cohesive identity as intimate as ours in the crew room. That Tubby was one of their group, that his wife was close to the other wives, meant inevitably he knew far more about the married officers' lives than he did ours, their slightest malaise or worry would reach him quickly via female links and he could take action without the pilot ever having spoken a word.

Our secrets could not be so discovered. Later on in May I suddenly began to have spasms of severe pain in the lower spine after three or four hours in the cockpit. I dared not tell anyone nor report to the medical officer lest it be considered psychosomatic, so I went in civilian clothes one afternoon to a doctor in Newquay, telling him I was an accountant and that this pain occurred after sitting several hours at my desk. He prodded about my spine, questioned me at length about symptoms, and decided it was merely a posture problem. He said I should get up from the chair every hour or so, walk about the office a few moments and do some limbering-up exercises. He charged me ten and sixpence. The attacks ceased a little later on – despite not following his advice.

Had I been one of the married group Tubby would have heard about my problem, the medical resources of St Eval would have been brought into play, I might have been off flying for weeks. This was probably the reason why the married men took longer to complete their tour of operations than we did: some who had started a month before me had still to complete their tour when we had finished. There was no differentiation in flying duties, just in the knowledge of fitness to carry them out. The only way this squadron division could have been avoided would have been to ban wives from the area, but this would have been a cruel sentence on married couples. So for all Tubby's efforts to blur the distinctness, the two groups remained a fact of social as well as physical life.

You could detect also a difference in attitudes. The bachelor pilots were more irresponsible as a group, we were the risk-seekers; the married men simply carried out their briefed tasks. A pilot who would make an illicit flight inland searching for a target rather than bring back bombs after a wasted anti-shipping patrol, one who would stay on to shoot up a searchlight or two after he had bombed, or do a dummy run over a dockyard just to savour the flak, was not likely to be one whose wife was waiting sleeplessly back in a silent house in Cornwall, listening tensely for the sound of returning planes. All that awaited us on return was an empty hotel room, and an enticing alternative to that was to range about in the night in search of thrill.

And we were also younger on average than the married men – giving the lie to Housman's poem about young men killed in war:

> Life to be sure is nothing much to lose,
> But young men think it is, and we were young.

That was not my experience. Those I knew during the war who were most eager to put life at risk were all young men.

The out-living group contained all the senior officers with their defined responsibilities, so we crew-room group had to develop tacit equivalents for our own needs – someone to organize our transport, another to chase up technical notices, and so on. I became the person expected to deal with authority. This was not because of seniority or age – there were several who exceeded me in both. The reason may simply have been that as I did not mind tackling authority about a problem or a request then it was little to ask of me anyway. And in the field of flying safety and accident prevention in particular, there was a real need at times to ensure that authority did take action. Such an instance occurred with us one night when off on a strike against Lorient.

It was a dark night, no moon, the sky almost completely covered in cloud. All was perfectly normal at the half-way mark on the runway, the tail lifted just as we crossed the ridge and the speed had moved steadily up to 70 m.p.h. but then, with the last light in view and committed to take-off, we were suddenly in desperate trouble.

Speed was not increasing fast enough. Take-off and landing patterns were fully established in mind by this time, at that runway stage we should have reached 90 m.p.h. with the needle still turning upwards, but it was still pointing below 80 as the last runway light flashed past on my left. This was barely flying speed with a full bomb load, but nevertheless I had to ease back the stick or we would have crashed into the perimeter gun-site. She did lift clear. Instantly I jerked up the wheels, but then kept forward pressure on the stick to get flying speed. Yet still the needle was quivering about the 80 mark.

In daylight or bright moonlight your inspection of the instruments in take-off is perfunctory, you have external visual checks to aid the aural and tactile senses that tell you all is well. On dark nights, however, you have to rely on the instruments, and of these the vital one was the ASI, the Air Speed Indicator; a wobbly artificial horizon, tilted turn-and-bank, spinning gyro, flickering rate-of-climb, altimeter that said you were underground, control column pressing you to climb or dive, could all be disregarded against the evidence of the ASI. To ignore its evidence on a black night was to ignore the challenge of a nervous sentry. It was imperative to act on its message.

I did so. We needed speed to survive. So I kept the stick pressed forward, giving us a flat trajectory, and the needle did waver up to the 90 mark. But while my eyes were locked on the ASI dial my arms were in rapid search for the fault. All those hours of cockpit drill meant the movements were automatic, speeding ahead of mental decision. Right hand down to check selector, wheels, trim, and up for boost control, then take over the control column . . . left hand check throttles, mixture, and up behind to pitch. With the experience of all those hours of practice back in the hangar at Andover my hands flicked over the seven marks with perfect accuracy in little more than a single second. No groping about, no panic, and no doubt remaining afterwards. All was correct. Time then to look out into the black night.

I saw the black shape and jerked the stick back violently just a fraction before John shouted. He had been looking out all the time, had suffered two or three seconds of hell as we smeared over the concrete roof of the bomb dump, and saw the blacker shape ahead a fraction after me. We were squashed into our seats when I jerked back the stick, and though I could not recall hearing anything nor feeling any spasm in the control column, we discovered later that the starboard aileron had been ripped open when we clipped through the top of a tree.

The result of my action was that the needle on the ASI dropped back, down below stalling speed . . . yet we went on soaring upwards into the black night sky. John went to check his instrument in the front compartment. That too was showing only 75 m.p.h. They must somehow be faulty. *Both* of them? I shut off the boost, eased back the throttles, and flew straight and level with hands lightly sensing the control column, feeling for the strength of response. It seemed perfectly normal. I threw the aircraft around for a few moments, climbed, dived, swerved on rudder, banked in steep turns to both sides, and it behaved perfectly despite the ASI hovering about the mid-seventies, at which speed with our bombs and full fuel tanks we should have fallen out of the sky.

What was so fiendish about the fault was that if it had been a complete failure of the ASI instrument I would have seen it quickly and stopped before the end of the runway, or climbed away on feel. But it had built up enough speed to deceive me into believing it was working normally, committed me to take-off, and then induced me to hold down for flying speed and so ensure we would crash into the slope on the far side of the valley.

We did not go out to sea and jettison the bombs, by then I was confident we could land without any difficulty, and so we did – a bit faster than normal of course, but never in danger of overrunning. In the morning they discovered a tiny piece of grit in the pitot head, the small projecting tube into which air can flow so as to calibrate speed for the ASI dials in the cockpit and in the nose compartment. Complete failure of the ASI caused by taking off with the pitot head protective cover still in position was not uncommon, and caused no great problem, but I had never heard of a pitot head giving murderous false readings, nor had any of the other pilots. However, the flight commander decided it was unlikely ever to happen again so no action was necessary. This annoyed me. I felt something must be done about such a menacing possibility.

After lunch that day I had taken my coffee outside with a naval pilot who wanted to show me some lapwings cavorting in the field outside the perimeter fence. There were about a dozen of them. They would take off in unison to climb up in a great sweeping turn, then suddenly falter in mid-air, and in a striking aerobatic display would come fluttering down with a loud throbbing sound like a car self-starter. On the ground they would run rapidly with crest held high, then stop statue-still for a moment, beautiful dark green plumage shot with purple, and the black crest like a little rococo flourish added by a tipsy artist. When Tubby came out of the mess with the group captain, heading for the operations room, I signalled him and they diverted to see what we found so interesting.

Before they could be distracted by the birds, however, I got in quickly with an account of the pitot head incident and they did show some interest in it, but then the lapwings went into their fluttering-throbbing act and Tubby was reminded into a long story about a bat smashing into someone's pitot head in a pre-war flight, despite the renown of the bat's radar. My argument was about to be swamped by reminiscence and technical discussion, so I brought it back immediately at the end of his story, declaring that some official attention should be given to a menace that nearly killed three of us – and may well have killed others in the past. At this the group captain reverted to his junior officer theme.

'You better pay attention to what he tells you,' he said to Tubby. 'He starts giving you orders otherwise.'

We did discuss it seriously then. What created most lively support was the naval lieutenant's argument that pilots would certainly be blamed, and probably had already been blamed, for fatal accidents caused by such defective readings. Engineer officers, who participate in all accident investigation, have greater faith in machines than in men, and were always quick to assess 'pilot error' as the cause of any accident – the pilot, being dead, could never respond to the accusation. The senior officers finally decided that day that I should write a report of the incident, and suggest how the danger might be avoided in future. I did this, and it was sent on to Command with additional comments by Tubby and the group captain. I never discovered if it had any consequence. The RAF handled this sort of field comment badly at that time; there was no organized procedure for discovering from pilots what potential for accidents they may have noted. Another year was to pass before they got around to that preventative measure.

One problem I was pressured by the others to take up with Tubby concerned our anti-shipping patrols in the Bay of Biscay. These were carried out a few miles off the French coast and were subject to cloud cover; if cloud cover was insufficient you had to return, as losses to patrolling enemy fighters had been severe. This did not present a problem on individual patrols – the order was subjectively interpreted and there was no alternative against which your decision could be judged. A problem did arise, however, when two or more were out together: in these joint sorties you flew the line several miles apart, out of sight and touch, and there could be different and embarrassing interpretations afterwards of what exactly constituted cloud cover. What was 'enough'?

There were as many answers to this question as there were pilots in the squadron. One pilot might accept three-tenths as sufficient, justifying this by saying it was made up of big cumulus blobs within which you could hang about for hours evading enemy fighters; another might say that even eight-tenths was not enough, arguing that it was mostly thin strata and offered no real cover at all.

On these joint separated patrols such decisions were independently reached and the outcome could provoke invidious comparisons afterwards. There would be ill-feeling in the crew room at times when someone had come back after only an hour or so declaring cloud cover had run out near Brest, then to discover another pilot on the sortie had continued down to the limit near La Pallice, telling the Controller on return that there had been ample cloud cover all the way.

We had an acrimonious discussion about this one day in the crew room. Although we had not been involved in the sortie that prompted it, I was hauled into the argument by Dobson, the other survivor of our Andover course – but only for a little while longer. Dobson was a precise character. He read carefully the instructions in Daily Routine Orders, always worked through his navigator's calculations with him, his locker was ordered as neatly as if for inspection at a drill depot. It was inevitable that he should fly these anti-shipping patrols to exact rules: six-tenths cloud cover to him was the 'enough' figure, being just over half and therefore the logical amount. He followed this himself and felt that it should be so decreed and enforced.

When he insisted I take up the matter with Tubby I pointed to the subjective element in assessing six-tenths, but he could not understand this argument. To Dobson six-tenths cloud was a matter of fact, not opinion; if in doubt you flew high above it or low below it, studied the evidence, arrived at the definite answer. However, he did concede that conditions could change with time, and this seemed to me to offer a solution. It was not specially effective for joint sorties to be run at exactly the same time; the same swathe of sea and the same chances of a strike would still be covered if there was a fifteen-minute gap between flights, and such a gap could mean different weather conditions, and so explain different pilot reactions.

I went up to Tubby's office that same morning and told him of the problem. When I explained why many pilots were unhappy with the current situation he saw the point at once, and agreed that a timing gap was the happy solution. He told me to pass the word that those who wished to be separated by a fifteen-minute interval on such joint sorties could arrange this between themselves. Why, he wondered, had not someone said something to him about this before?

It is quite possible that none of the married group happened to have been involved in such a situation, but the main reason for his ignorance was that the squadron hierarchy was so disorganized at that time. Normally a squadron such as ours would have two squadron leaders to command the flights, in both of them would be a few flight lieutenants and flying officers, and at the bottom of the ladder would be the majority, pilot officers like us commissioned within the previous twelve months. But this neat structure went awry during periods of heavy losses; squadrons would finish with a number of pilot officers fresh from operational training school, and few of the intermediate ranks before the wing commander at the top. The Blenheim bomber aircrews of Number 2 Group operating over the North Sea that summer, for example, had a life expectancy of only twelve sorties; fighter pilots in southern England during the Battle of Britain were only three or four better. We did not suffer quite so severely: our life expectancy in that spring of 1941 was about eighteen sorties, but you could in principle complete those in less than four weeks and so become one of the most experienced pilots on the squadron, even though you might only be a pilot officer, like me, commissioned just seven months previously.

We needed a flight commander to tidy up our squadron organization. This was a squadron-leader post and we were awaiting a particular man who had flown on the same squadron as the group captain. But he would not be arriving for another month, so we in the crew-room group lacked even an official bridge to the senior out-living group. Not for long, however, after that meeting with Tubby about cloud-cover sorties. The next morning I was called up to station headquarters to see the group captain. Tubby was with him in his office.

They would like me, they said, to take over command of 'A' Flight until such time as the squadron leader became available. How did I feel about it?

I agreed. The group captain seemed to have expected a more enthusiastic response.

Chapter 10

———o———

With its variety of institutions, its bank and post office and food stores, its social activities and services, a battleship is like a village. There were 1300 men living in the *Hood* community, all going about their different tasks every day, and even when the alarm signal called the community into action some continued with their work, as in any village during an air raid. Then, in one appalling clap of thunder on 24 May 1941, almost the whole thriving community of the *Hood* was wiped off the face of the earth – just three men left floating in the empty sea. No shattered buildings as in a town devastated by bombers, no liferafts crammed with survivors as after the sinking of the *Bismarck*. Nothing but the echo of the explosion and a column of smoke over the grey North Sea.

We became immediately involved. Patrols were sent out into the Atlantic westwards of Brest where we carried out extensive searches for the *Bismarck* and the *Prinz Eugen*. They were found by a Catalina flying boat, far out of our range, and the Royal Navy pursuers guided into vengeful action. In a battle spread over twenty-four hours, the *Bismarck* was first halted by torpedoes from navy planes, then shattered by shellfire from the pursuing force, and finally sunk by torpedoes fired from a cruiser. The *Prinz Eugen* escaped, made a wide detour south beyond the limit of our patrols, and eventually came up the coast by night into Brest harbour. Then there were three of them in that AA fortress, the *Scharnhorst*, the *Gneisenau* and the *Prinz Eugen*.

For some reason the RAF never did make a determined effort to destroy the ships in harbour, as they did successfully to the *Tirpitz* later. The effort by Bomber Command against Brest was irrationally small, considering the importance of the targets; they used it as a training ground for what they considered to be their proper business of deep penetrating attacks into Germany, sending new units out occasionally so as to give them a short-range blooding over the most heavily defended target in the world. We in 53 Squadron alone had no hope of causing serious disturbance to the German plans for the ships, the total payload of our sixteen Blenheims was only about one per cent of a single Bomber Command group. However, we were close at hand so were used for harassing attacks, along with Spitfires for daily observation, and Hudsons for 'Stopper' patrols; these were carried out nightly by the comparatively luxurious Hudson aircraft, carefree flights well outside the harbour, to ensure that we knew at once if the ships tried to escape under cover of darkness.

Day offensive patrols off the harbour entrance, a task given to the Blenheims occasionally, were not so carefree – they cost us three crews that June. And for a Blenheim to go *inside* the harbour in daylight was reckoned to be fatal – we could not approach the rarefied heights and had only half the speed of the stripped-down Spitfires. Yet one of our pilots did go in one day that spring when cloud prevented the Spitfire checking a report that the *Gneisenau* had moved. Miraculously he survived, protected from fighters by cloud under which he took photographs showing the ship still in place. The aircraft was hit by AA but the crew returned unscathed, only to be killed later on a night raid.

By this time the night raids on Brest had become so commonplace we had ceased to have normal briefing procedures. We went into the crew room in the morning and there on the blackboard in the squadron leader's writing was the simple announcement:

> BREST   T'O 2100   4 x 250
>   P'O Herrick
>   P'O Buck
>   P'O Dobson
>   P'O O'Brien

It was up to each individual to contact the operations room for weather forecast, beacon letters and colour recognition signals of the day, then you took off (T'O) before nine o'clock with your four 250-pound bombs. Anyone passing the crew room could see the notice on the board.

It was a warm dry May that year, we had opened the crew-room windows and spent our waiting time outside within sound of the phone. The grass was covered in enormous dandelions, yellow bright as the sun in enamelist art, and the bumble bees would come zooming in to bounce from one flower head to another till they found one to their liking. I licked some sugar wet on my finger one day, held it beside a dandelion, and within seconds had one moving with furry tickles over my hand as he dabbed up the nectar. From the grassy bank we could see the blackboard clearly just inside the window and we reckoned a low-flying German pilot could even photograph it.

The information was of no import, however. The guns would be ready without any prompting. They now had the *Prinz Eugen* guns added to their barrage, another eighteen AA guns had been fitted to the *Scharnhorst*, fourteen more to the *Gneisenau*. This was the sort of precise information that Jean Pitillon, the Resistance officer, was passing through at this time; little wonder he later rose to become Commander-in-Chief of the post-war French navy.

Our standard instructions for Brest raids were simple enough, but the response from individual pilots varied. At first, if Brest was covered in cloud, we were allowed to try for an alternative target such as the submarine pens at Lorient, but group headquarters had not been happy about this – maybe some staff officer, who would himself have taken such an easy option, decided we were doing it for his reason, so alternatives were abolished. If Brest was clouded over we had to drop our bombs blind at ETA, and even if there was no gunfire to indicate that we were actually over the target area the bombs still had to go down. The declared justification for this was that the more bombs we dropped the better the chances of a hit, and bombs anywhere in the Brest area would affect the performance of the dock workers by depriving them of sleep, and so contribute towards keeping the battleships out of action.

Naturally, the policy was not popular with us; with me particularly, because, as their equally-ranking flight commander, I got all the complaints about it. It raised all sorts of problems – moral, emotional and professional. Should you drop bombs when you might be over a residential area miles from the docks? Did you believe you were really over the target, or did you know in your heart you were miles away, after such careless (or calculated) compass flying? Had we had all that practice on the range just to finish up slapping bombs down from inside a cloud? I told the naggers to make up their own minds, and leave me alone. So each dealt with these problems in his own way, and there was little talk about the solutions adopted. The reports given in debriefing after such blind drops can now be read in the archives, but I would advise historians not to trust them.

We ourselves never did have a completely flak-free drop, but on one I feel sure we did not bomb the dock area. From the moment we rose into cloud on take-off that night until we trembled down through it over base on return, we saw neither earth nor sky. When estimated to be over Brest we were in peaceful cloud and only after dropping a second flare did we raise some heavy AA – separate flashes in the cloud, perhaps only a single battery firing at us. It was unlikely just a section of the Brest defences would open fire, but it was all we had. The cloud about us lit up with each explosion, but as with lightning in cloud it was difficult to decide upon the centre of action, so we finally let them go on an estimate then turned for home with scarcely a word between us.

You felt angry after such a sortie. After being so tensely ready for action, looking forward to the moment of triumph when danger had again been successfully taunted, it was shaming, and disturbing, to finish up attacking what was little more dangerous than flashes of lightning. In the operations room that night I was still so wrought up about it that the group captain, happening in during interrogation, asked coldly if I thought Churchill and the Air Ministry should consult Pilot Officer O'Brien before deciding upon bombing policy.

Another night after vain provocation for an hour, we thought we might have to bomb whatever was below, when, to my apprehensive relief, the barrage suddenly started up ahead of us so we were able to home in on the centre of the inferno – the Germans, of course, did not open fire until certain we had found them. But 'the centre of the barrage' on cloudy nights was a vague concept, so God knows where our bombs landed on some cloud-confused nights. I wanted to ignore the stupid order, go to another target on such nights and not disclose this at debriefing. The lie would not have troubled me, but unfortunately John would never cooperate in any such deceit, so we had no escape from the blind-bomb dictate.

Some crews could manage such evasive collusion. Tony Buck was quite frank in the crew room about having dropped his bombs in the Atlantic on occasion. He said he was not going to risk the lives of his crew and himself by flying into a gunlit cloud mass to drop bombs that could fall on innocent French people, and his navigator was happy enough to back him up in the debriefing lie. You could tell from the muted reaction to his admission that day in the crew room that he was not the only one to have dropped bombs into the broad Atlantic.

The coolness between the group captain and myself manifested in the blind-bombing policy was followed by a further fall in his favour when we were called one morning for a daylight sortie over Brest. This operation started off with the same sequence of events that had led to that other Blenheim being sent over the harbour in daylight; again the PRU Spitfires had not been able for some reason to check on a report that the *Prinz Eugen* had moved towards the harbour entrance, so a Blenheim had to go immediately to discover the facts.

I was over in dispersal that morning conniving in a fiddle to get another tin helmet for the flight sergeant, because a robin had built a nest in his when it was hanging with his gas mask from our hawthorn bush the previous day. The speed at which the bird had built the nest was surprising; the flight sergeant had hung his helmet there at twelve-thirty on return from lunch, and the nest had been completed by six when he was going off duty. I went over to the little hawthorn bush, which was smothered in white blossom, and saw that the helmet was not squarely upturned but hanging by its strap at an angle, so the nest was built on one side, but it looked safe enough. The robin, perched above it within the blossom, watched with shiny black eyes our every move. I had just finished writing the indent for a helmet to replace one 'lost when aircraft was holed over enemy territory', when Tubby's car came bumping over the grass to our tent.

'They want someone over Brest right away,' he said.

The next half hour was a whirl of events. Although I knew well enough the enormity of the risk, I either had no time to dwell on it or was excited beyond care. The operations room lavished attention upon us, but Tubby was obviously jittery; he tried, and failed, to get us permission to go without a bomb load (so as to get maximum speed) but did win the argument for a hand-held camera, more flexible than the installed type that would force us into a direct line over the battleship. The Met people expected about three-tenths cloud at six thousand feet, so I reckoned to make our run at that height. It was vital that the radio be working, so Dennis, our gunner at that time, stayed down at dispersal checking ours in PZ-H and also the one in our stand-by aircraft. We were to send a simple 'OK' if all the ships were still in position, transmit in clear if any had moved.

Tubby drove us down to the flight room, then suddenly left us, telling me to taxi out to the perimeter track when ready but under no circumstances to take off until he returned. Down at dispersal I checked the service details on the Form 700, heard the latest robin news from the flight sergeant, and told him if there was any problem with stores about his helmet replacement I would sort it out on my return. As I left him to walk across to join John at PZ-H, I remember suppressing a quibble that arose in mind about that word 'return'.

Once at the aircraft we were back in business. It was a warm day, the sun high and clear in the sky, the cockpit so hot I took off the Mae West to get rid of my jacket. When about to pass it through the hatch to the airman, however, I did think consciously about our chances, surviving perhaps to become a prisoner of war, and decided the jacket would be useful. But when I threw it into the well, ready to grab if we baled out, I felt the need to ridicule such optimism: 'Bale out? You'll be lucky!' It was only a fleeting thought, swept away again by action. I had to buckle up, sense the controls, start the engines, do all the usual checks, then taxi out on to the perimeter track. There I halted, keeping the engines on a lively tick-over, looking towards the hangar for Tubby's car.

The next few minutes, which turned out to be so important, are clear in my memory because I had nothing to do. My hands were wet in the leather gloves so I decided to risk torn flesh, tried to stuff them into my pocket but couldn't do it past the harness, so threw them behind into the well. John was back beside me. I asked him for the first course, and was locking the compass ring on to it when he tapped my arm. Tubby's car was racing along the perimeter track towards us. I called to the gunner to pop his head out to take the message, but then he called back that Tubby was climbing up the wing. I throttled down the port engine and slid the hatch open. Tubby appeared, leaned in through the hatch, plump face glistening with sweat, and I raised one side of my helmet to hear him. John was not wearing a helmet, so he too heard every word that was said.

'They've changed it,' Tubby called. 'You're not to go over the harbour. Just make a check as near round the entrance as cloud will let you. See if any of them have come out. Take oblique photos from there. That clear?'

'Okay, sir.'

'Stay *outside* the harbour entrance. About the line of the "Stopper" patrol.' And when I gave him a thumbs-up sign he repeated finally, 'Take the photos from there.'

He patted me on the helmet and left. Later on John and I had good reason to discuss this last-minute contact. We agreed that those were more or less his exact words, and John wrote them down – I still have the piece of paper on which he wrote them. We never discussed his final orders as we set off, for neither of us had any doubt about them: our task was to see if there was any sign of a battleship in the offshore area and take obliques of the harbour from as close to the entrance as cloud allowed, staying outside about the distance of the 'Stopper' night patrols. The primary purpose remained much as before, to check if any ship was on the move, but the vital difference now was that this check was to be done from outside the harbour, the actual distance being dependent on cloud cover. So now we could reasonably think about a possible return journey.

It was just after midday when we set course from Lizard Point, directly over a field where a tractor was being followed closely by seagulls in such swirling numbers it looked as if the plough was flinging them up out of the dark soil. We travelled across the western approaches under a hazy sky, then chunks of solid cumulus began to close in from the west. By the time the rock-ringed green plaque of Ushant came into sight we had about four-tenths cloud, with base at five thousand feet; we were flying above, and now tracking from clump to clump.

Our approach to the harbour entrance was along the line of broken water, black rocks, and islets that link Ushant with the mainland, and we finished up circling between two great chunks of cumulus about a mile off the harbour entrance. The sea surface looked glassy smooth, pure ultramarine with just a lacy white collar about the rocky headland; we could see a scattering of very small fishing craft, the large red-hulled lightship near the harbour entrance, and on land discern the line of the road running east towards Brest, but it was impossible to see any detail in the town area or the inner harbour – we must have been nearly ten miles away from the docks.

There was no sign of any large ship, no major activity whatsoever over the whole sunlit expanse of the hundreds of square miles we could see from just below cloud base. The lightship and the scattered fishing boats were stilled models on a wide blue floor. We had no binoculars, this offshore check had not been the original plan, but the magnification of the hand-held camera would show up the harbour better than we could observe, so I told the gunner to tap out the negative signal and John prepared to take oblique shots of the harbour. I kept a close watch in the direction of Lanveoc airfield, and once the gunner had sent his message I kept checking with him for reassurance of all-clear reports.

For the actual photographs I made two swoops to pass over the tip of the headland, and also did a series of turns within the clear area between our two big chunks of cumulus. The whole operation lasted six minutes. It took so long because John had to pause in his photography each time I turned back towards the clouds. I was beginning to grow a little anxious when he suddenly lowered the camera, swiped his window shut and urged we leave. I climbed well above the peak of our seaward cumulus cloud to get diving speed in the getaway, and when we slanted down we were heading not northwards towards England, because the sky was terribly clear in that direction, but westwards into the Atlantic where the cumulus was lumpy across the horizon. We had quitted our immediate cover and were still a few miles short of the next big cloud when the carrier wave of the gunner's transmitter struck a chill in my heart.

'There's something – Jerries! Four o'clock high.'

That made them down sun. John twisted around in his seat to look for them as I pulled the 9-boost and steepened our dive across the gap, heading for the very bottom rim of the huge white mound of our safety cloud. Two fighters at least, the gunner called. I told him to check up sun, in case these were acting as decoys, but after a brief pause he came through again:

'Nothing up sun. One is turning in for us. Me 109, I think. Still high.'

John had also seen it, and he jabbed his finger forward at the cloud mass. But I knew we could reach it by then. A few seconds later, before the gunner could report again, we were there, plunging into the enveloping whiteness, confidence surging in the security of its massive bulk. I reduced speed and settled into instrument flying as we spiralled up more than a thousand feet in our sanctuary, John and the gunner exchanging opinions about the track of the turning fighter. When we did burst out of the churning whiteness into the clear there were no aircraft in sight, so I climbed higher directly above its shelter to get diving speed towards our next cloud. This, too, was to the west, and we reached it without further sight of the enemy aircraft, there to stream along its wispy flat base, then across in level flight to another close by, then climb above that to pick out our next refuge. And so, using the clouds as stepping stones for the next thirty minutes or so, we flew roughly westwards out into the wide Atlantic, until at last, confident we had won the game, I turned north into the clear skies that stretched away towards England.

There was no fuss on our return. It appeared that while we were away group headquarters had decided, or discovered from an intelligence report, that the rumour about the *Prinz Eugen* being on the move was false, so there was little interest in a sortie already written off as unnecessary reconnaissance. The debriefing was perfunctory, we had a few drinks in the mess before dinner, answered a question or two from a jovial Tubby, and thought that was the end of the story. However, some officious staff officer at group HQ, perhaps the man who had been pressured to modify his dangerous original order, seems to have been waiting to examine our report.

We had dined back at the hotel, not intending to go into Newquay that night, but just after dinner a naval lieutenant we all knew called in with three girls, en route to the Club and happy to share his riches. One of them was a naval captain's attractive daughter who had just come from an extended cocktail party; she was wearing a sinuous body-clinging dress of peacock-blue satin, and I had just accepted a personal and prolonged hand-holding-stroking invitation from her to join them when the corporal batman coughed to announce his intrusion. I was wanted at the operations room immediately. They had sent a van for me.

So, instead of a joyous singing drive over to Newquay I had a worrying silent one up the winding dark lanes to the airfield. There I discovered from an embarrassed Controller that an imperious order had been received from Group that I was to give 'a full and immediate explanation for not staying on "Stopper" patrol until PLE [Prudent Limit of Endurance]'. Having had enough alcohol by then to blur all badges of rank I flared up at the implied criticism.

'We weren't on a bloody "Stopper",' I declared.

The Controller was a Canadian squadron leader, and he treated me gently. I should go back to the hotel, to bed, and report to him next morning. But I was so mutinous about the reproof that I went to the mess and rang Tubby at home to tell him what was happening. He assured me we had carried out his orders – 'to the letter, Pat' – told me not to worry, and promised he would sort it out next day.

I never did discover the whole background to this incident – how or why our briefing had been changed at the last minute, and how the confusion arose about the final orders. I do know there was some discussion the following day between the Controller, the group captain, and Tubby, about the explanation to be tendered to the dignitary at group headquarters whom I had offended, and I saw the outcome when called there and given a short report to sign. This said there had been a misunderstanding about the last-minute alteration given to me in the aircraft, perhaps because of 'engine noise and the urgent circumstances', and that I regretted it if we had not carried out the operation exactly as intended.

Naturally, I was not happy about the explanation that had been concocted, but Tubby was clearly anxious for the settlement so I signed without a murmur. For some reason or other in the tangled background of this affair the group captain was distinctly cool when he called in just after I had signed the report. He glanced at it, turned his back on me to engage the Controller, and presently left without saying a word to me.

It was not unusual to come across staff officers who were quite unaware how sensitive pilots could be to any comment which insinuated a lack of courage. I never heard anyone in our squadron ever speak seriously about fear of death. They joked about the subject, laughed when they said: 'I was shit scared when I saw the stuff they were pumping at us,' downgrading their own acts of courage so as not to admit the fear that made them so valuable. But when you are striving to control the delicate balance between excitement at danger and fear of death, you become extremely sensitive to any suggestion that fear was in control. Some senior officers would assume that your angry reaction was a gratuitous impertinence. It was not. It was an act of self-defence.

There was a second, more serious, censure from group headquarters at the beginning of June. We were sent out alone one night to bomb the submarine depot at St Nazaire, despite a weather report that indicated we had no realistic chance of ever finding the place. In view of this cheerless forecast, we were given alternatives of

Lorient, Lanveoc-Poulmic air bases, Brest itself, or 'any other suitable target' in those areas. We travelled over land on the way down because the direct route left us with more fuel to hunt for an alternative in the likely event of failure to find our primary target. Surprisingly on such a black night, when the defences would usually not disclose themselves, we met gunfire at a place which must have been at least fifty miles inland of Brest; a battery of heavy guns opened up on us as we passed in broken cloud, the shells exploding at our height, and not that far off to starboard. John marked the position for intelligence – and also as a last resort for our bombs that night.

As we continued on south the cloud kept increasing steadily. A wide layer of stratus developed at our height so we dropped down into the blackness underneath, and then presently were flying through blocks of thunderous rain that whitened the perspex and set the fuselage ringing, and even between these disturbances the darkness was so complete we could see nothing below. We were in rain approaching St Nazaire, and it must have extended wide about the whole town. For a quarter of an hour we cruised about, jiggling the throttles in the hope that someone would fire at us, and when this failed we finally dropped a flare. There was no reaction whatsoever – not surprising, for when we followed the flare down we saw only a curving hillside covered in forest.

We then spent a long time trying to find the coastline, travelling roughly north-east, until at last, in a cloud break, we caught sight of a glint of water. We circled down in the clear to about a thousand feet, but it was hopeless trying to get a pinpoint from the little we could see, then the rain closed in on us and we had to climb once more to a safe height. When John reckoned we must be in the Lorient area, we dropped a flare which showed broken cloud all about us, so we abandoned that one and flew on to where we reckoned Lanveoc to be, but had no response there either. We continued on for Brest, dropped a flare and circled down with it to see a pallid cultivated field, a cereal crop of some sort. We did a square search that lasted almost an hour, giving frequent flashes of the landing lights, but could get not a flicker from the ground. So then, with only one flare left, we took our bombs north for a coastal pinpoint that would enable us to find the guns that had fired on us on the outward journey.

It was a worrying search. Early on we ran into a bank of cumulo-nimbus, and for a moment the lightning deceived me into thinking we had found the Brest barrage at last, but realized the mistake when the aircraft began to be hurled about in the violent natural turbulence of the cu-nim, nothing like the single air-thump you feel from an AA shell burst. I banked away steeply to escape the dangerous illusion, but it took us several boisterous minutes to get out of the storm; the lightning was continuous, flickering like a lamp with a faulty connection and showing immense cloud valleys and chasms like a Doré vision of the world of the damned.

We had to use our last flare to get down below cloud and with its help did discern what might have been a coastline. So from there we set off on the course we had been following when we met the gunfire. This time, however, we had no reception. With no flares to help provoke fire I had to rely on what I hoped were a threatening burst of throttle and occasional flashes of our landing lights, but it was all to no avail. The ragged peripheral cloud of the storm was scattered about at varying heights, and, with the Monts d'Arrée rising to two thousand feet somewhere in the area, it was far too dangerous to try and get close to ground in search for opposition. Just when we were thinking of abandoning the search we had luck of a sort. The gunner got through to base and was told the weather there had also closed in, that we would have to divert to Boscombe Down. But when he tried to get a line bearing he failed to make contact.

I reckoned we had fuel enough to try for Cherbourg docks, only slightly off the direct line to Boscombe, but we were in rain over most of the Normandy peninsula and had no idea when we ran out of land and had reached the English Channel. We continued on blind until well over England and finally found a way down through cloud almost directly over the cathedral at Salisbury, and thence easily to Boscombe Down flare path, by then its lights fading in the approach of dawn. There we refuelled, and after waiting an hour or so to get the all-clear from St Eval, we took off in daylight, climbing away above an avenue of laburnums in golden flower and westwards to Cornwall where we landed with our bombs still intact. There we were briefly debriefed about the fruitless sortie and made our way back down to the Watergate Hotel for our usual day of rest after two successive night operations.

The morning after our day off we arrived up at the crew room to find a chalked message on the blackboard:

P'O O'BRIEN REPORT TO OPS IMMEDIATELY.

It was not the Canadian squadron leader, who had been so tolerant previously, at the desk that morning. This Controller was older in years and, at first, far more distant in sympathy. He did not say he had an instruction from Group but asked outright, as if it were his personal demand for explanation:

'Why didn't you go to an alternative target the night before last?'

He spoke in a loud voice that caused the others in the operations room to lower their heads in busy embarrassment at the public rebuke. It was the form of the question that made me flare. After all that effort to get rid of the bloody bombs! I pointed that out to him, said we were so desperate in the end we would have dropped the whole thousand pounds on a single searchlight if we had seen one. But we saw nothing, exactly as reported in debriefing. This final comment surprised him – and probably stopped a reprimand for insubordination.

Had I given these details at debriefing? I assured him we had. He looked puzzled, picked up a note on his desk and read it, then began to flip through some other papers. With everyone else in the operations room studiously intent on not looking our way, I could feel myself close to revolt as I stood there waiting for him to continue the criticism. But then Shackleton came hurrying across from his cubby hole to support my story with his word and documented proof and when the Controller spoke again his tone and manner were sympathetic. He could not understand why Group had called for a report. Well, would I mind giving him something to pacify them? There's a good chap! Some details about our effort to find a target?

He was so much on my side I had to agree. But when I started on the report down in the crew room it was at group headquarters that it was angrily aimed, so the tone was far from conciliatory. Apart from John, who busied himself with his own notes, the others in the crew were eager to participate. What could be included in that waffly direction 'or-any-suitable-target' they had as usual given us at the original briefing? Rather than bring back bombs should we then drop them on isolated farmhouses in France? Or on crops of cereal? Or on the factory that made the soya-links they served in our mess? Or could we perhaps land and sell off the bombs to Cornish fishermen for explosive catches, so helping provide valuable food during the national shortage?

We continued this play for some time, during which three of us went across to the escallonia bush beside the ambulance shed to see the vivid sky-blue eggs of a hedge sparrow in a mossy little nest that one of the airmen had discovered. John, meanwhile, stayed at the table in the crew room writing. With the advantage of his own calm temperament, and experience of official reports and official language in the Royal Canadian Mounted Police force, he finished the task with not a single correction and handed me the result. It was severely factual: time of arrival over each search area . . . time spent on each search . . . plot location of each . . . time flares dropped . . . time forced to abandon last search . . . time of landing. I took it later to the operations room where the Controller read it, gave a pleasant word of thanks, and presumably passed it on to Group Headquarters. We heard nothing further.

Chapter 11

———o———

The length of an operational tour varied according to Command (Bomber, Fighter or Coastal) and to type of work within that Command. We in Blenheims of 53 Squadron then had a tour of thirty operations. Sorties aborted within England because of radio or mechanical failure did not, of course, count, but less reasonably a double strike counted as only one. These occurred when you split a bomb load between two targets, in effect flew two separate strikes from a single take-off – for example, in the 10 May entry below we dropped two bombs on the pens at Lorient, then had to fly on to Donges and drop the other two on the docks there. Here is an excerpt from my log book of that period:

7 May	Blenheim PZ-H Night Strike Brest	3 hrs 15 min.
8	Blenheim PZ-H Test	20 min.
8	Blenheim PZ-H Anti-ship patrol Biscay	4 hrs 20 min.
10	Blenheim PZ-H Test	35 min.
10	Blenheim PZ-H Night Strike Lorient	5 hrs 10 min.
11	Blenheim PZ-H Test	20 min.
11	Blenheim PZ-H Night Strike La Pallice	5 hrs 45 min.

Had we been able to continue at that rate all the time we would have finished our tour in about two months. However, no one was able to keep up the theoretical standard of two operations every three nights; apart from losing so many flights through technical and W'T-go failures, and no job turning up when you were on a day stand-by, you would also fall behind because of sickness or leave. We were lucky in that we lost no time through these latter reasons; failed W'T-go cost us five sorties, that ASI failure another, and we had a good share of futile stand-bys.

It took us seventy-one days to complete our thirty operations – during which period sixteen crews were killed. Though this was much longer than the theoretical minimum it was still a lot of action in a comparatively short time, so it was not always easy afterwards to distinguish in mind the details of every one of those operational flights. I often wrote in my notebook when on stand-by in the crew room, but mainly about scenes and personal feelings and thoughts and dreams. Many operations were not noted in any detail at all. Some notes were a mélange of several trips. The following entry, reproduced here exactly as written in the exercise book, deals with a St Nazaire raid on 18 May.

We saw a fighter last night over St Nazaire. Reported it in ops. It was useful gen. Report such things, but never your private thoughts about the sortie. I know I made a mess of it. Clear night, moon almost full, we circled north of town, both J and I saw Me 110 cross in front of us, then turn as if he was going to get behind us so I opened taps and dived down moon. That buggered plan we'd made for J to bomb. I took over. In down-moon dive we could see ground fairly well, town like crumpled graph-paper, dark silvery water of Loire.

Gunfire died down just before we started the dive, maybe F just finished his attack, but it picked us up quickly and all the searchlights swung north for us; they move like light flak, slow at first and then flashing past (you hope) at blink speed. An amber one making great sweeps across the sky. The town stretched away from docks further than I'd calculated, we were still miles short of docks when down to five thousand.

Flatten out or plunge on down? Flatten out, you lose speed, give gunners time to catch up. Now you want to finish quickly, quell fear with excitement (or do you *seek* fear?). Anyway you decide go on down, faster, faster, and lower all time. Concentrate on the sharply angled slab of blackness against broad silvered patch, that's the dock. You urge PZ-H through the swaying lights, all around you are coloured streamers (there was a pinkish one, firing slower than the others). They float up in lazy curves towards you then whizz past like lightning – but no heavy stuff thumping you around in their smoke, no stink of cordite. Light stuff mostly silent, just sometimes a wail, and when close you get vicious pok-pok-pok, makes you wince. So many coloured lines in front you think it impossible to get through without contact, you're a fly in a three-dimensional web. You try and shut out sight and sound of it all as you keep jabbing stick forward, trying to urge more speed, crash a way through it, cursing the aircraft, the defences, God knows what. The sharply angled block closer now, one side irregular. Ah! It's a separate block beyond. Actual buildings visible up-moon on left. We're going to overshoot. Stick further forward. Crimson flak flowing up from flat roof. Black water with reflections of flak like shivering film of oil. Scaffolding? Cranes! That's it! Bang the bomb tit. Too late, I think. Overshot into water.

A thud when they go. She leaps forward, still diving. Back on the stick. Back and back – come on, PZ-H, for Christ's sake! Squash into seat. Up she comes! Level now. Battery of light flak opening up from far shore, one of the green-tinted stuff amongst it, going across in front, pok-pok-pok but no flashes. An explosion in the water off to right – someone's bombs? No more flak ahead, but bloody stuff arching over us from behind. Bastards never give up. That's it! Now only stars ahead over gleaming water. A great gasping breath, and then you laugh. Bloody marvellous! Let PZ-H come up slowly, slowly. Keep on out to sea. Okay – enough. Now split-arse turn over water, see if they're still raging. Yes. Someone else getting it now.

'See the bombs, G?' (Graham, our current gunner.)

'Yes, sir. On the docks.'

Good old G. Never lets you down. Bombs always right in centre of target. Never press him for details, forget what you thought yourself, let his story stand at debriefing. Cheating? What the hell!

And so, once more, away, away, away. Far away out into moonlit Atlantic. Plenty of petrol to enjoy ourselves. The lovely time. J goes forward to perfect his provisional course. Set the throttles so she runs with a sweet ringing sound, and sing about the night being filled with music, the splendour that falls on castle walls and snowy summits old in story. Marvellous to be alive, free in the beautiful night, flying on and on forever over the velvet-blue sea.

Back in the ops room, lights and pencils and telephones and strong tea. All that excitement and fear and exultation becomes just a few lines on Shackleton's form. St Nazaire . . . O'Brien

. . . dive attack down to 300 ft . . . medium flak . . . bombed at 0130 hours . . . gunner reported all fell in target area . . . landed 0335 hours. Good night.

The new flight commander, Squadron Leader Peter Lilly, arrived on 19 May and took over my flight. He was a New Zealander who had flown with the station commander on Ansons when they were used on convoy escort early in the war. He was unmarried, so lived with us at the Watergate and that did help merge the two groups. I was glad to hand over to him, the command had never carried any real responsibility. Assignment of crews and aircraft, and planning of operations, had remained under the control of the other flight commander; my duties had been mainly concerned with airmen's discipline, dealing with men brought up on a charge, and I always found that difficult to take seriously.

There was a prolonged spell of bad weather at the beginning of June, and they kept offering alternative targets at almost every briefing. We would go out to bomb La Pallice, and finish up having to bomb Lorient hundreds of miles away because it was the only place we could find in the cloud-filled darkness. You would find yourself sometimes wandering about in the black night, jiggling the throttles and swearing aloud at the guns for not opening fire – 'Wake up, you stupid bastards! Can't you hear?' And you would let off a flare, or even flash of landing light, to try and rouse some opposition and so let you know you were in fact over the target.

We saw a great array of lights one black night when searching for St Nazaire, and headed towards the spectacle in wary approach. What on earth could it be? It was a ship. A big one, maybe ten thousand tons, completely lit up as if in some festive celebration – actually decorated with lights, not just riding lights and a working arc, but great strings of lights from bow to masthead, across the central superstructure, curving down to the stern. You could see the pale blue bridge and an expanse of yellowish decking forward, there was a derrick working aft loading on to a barge, circles of light from portholes, and on the wharf were trucks with headlights in full blaze. A ship that size would have been an overriding target at sea, or at St Nazaire itself, but we had never bombed anything at Nantes, and anyway I had no intention of bombing a ship that so advertised its presence.

That was the first time I had ever seen lights at night, apart from a flare path and beacons. I used to wonder sometimes what the peacetime world would look like at night. I had a picture like an intricate pattern of diamonds set out on a black cloth, pulsing with coloured flak-like flashes from neon advertising signs and being swept by low searchlights from hundreds of cars. John had flown over Canadian cities on night training exercises but was no help in creating the scene; he said towns at night were just like towns in daylight, the main difference being that they showed their size by lights instead of by houses. I thought they must be magical sights.

We were all sure we had been hit badly one night on Brest when a heavy AA shell exploded nearby just as we dropped our bombs. There was a brilliant sun-like flash just below our port wing, the aircraft was smashed up, almost turned on its back. It was difficult to level out afterwards, we were flying powerfully left wing low, but neither we nor the gunner could see any sign of damage in the rudder or the wings. On return I decided to wait till daylight to land, so we flew up and down the Cornish coast for something like two hours all the time with that heavy drag to port, and worrying about what it could be.

Dawn was a long time coming. The stars stayed twinkling bright, a crescent moon hung poised over the ebony cliffs at Watergate Bay, and the hills beyond were still vague and formless in the lack of light. Then at last the dawn began to caress the slopes, moulding them into familiar shape; the darkness faded first into grey, then to a deep purple over the Atlantic, and to our starboard a pink line of cirrus appeared above the orange glow of approaching sunrise on the eastern horizon. I turned in that direction, towards St Eval and the dawn.

I had already tested the flaps and wheels thoroughly, and they seemed intact, but at lower speed the left-wing-low attitude became very difficult to counteract, so we came in fast for a wheeled landing with need for powerful rudder and brake-jabs to keep us on the runway. The first indication we had of the source of our problem was when the airman who was guiding us into dispersal kept pointing at the underside of the fuselage and waving an arm up and down. A few minutes later we saw what he was trying to signify. One of our spring-loaded bomb doors was jammed open by a chunk of shrapnel; it must have hit us at the very instant we dropped our load, when the bomb doors were open.

Another black night, forced to come back over land after a raid on La Pallice, we finished blundering over Brest and were hit, but without damage, in the port wing. It made us realize how lucky we were compared to Bomber Command crews who had to go over land all the way out *and* back on their raids – never any safe sweet times over the Atlantic for them. And one moonlit night, after an attack on La Rochelle, we saw a steam train and dropped down low to fly over it – for fun, not aggressively. We never shot up trains. It left a roll of pallid smoke clinging to the dark trees behind it. We seared through this to see the blobs of ventilators on top of the carriages, and a ruby glint of fire from the engine, and when we sped low over it we felt a bumped uplift from the funnel hot air, then we were beyond, out in the clear with clean sharp moonlit railway lines streaming towards us to flash past under the fuselage like silver flak.

By the beginning of June, when we had flown twenty-five operations, it looked as if we might complete the tour and Tubby began to concern himself about my future. He dragged me away one night into the kitchen of his house and urged me to live up to my grey hair – it had started to whiten noticeably at that time – and become a little more responsible. He wanted me to move to a staff job, and said he could arrange this. John was going back to Canada – it was a Canadian rule that all those who survived a tour should return home. I wanted to team up with a new crew and start a second tour after leave, but Tubby refused to consider this; he wanted me to build a career in the RAF. He had enjoyed his life in the service, wanted me to share its pleasures.

One evening in the mess that June I was alone with Tubby, all very jovial and boisterous with tankard in his hand; but there was a persistent line in his questions that I failed to note at the time. He discovered I was going to stay on at the Watergate for my fourteen days' leave which was granted at the end of the operational tour. I had tried to get some of the balance of the share-sale money from Australia but this was refused, and, not having saved enough to go anywhere for leave, I had decided to swim and read and watch the seagulls on the cliff. But before Tubby finished with me that night he had learned that I did actually have an English civilian acquaintance; Liz Layton, the wife of a stockbroker to whom I had had a letter of introduction from a friend in Sydney. She had invited me out to tea in her Hampstead house when I was at Uxbridge eighteen months earlier, we had gone for a walk in the park with her five-year-old daughter, fed the mallards and talked about her concern with Jewish refugees, war aims, English politics, and the farm in Sussex where she rented a cottage. Tubby professed interest in the stockbroker, said he dabbled in shares and perhaps knew him – what was the firm?

A few days later I received a letter from Liz Layton inviting me to spend leave with them. When the bombing became severe she had moved out of London with her child and 'my young friend Timmie, a daughter of an old family friend, who would love to hear your stories about Pacific Islands and koala bears'. There was a separate letter from Timmie, in childish semi-print script, saying she hoped I would join them for my leave. I wrote back at once to accept the offer, I had enjoyed that afternoon with Liz and her daughter in the park, and the letter from her little girl friend was a charming invitation impossible to resist. It was only when I began to wonder how Liz came to get my St Eval address – we had not exchanged letters for nearly a year – that I recalled that conversation with Tubby.

He admitted the charge when I raised it, he had written to her care of the firm. I was lucky to have friends like that, he said. And like him, I thought.

Our final operation was on the Lanveoc-Poulmic air base. When the Intelligence Officer gave us details of the task we had to carry out that night, John turned to me and said quietly, 'They've given us a raw deal on this one, Pat.'

It was the only time he ever made a complaint about an operation that had been allotted to us. Certainly there were easier targets we might have had for that final sortie, but it was not the target itself that provoked his quiet resentment that day. It was the nature of the task.

We had to make eight separate runs over the air base. These were to be done at half-hourly intervals; on four of them we would drop a bomb, on the other four runs we would drop a flare. In the intervals we were to stay in the vicinity, make 'threatening runs' at the airfield, fire occasional Very pistol lights, and 'use imagination' to give the impression that the airfield was under continuous threat. The sortie promised, and in the event proved, to be the longest operational sortie carried out by a Blenheim from St Eval, lasting nearly seven hours – to a target barely an hour away from the field.

The reason for our game of Russian roulette with the enemy barrage was that Bomber Command was to make one of its rare raids on the battleships. Lanveoc airfield was only about three miles away from the anchored *Prinz Eugen*, perhaps a mile further from the dock area where the other two battleships were then located, so the German night fighters stationed at Lanveoc were able to take off at once whenever a serious attack seemed to be developing on the ships. Our job was to 'delay, discourage, and harass' any such attempts. A month earlier three of us had been sent out at half-hour intervals on a similar obstructive task, but had then each made just the one bombing run on the airfield – and had observed, incidentally, bombs exploding in the Lanveoc area by aimers either genuinely unsighted by the barrage or preferring to avoid the core of the inferno.

This time Coastal Command had decided to economize; one aircraft alone could not merely do the exercise but could double the work load. The idea was that by repeated attacks over four hours one Blenheim would inhibit all take-offs for a period starting half an hour before the first bomber arrived, and continuing till half an hour after the last one departed. This was the single operation needed to complete our tour; a cynic might think that fate, or a frustrated staff, was clearly desperate at this final stage of their game with us.

The weather was all gloom over Cornwall that night, and forecast to be so on return, but the front extended only to mid-Channel and in the Brest area we found not a wisp of cloud in a night sky lit up by a near full moon. Despite such good visibility, the guns did not open fire on our approach over the white beach in Douarnenez Bay, but as soon as the first bomb went down all the southern section of the Brest defences exploded into action against us. It was as though we had entered on stage in a huge assembly and the mass of waiting photographers suddenly all started flashing in a mad scramble for pictures. We were at twelve thousand feet when John let it go, and I swung immediately into a diving turn to the left so as to avoid passing directly over a flak ship pumping up coloured streamers ahead of us. Nothing of all this came close enough for us to hear, however, nor feel through shaken air.

'Three more for me, four for you,' John called.

We had planned he would drop the bombs, I would do diving runs with the flares and also devise the threats required. After that first run we flew back to the white crescent of beach to catch our breath and observe activity. The guns stopped, but isolated searchlights kept wavering about in vague hunt for us, and after a few minutes I flew across to the nearest one and let Brooks, our current gunner, have a burst at it. We were much too high to hope for success, but we were making a threat as briefed. And the light flak snapped back at us.

Visibility was so good we could pick out the blocks of buildings on the southern side of the airfield, and see at nearby Poulmic the seaplane ramp jutting out into the dark water of the harbour which flickered with explosive reflections when we came under fire. When the bombers arrived the guns on the other side of the harbour opened so rapidly in turn it was like a short in a monstrous high-tension cable over there, sudden blinding flashes that made a spluttering crackling jagged line across the star-filled sky. It started with bursts at about fifteen thousand feet over the town, then spread quick as a fuse-trail right across to the entrance of the Rade. A few moments later the light flak joined in the barrage; it seemed to be streaming up almost to our level, all of it looking the same pearly colour when we circled south of Lanveoc, but when we approached within a mile or so we could begin to see the colours. The beam of one of those bluish searchlights, however, remained noticeably distinct even from the extreme distance.

Within the barrage the light flak was colourfully clear in awful splendour. The lines streaked and wavered about us like a spray. I could pick out two definite sequences from a battery near the harbour entrance; one shot up green, flame-red, then orange, the other had a sequence of green, yellow, and then flame-red – the green was reddish green, like on a ripening Cox's apple. The height band of the heavy AA widened as the attack developed, from our side of the harbour the bursts appeared to form a rectangle several miles long and three or four thousand feet high, ranging in colour from deep orange to mirror-flash white, dependent on distance perhaps. A few heavy AA shells were fused at low height, merging into the cascades of coloured flak, and the whole picture gave the impression of a fantastic machine at work, as if the big flashes of bright explosions at the top were being produced by coloured pistons thrusting up and down with a sort of throbbing slowness that was curiously mesmerizing – once you were through it again and could observe from a safe distance.

The southern guns opened up on us again as we went in to drop the first flare. It was mostly heavy AA because I went across in a shallow dive that had us over nine thousand feet even at the end of the run. Six searchlights were located south of the aerodrome, shining up at different angles across it. They remained oddly static during our run. I weaved a passage through and only when we were in the clear did they start to sweep again. The heavy AA was well set for height but exploding ahead of us; we were jarred as we passed through the blobs of smoke and had to slide open the windows to clear the stink. John and I made separate checks on the drift of the flare; my marker was a flak ship quite distinct in the harbour area as it kept up its stabbing fire at the bombers, and when we came back in a wide run three minutes later the flare was still so clearly visible I even caught a glimpse of its parachute. It continued dropping towards the docks until we lost it in the turmoil of light flak.

Just after John dropped our second bomb, while we were still under fire, we heard the chilling note of the gunner's transmitter – you always thought of fighters at that sound over enemy territory. But he had only a spectacle to report: 'There's a big flare. Three o'clock high.'

I gave it merely a brief glance at that stressful moment, but when we were safely through the barrage again I banked to bring the object into easy view. It was down to our height by then, a comet-shaped flame, fiery red, huge, diving down fast against the backdrop of the flashing explosions of heavy AA; but a flare is a blob of light, whitish light, it hangs in the sky under its parachute. This was a blazing aircraft. The dive steepened as it seared westwards across the harbour some five miles from us, then a large chunk broke away to streak vertically and plunge into the flak. The main part continued at an angle and there was a bright flash when it hit what was probably water, because the light disappeared almost at once. Later we saw another one go down in fiery descent east of Lanveoc, heading inland, but never saw the final explosion.

The guns had stopped firing over the docks when we made our second bomb run, just searchlights over there sweeping aimlessly about, but afterwards when we made one of the stipulated threatening runs a battery of light flak opened up at us from Camaret, south of the harbour entrance. Perhaps a bomber had come in on that line because the full barrage burst into action again, and continued for some time as the attack developed. One aircraft dropped four large bombs, four bright shivers of light, near our white beach at Douarnenez.

Our third bomb hung up. As soon as I knew it had not gone, I took over from John, banked sharply and put the nose down in a steep dive back towards the airfield. When we were down to six thousand feet, light flak converging towards us from all quarters, I hauled back sharply on the stick as I pressed the bomb switch, but the blasted thing still did not drop. I swung away towards the coast, diving till out of the flak, and when clear we discussed the problem. It would be a waste to shake it clear over the sea, but stupid to go back and keep trying under fire – when it was unlikely to hit the airfield anyway. So we went back at about twelve thousand feet above that light flak battery at Camaret, and sure enough they opened fire, but their bright orange streaks curved away below us. For about five minutes we dived and climbed and banked above them, fusing and unfusing the bomb, pressing our releases, then suddenly it thumped clear. We saw it explode, wide of the flak battery – but they did stop firing.

By the time we came with our third flare the gunfire over the dock area had stopped altogether, but still the southern section enveloped us in their fury, and the searchlights across the harbour joined in the sweeps for us. When we finished the run the barrage stopped as if on a signal, except for a single gun from a flak ship. It was firing that reddish-green flak, aiming for our flare, but although they continued firing at it for more than a minute they still failed to hit either the flare or the parachute. It went on floating slowly down, still alight, to disappear about five minutes later into water.

For the next forty minutes the defences were stilled when we were out of AA range, just a few searchlights in play, and only the southern barrage blazed to furious life when we made a run. I was growing uneasy by this time. We were all alone in a mist-clear cloudless sky, there had been plenty of time for German fighters to come from miles away, so even if we managed to keep Lanveoc closed that was of little comfort. The last quarter of an hour waiting to go in and drop the final flare seemed a particularly long time passing. We made a dummy run at one stage, but had provoked no action when almost above the airfield, so I swung away again – it was stupid to risk being hit whilst doing nothing. I was also worrying about the amount of fuel we had used in all the fiddling with the throttles, so when John called to say we had seven minutes to go I cried halt. The bombers were long finished. There was no point in hanging around further.

'Bugger their seven minutes,' I said. 'I'll do it now.'

He grunted approval. We made a fast dive across the airfield, the guns all exploded into action for thirty seconds or so, the last flare went down, streaks of coloured flame came lazily up to go zipping away behind us, searchlights jerked and swept across the lightening sky, then we were through. We continued the dive down to two thousand feet over the sea, and then swung on to course for Cornwall as the stars began to blink out of sight in the approach of dawn.

Once safe out in the Atlantic, the gunner called base for a weather report; this was urgent because our fuel was now too low for any of the normal diversions. In our need, however, the radio, as expected, was a dead loss. He went on tapping for about half an hour but could raise not a single dot in response. We were not worried about finding base, it would be light enough to get a visual pinpoint once we hit the English coast. My worry was that St Eval might be closed out by low cloud. This worry intensified when we ran into the cloud front about half-way across the Channel, just about where we had left it the previous night. And just as bad. Gradually it forced us lower and lower as we neared the coast, passing through frequent grey curtains of rain.

It was light enough by then to see dark white-striped water below, so I decided to check the altimeter while we had the opportunity, as it seemed likely we might need accuracy when we reached cloud-covered land. Descending close to sea level, the propeller tips almost flicking the furrowed water for a careful instant, I re-set the altimeter, then eased up again near cloud base which was then about five hundred feet. We continued on course with both of us peering through the grey dawn for first sight of land.

True to John's form we came out almost exactly as planned at Nare Head, the landfall being confirmed by the flashing beacon near Truro. In the grey dawn we could see the glisten of rain-washed streets as we flew low across the rooftops on the eastern edge of the town. The further we went inland, however, the closer our ceiling came to the rising ground, but I felt we had to press on for St Eval because we had too little petrol to hunt for a diversion where, in addition, I would have to deal with unknown topography. After nearly seven hours' flying our fuel was by this time down to a level that would have been of some concern had we been up on a local air test, and because of this we flew on a direct course to St Eval for the last twenty miles, not wasting petrol to follow the rolling English drunkard's route of the main road.

We were lucky with the first cloud-high hill on our track, for it came up within a break in the overcast, so we could climb over in the clear and drop down below cloud again the other side. But after that the cloud base became solid again, and the gap between it and the curving hills grew less and less, until at last, when just four miles short of St Eval, we were blocked by the hill on the far side of the Vale of Mawgan. The moment I saw the block I swung the aircraft into a turn back on track, circling in tight safety for a minute or so to consider the situation.

We had four obvious options: we could continue towards St Eval and hope to find it clear for landing, search for Perranporth fighter airfield with the same hope, look for a field big enough to make a belly landing, or climb into cloud and jump. The other two opted to try for St Eval. That meant we had first to get over the cloud-covered hill and down into clear space the other side of it – if such a clear space existed over there. John had the map on his knees, had been finger-following our track since landfall, and as we circled tightly in the clear he spoke before I asked the question.

'Nine hundred feet will clear it easily.'

Having made that altimeter check out at sea I was now prepared to bet our lives on its accuracy. I turned on to course again, aiming for the cloud-covered hillside, and when half-way across the valley I climbed steeply into cloud, levelling out at a thousand feet. And prayed. John had reckoned that thirty seconds would see us past the top of the hill. He was doing the timing, I concentrated on flying level, exactly on course and height. The cloud, grey and damp, came wisping through the open window and flitted about the engine nacelle. After a long, long, long, thirty seconds John called:

'That's it.'

This was the worst moment of the whole trip, and as memorably tense as any moment in our whole operational tour – when I was writing about it in my notebook that afternoon I felt a retrospective chill at what we had done. The descent through the fleeting wispy grey silence was terrifyingly slow. The altimeter turned unwillingly, from a thousand feet down to nine hundred, to eight, and then to seven with still the grey swirling dampness all about us – window open, peering down past the yellow circle of the propeller tips, eyes straining to pierce the cloud, breath stilled.

Then suddenly, for an instant, like a hope you dare not trust, there seemed a smear of darkness below. Come on! Come on! You begin to believe the eddying greyness is truly starting to disintegrate. Then the shivering tension suddenly collapses at the realization. You're through. No doubt left, it *is* the darkness of ground . . . stone-walled fields . . . a heart-shaped patch of gorse in golden flower . . . white-walled house . . . a man harnessing horse to cart in a gleaming cobbled courtyard, pale face upraised as we thunder over the slate roof, cluster of steaming cows around gateway to field. And now ahead is a clear gap again between the grey base of cloud and the dark green glisten of wet grass.

The rest was easy because it was so familiar. This was home ground. The hill south of the bomb dump was in cloud as expected, so we flew out to sea and came back in at the low point north of the Watergate Hotel. We were safe then, but I was still darting anxious glances down at the petrol gauge as we crossed the dispersal of the naval airfield and saw our control tower of St Eval. Then we were flicking through cloud over the hangars in a circuit almost as tight as the perimeter track, catching sight of a little brown car near the crew room with a podgy figure beside it, still tightly turning over dispersal, then levelling off sharply, slamming back the throttles, and smoothing down at last to sweet, sweet ground, with a popping and a flaring from exhaust stubs as we let her rumble on to the end of the runway.

Tubby met us in dispersal, waving a welcome as we taxied in, waiting in the mud as we descended the wing. He had been worried when they failed to contact us with the diversion signal, for the airfield had been closed out; he had no idea if we had ever reached the target let alone got away from it, and had reckoned some time before hearing our approach that our petrol must surely be exhausted. We were the only aircraft to land at St Eval during the night, and for the next twenty hours.

As we were about to start off towards Tubby's car, John asked us to wait a moment. He went back to the Blenheim, then patted the fuselage of PZ-H just aft of the gun turret:

'Thanks, pal,' he said.

The following day he was on his way back to Canada.

Chapter 12

———◦———

Tubby came on leave with me. The New Zealander Herrick flew us up to Hendon, and returned to his death over Brest two nights later. We arrived two days after London suffered one of the heaviest air raids of the whole war. Immense fires raged throughout the central area, all the main-line stations were put out of action, Westminster Abbey, St Paul's, the Houses of Parliament and four of the Thames bridges were hit, and more than two thousand people were killed outright during the capital's night of agony. There had been a reduction in the number and intensity of raids in the previous six months, thousands who had previously thronged to the tube stations for a night's rest had begun to risk staying at home, but that raid at the end of May 1941 reversed the trend sharply.

We travelled by tube into town, it was late afternoon by then and already people were laying out blankets by the platform wall, putting down suitcases to reserve sleeping areas, bottle-feeding babies. When we reached the centre of London it was after five o'clock, and here the tube sleepers were gathered in great numbers. There was evidence of considerable organization; three-tier bunks were aligned along the walls, there was a canteen at the bottom of the escalators, toilet facilities (we saw men with towels around their necks, a girl vigorously drying her wet hair), and in a cleared space between platforms a large crowd was sitting down waiting for some sort of entertainment to start.

Tubby had arranged rooms for both of us at the RAF Club and we spent the evening there together. During the long convivial sessions that night at the bar and in the dining room, I gained the impression that peacetime RAF must have been like an intimate club. Tubby seemed to have memories to recall with everyone who came in that evening, they all knew one another, had shared experiences together, and when you thought the group had exhausted the review of their log books there would be a cry from a newcomer at the door:

'Good God! Tubby Grant!'

The next day we walked down to the Air Ministry, passing some old bomb sites where wild flowers were now growing quite profusely, the purple rosebay willow herb being particularly common. The visit was a revelation to me. I had no idea we possessed such precise details of German units. Tubby, who had been in Air Intelligence before taking over the squadron, kept asking questions like 'Where is Gruppen Kommander so and so now?' . . . 'What happened to the fighter squadron they had at Morlaix?' . . . 'Who's Kommandant of Lanveoc now?' When he told of my attack on Lanveoc we learned that two fighter squadrons had moved from there the previous week, transferred like so many other units to the east.

These large-scale eastward movements were explained when we had a session with his old chief, an air commodore. In his office one wall was given over to a huge map covering most of Europe, with little coloured flags marking location and aircraft type of enemy squadrons. A mere glance at it showed a massive build-up against the Russian border, pockmarks all over northern France and the Low Countries being left by pins that had been moved across to the right near Russia. When the air commodore said the attack was expected at any moment, I asked if the Russians were aware of this treacherous intent by their ally.

'We've told them,' he said. 'I don't think they believe us, though.'

I had imagined the sort of information conveyed on the map would have been visible only in a deep cellar reserved for the Prime Minister and the Chiefs of Staff. The implications of Russia as an ally were staggering, but, despite its momentous import, the air commodore and Tubby went on talking about old acquaintances and situations without any further reference to the subject. We were with him for more than half an hour, during which time a number of people came in and out of the room, some on business and some who had heard Tubby was in the building, and no one showed interest in the map. It was clearly an old story to all of them, yet it was totally unreported in the outside world.

Afterwards we walked back across the park, passing an elderly woman feeding the mallards who felt impelled to tell us that the bread was mouldy – you could be prosecuted for wasting food, and some councils checked through dustbins to discover offenders. At lunch I tackled Tubby again about doing a second tour of operations.

He still refused, and suggested alternatives: an instructor on Blenheims . . . a ferrying job with Transport Command . . . something in Air Ministry perhaps? He had wide contacts, was confident he could arrange such postings, but none appealed to me, so he finally agreed to defer decision. I would stay on temporarily, without a crew, carry out non-operational flying and odd jobs, and we could resolve the problem at leisure. I was happy to accept this, well aware of my luck in having a commander who would allow a mere pilot officer to quibble about his posting.

My hostess for the leave, Liz Layton, lived in a Buckinghamshire village and her 'young friend Timmie' turned out to be not a child but a delightful girl just a couple of years younger than me. Liz was working in London with a group led by Sir Richard Acland and Priestley who were setting up a new party called the Common Wealth Party. She gave to these political activities that same intensity she had shown when we met the previous year; whereas then I had thought her concern for Jewish refugees from Europe was because she herself was Jewish, I came to realize that such passionate involvement was typical of her attachment to almost any cause.

'How can I be tolerant when I feel so strongly about it?' she demanded, when we were talking about the government failure to specify war aims.

She asserted that the vast majority of people were now demanding to know the future for which lives were being sacrificed. Timmie and I had an argument with her about this that first evening. I had never heard anyone in the services claim, except ironically, he was fighting for those noble concepts you read in the press: 'freedom to worship how you wish' . . . 'a new social system in Great Britain' . . . 'the defence of democracy', and so on. Many may have seized some such excuse if questioned, but the real reasons were far more personal, and far less precise. My own must have been shared by many who had come to England to join the RAF – or to Germany to join the Luftwaffe. It was best noted by Yeats in 'An Irish Airman Foresees his Death':

> Nor law, nor duty bade me fight,
> Nor public men, nor cheering crowds,
> A lonely impulse of delight
> Drove me to this tumult in the clouds;

> . . . The years to come seemed waste of breath,
> A waste of breath the years behind.
> In balance with this life, this death.

After that first night Timmie and I lost interest in war aims, and for the next ten days we took no part, and little interest, in the war. She had been a driver in the ambulance service during the blitz, and because of her facility with the language had now been released to work with the French section of SOE, the organization that liaised with resistance groups in the occupied countries, but happily had not to report for duty till after my return. She had a little green Austin Seven saloon, and I had a leave allowance of ten petrol coupons – ten gallons cost less than a pound, and was enough to take us the length of England had we wished. But the Buckinghamshire countryside was delight enough for us in love that summer, as we watched the parting day from the churchyard at Stoke Poges with never a ploughman in sight, trailed hands in the rippling Thames at Bourne End, and one golden afternoon at Burnham Beeches saw a mallard drake land perfectly on the tiled ridge of a house, balance there without any apparent problem for several minutes, then fly off into the setting sun.

The traffic we met was nearly all military. There would be long convoys of canvas-topped camouflaged trucks weaving through the country roads with troops crowded at the tailboard, whistling and waving and shouting to Timmie as we ducked in behind each successive vehicle. There were staff cars, mobile AA guns, generators, amphibians with hissing tyres, tank transporters, and above all there were the tanks themselves; in the fragile little Austin you felt terribly vulnerable as these lumbered zigzagging towards you down a narrow leafy lane, clanking and squealing, monstrous front gun waving about in antenna-like search. We would pull up crammed against the hedgerow, and the great steel beast would lumber past in a clattering din, flabby tracks bouncing over wheels and flopping down on the road, the exhaust flattening in tone as it passed. Afterwards you would continue through a miasma of fumes over a tarred road surface now frosted with corrugated gougings left by the monsters.

The return from leave was depressing, not only because our holiday from war had ended but also because of the limbo that awaited me on return. It was almost midnight when the train arrived at Newquay, and I went straight to the Club for squadron news of the fortnight's events. Normally there would be up to fifty people crowded into the big room with its mahogany bar, red-tasselled lampshades on the wall lights, and rustic tables made from sections cut through the trunk of an ash, but this gloomy night there were only about a dozen there. I began to feel I had come to the wrong building – I had this sudden mental confusion, like when you have done all the normal things yet finish in an unreal world. Then I heard my name shouted from the far corner.

It was Tony Buck, sitting alone with several empty glasses on the table in front of him, bleak with news. Three aircraft had been shot down during the fortnight but the cause for his gloom was more personal. The squadron had been finally transferred from Army Cooperation to Coastal Command, Tubby had been recalled from leave to be told we were to convert to Hudson aircraft, and most of the squadron had already left for the conversion course in Norfolk. We had seen Hudsons working out of St Eval on that nightly 'Stopper' patrol off the entrance to Brest harbour, and that they were employed on this kind of placid operation indicated their nature. They were matronly things, plump and amiable, a converted civil type with padded seats and doorway entrance, designed to carry passengers comfortably at a steady speed. The Blenheim was a fighting machine, bare metal, almost half as fast again; to be switched from such a machine to a Hudson seemed almost the same as being switched to civil aviation.

So I was not surprised, nor excited, when Tubby told me next morning that in view of the changeover he had decided to let me do a second tour of operations. It promised to be long and dull, fifty sorties perhaps, for at that time the loss rate on submarine hunts far out in the Atlantic was nil from enemy action. Some Hudson pilots had finished their tour of operations without ever having caught a glimpse of anti-aircraft fire, never dropped a bomb, never fired a gun. Theirs was a stolid role remote from that vision of dashing duels in the sky that had drawn me away from the Solomon Islands. And Buck, with whom I had gone roistering about the Île de Ré one cloudy afternoon looking for an enemy presence to attack, was another who was desolate at the changeover. He was thinking of trying to transfer to Bomber Command.

My Blenheim, PZ-H, had been left for me to fly up to Norfolk where we were to do our conversion course, but Tubby asked me to wait a few days to see off the last of the ground crews. Left behind to help was a new arrival, Stanley Mayhew, not yet in his twenties. His brother commanded the torpedo-carrying Beauforts of 22 Squadron and was killed later that summer. Back in April when visiting Andover to collect a gunner, I had delivered a note to Stanley from his brother, and, so he told me years later, had made a heroic impression as a battle-hardened veteran from the fighting station out west. Now that I had finished a tour of operations he had me at Olympian level. I knew nothing of this at the time, but it was impossible not to notice the deference he accorded me during his first few days on the squadron – he even tried to carry my flight bag when we left the mess the following morning to walk down to the hangar.

Such was his respect that he was probably not surprised when the squadron commander himself, happening to emerge from the operations room just as we were passing, cried out 'Pat!' in obvious pleasure at sight of me. The reason for Tubby's pleasure was simply that I had saved him a search. A dinghy had been reported south of Ireland, it had to be checked for signs of life, and as he hustled me into the operations room the question of a navigator arose. I turned to Stanley, who had followed dog-like behind, he nodded eagerly, and Tubby agreed – the reported position was only half an hour away, so a specialist navigator was not needed. We rang the sergeants' mess, found a gunner, and in a matter of minutes were on our way down to our Blenheim in dispersal.

It was a day of hazy sunshine about the Cornish coast, so warm that I was flying in shirtsleeves, and the harness was already clammy on my shoulders by the time we were clear of the circuit. We climbed up to five thousand feet for a comfortable temperature and headed out westward over a huge flock of sea birds milling about a bountiful patch of sea which was being shrapnel-splashed by plunging gannets. There was no point in precise navigation, lookout was more important, so I told Stanley to come back beside me. He did so, but kept the chart on his knee, drew in track and wind vector, then presently gave me a course for the reported position. He locked the compass ring on it but I did not bother to get the needle parallel; it was an unnecessary bore to fly an exact course, and to avoid him checking the compass I told him to keep a keen lookout.

The haze cleared over the Irish Sea and visibility steadily improved, until, at about the time we reached the search area, we could see the sharp sea-line on the southern horizon, and to our north the Irish coast was colour-clear in brown rock, green field and white speckled houses. There were only a few mounds of cumulus scattered about the pale blue sky and the sea was smoothly calm, just breathing gently, one large fishing boat lolling on the surface, and not a sign of a yellow dinghy anywhere in the whole wide blue.

We set off southwards on a square search but after only fifteen minutes or so the gunner came through to say we were recalled. The navy had picked up the dinghy. So there we were, about fifty miles off the Irish coast on a bright sunny day, in an aeroplane practically full of petrol, and with nothing to do. I decided to visit Ireland.

There were a variety of reasons for this unauthorized intrusion over a neutral country. As I told Stanley afterwards, and truthfully, the prime one was simple curiosity – someone called Terence Patrick O'Brien was bound to have a look at Ireland for the first time when the opportunity was suddenly offered. It was fun, too; not the same pitch of excitement as flying over Ushant, for there was no risk of gunfire or enemy aircraft, but it was forbidden territory and therefore attractive. But vanity contributed to the decision also; I would have gone over Ireland that day without Stanley, certainly, but his hero-worshipping attendance was an attractive bonus.

He thought I was joking when I told him, then became concerned to find I meant it. Suppose we were shot down? We would be court-martialled. I burst out laughing at this. Worrying about a court martial struck me as an unlikely thought when plunging down in flames. Anyway, the only realistic chance of being shot down was by a German Me 110, and we were safer from them over Ireland than over the open sea. But Stanley remained anxious as I swung the aircraft around to the north, put down the nose, and we went slanting down across the glistening sunlit sea to the green coast of Ireland.

We had no map of the country, of course, so had no idea where we hit the coast, but some time afterwards we checked and decided we had crossed somewhere south of Cork. The coast was rugged, low cliffs and rocky inlets, and as we approached I pulled up briefly a thousand feet or so to check what was ahead – it was unwise to pass over a town, for the big PZ-H lettering on the fuselage would identify us positively. As we continued inland I kept zooming up every now and then to check the track ahead was clear.

The terrain could have been Cornish, small fields of various shapes defined by bulging hedgerows or stone walls, fitted together like a child's jigsaw, and frequently including a white-walled cottage; but there was one beautiful Georgian house with sash windows in perfect symmetry about a pillared central doorway, the approach drive lined with two soldierly ranks of lombardy poplars in fluttering leaf. There was little livestock in the fields, just a few head of cattle, but on the road we saw quite a lot of horse traffic including a light trap driven by a man who waved his whip at us as we swept past him along a slope. The other vehicle we passed on the road was a purple charabanc with five rows of pink seats stretching full across the width of the vehicle; it was empty except for the bald-headed driver, and looked like an exotic beetle crawling along the narrow road. There were hills ahead as we continued inland, so I turned away slightly to port and flew very low down a wide emerald valley for a few miles before turning south again to avoid a small town. We came back to the coast near a headland where a grey donkey was scampering down the length of a narrow field and kicking its legs in the air.

We were probably over the country for only about five minutes and Stanley had not spoken a word the whole time. I had assumed he was too worried about his involvement in the escapade, but once we were clear and out to sea I turned to ask his reaction and saw his brown eyes bright in excitement; the forbidden fruit had obviously tasted delicious. As we neared the English coast, however, he confessed he felt apprehensive about debriefing, wondering what he should say if questioned. I made sure he got nowhere near the operations room when we landed. There were never any repercussions, so presumably no substantiated complaint was ever lodged by the Irish government.

The following day I flew the Blenheim up to Norfolk, crossing low over the Fens where the willows were in yellowy green leaf, graceful light branches dropping into their own reflections in the placid waterways of the Broads. Bircham Newton, unlike St Eval, was not immediately involved in the war; their air-sea rescue flights were carried out from a satellite field, and not only were the aerodrome and buildings untouched by enemy action but so too were the station personnel, who frowned on our wartime standards of discipline and noisy activities in the mess. I don't know if it was Tubby who arranged the operational sorties for us so as to utilize our energy in fighting, or whether the station commander fixed it in the hope that the lot of us would be shot down and so relieve him and his staff of our pestilential presence, but presently we were being sent out in Hudsons and Blenheims to attack shipping or raid airfields in Holland.

Daylight strikes against shipping in the North Sea were more dangerous than those on the Atlantic coast because the ships travelled in defended convoys and usually with air cover. Buck was shot down attacking a convoy that was being escorted by three destroyers and five German fighters. Tom Waters, following close behind in the attack, hit the sea trying to avoid the exploding aircraft but managed to pull up with a damaged wing, drop his bombs on one of the destroyers, then evade the fighter escort by cloud hopping – or as Waters put it, 'I played pussy for ten minutes and lost them.'

I put off converting for as long as possible. In the meantime, using Blenheim operations to check out a possible new crew, I flew three night strikes against the Dutch airfields with three different navigators before meeting Peter Gibb, and at once struck a happy relationship. Peter was English, about twenty years of age, blond hair and blue eyes, and a little unsure of himself as a newcomer to our established group. It took us three attempts to get off on our first operation together because the new gunners were having familiar trouble obtaining W'T go, but in early July we finally managed to get clearance one night when due out on an anti-shipping patrol.

It was a thinly clear night, and climbing away from the satellite field I could see the shimmer of moonlight on corn that was rippling in a gentle breeze, and the waterways of the Broads showed up like pallid veins on a huge dark leaf. We climbed gently as we crossed the North Sea, and saw a shooting star come sweeping up from the eastern horizon to streak right across the sky in a great rainbow arch to disappear below the opposite horizon, and I half expected to see it rise again in the east on another scintillating circuit of our world. When within sight of the Dutch coast at about five thousand feet, I happened to look back on the port side and there on the silver ribbon of moonlight were set out three lines of ships which we must have almost passed over a moment earlier. You see best at night when looking up moon, the difference with ships in particular being that they stand out clearly in the lane of moonlit sea, black silhouettes sharply defined by the silver background; looking down moon it is difficult to see even a wake-producing target.

There were four ships in the centre line, the escort in the two outer lines comprised two destroyers and three very small vessels I guessed from the wakes to be MTBs. We kept steadily on course towards the coast, as if en route to some continental target and uninterested in marine activities, but called the gunner with the information and warned him to keep a specially keen lookout for night-fighter cover. We continued on course until about four or five miles away, by then over a grey curve of beach sands, and there we made our move. With throttles almost closed, bombs now fused, we slanted back down in a semicircular turn that left us heading up moon and on a line we reckoned to bring the convoy directly ahead of us in the silver shaft of sea.

They came up exactly as planned. We were still a few hundred feet above sea level, planing down fast, when we saw the three lines directly ahead – merchant ships in the centre, MTBs nearer to us, destroyers on the far side. We steepened the dive until almost within prop-tip touch of the deep blue silvered surface, then slammed on full throttle, together with the boost, and charged in towards the second merchant ship in the centre of our moonlit track. You do not just drop the bombs in such attacks, there is a feeling of positively ejecting them when you pull up sharply at the moment of release to hurl them against the black wall of the ship's hull. We passed so low between the masts we could have cut their aerial, and I saw clearly a light move quickly across the forward hatches, far too quickly to have been carried. Thrown? We dived down to sea level on the far side, skimmed through the gap between the two destroyers and then away down the moonlit trail across the calm sea. Not a single shot was fired at us.

The bombs were fused at ten-second delay by which time we were nearly a mile away. I am sure at least one of the four bombs must have skipped into the ship's side, and the fact that the gunner declared only that he 'thought' he saw a flash made no difference to that conviction. A bomb that explodes inside the hold of a ship might well show little or no external flash, particularly to a viewer a mile away at very low level. I considered it a copy-book attack.

The Controller in the operations room did not think so. He was a namesake, Charles O'Brien, a first-war pilot, and at debriefing he told me we should have gone back to observe results. I just shrugged, but he kept on nagging about it so finally I told him that if he considered the record so important he should fly out himself to the awakened escort and look around. He became testy at this, said he would 'speak with' my commanding officer. There was no chance of any useful dialogue after that and we parted in scowling antagonism. He had said nothing that persuaded me we should have hung around to check results; we would not only have come under fire from the escort ships, but also probably from the night fighters normally associated with these convoys. The essential job had been done; a big ship had been hit, and His Majesty's aircraft and crew were back at base ready to do another strike. That was the way to win wars, surely?

I had a second skirmish with Charles O'Brien a week or so later. We had been sent out on a convoy escort, taking off in the pearly blue dawn as the veils of mist over the Fens were drifting up to caress the sky, and we assumed the sea mist would also thin out with the onset of daylight. But it did not. When the sun had finally broken clear of the horizon, and the sky above was a limpid egg-shell blue with not a single cloud to mar its purity, down below us the mist still remained in solid cover as far as the eye could see. It was about three hundred feet thick, laid on the surface of the sea like woolly strips of fleece that dipped down slightly at regular joins in the vast white layer; visibility down inside it was little more than a hundred yards, as I discovered in a brief check, so I shot up again into the safe clear.

In such conditions I doubted if we would ever find the convoy, let alone escort it, but it had solved the problem for us. Approaching the position given to us, we suddenly came upon five silver barrage balloons poised about four hundred feet clear above the corrugated roofing of mist, spaced out neatly in line against the horizon. From a distance you could not even see the cables, let alone the ships to which they were tethered, just that line of free-floating balloons, and I suppose I should have been grateful for these markers; now, all we had to do for the next three or four hours was to circle about them gently in the sunlight, instead of trying to get down among ships and balloon cables and trigger-happy destroyers inside the murk that was settled on the sea.

I could not relax, however. The folly in not close-hauling the balloons in such circumstances struck me as incredible. Having learned something of balloon tactics in those early months of the war, I felt the man in charge of that unit should either be court-martialled for treason or dismissed from the service for gross incompetence. The ships were hidden in the mist, he then proceeds to fly his balloons not merely to advertise their existence but to provide actual aiming points for enemy aircraft. Had it been a German convoy, I would have dive-bombed from the clear above in four different directions, one bomb through each of four balloons so that at the very least I would have destroyed them – the gunner finishing off the others – and on probability hit at least one ship.

Had we been able to contact the convoy I would have told them to close-haul the balloons, but I had no intention of blundering about in that murk where there was little chance of getting a message through on the Aldis to any ship at all, let alone that of the convoy commander. So it was not until our return that I could do anything about the situation, and it was unfortunate I then had to deal with Charles O'Brien in the operations room. When I said that the navy should be informed about this stupidity, he told me rather pompously that it was not for me to tell a convoy commander how to do his job. He would not even include my criticism in the intelligence report until I threatened to call in Tubby to adjudicate. We parted in mutual disagreement for the second time.

The battleships in Brest finally prised us away from Norfolk. Their continued presence so close to the vital Atlantic link was like having a landmine caught insecurely in a tree beside your house – any moment it might slip with catastrophic consequences. The slightest movement of the battleships, or any suspicious local activity, sent tremors quivering through to London, shocking the Admiralty and the Air Ministry to instant action – panic action occasionally. I don't know why, on 29 August 1941, we were all ordered into the air at short notice; maybe it was a Spitfire photograph showing a wisp of smoke rising from the *Scharnhorst* funnel, or an agent's report of a *Gneisenau* sailor buying a panama hat, but the consequence was that we flew off instantly to Northern Ireland to prepare for battle. By the following day, however, the tremors had passed, the ships were still solidly Brest-locked, so we returned to England. They settled us back at St Eval in Cornwall, now as a fully operational squadron of Hudsons.

Once or twice over the next few weeks I took out new crews on introductory night 'Stopper' patrols outside Brest harbour, but the vast majority of the squadron flights were anti-submarine patrols. These were done miles out in the Atlantic, sometimes over the gently breathing sea at the centre of a great atmospheric high, sometimes over the turbulent gale-streaked waves of a deep low, but almost invariably without enemy contact. During the three months of this work only five submarines were sighted and attacked, and none were claimed as definite kills. And we did not lose a single aircraft.

Only once did I ever come close to offensive action, when we sighted a boat much bigger than any trawler we had ever seen in the Bay. It had cabins, bridge superstructure, and a lifeboat, and we thought it might be one of the German 'mystery' ships we had been warned about, but we were finally able to identify it as a Spanish trawler, venturing dangerously into the war area. It was a lovely day, the sea surface perfectly smooth with just a gentle heaving like a great blue jelly that had been wobbled and was settling back into stillness, and there in the middle of it was this boat with two shirts hanging out to dry over the front hatch, a small brown and white dog rushing about the deck and obviously barking furiously as we kept roaring past, and four of the crew waving at us.

I was glad they were innocent. Never before had I seen the Atlantic so blue, the Bay so glassy smooth, just here and there those faint ripples made by detached eddies of wind that moved like wayward spirits across the empty seas. After speeding across the heaving surface for a while, I felt induced to participate in the movement, relaxing into a gentle easing backwards and forwards of the control column as I and the aircraft moved in slow undulating flight as though part of the very sea itself.

It was not a day for dropping bombs.

Chapter 13

―o―

That second operational tour in the autumn of 1941 was a broken one. I was used as an odd-job man, being pulled in for a sortie when there was an emergency shortfall, taking out a new crew on their first night-bombing operation, doing flying tests on specialist equipment. In addition I was sent flitting about the country on a variety of non-squadron tasks in a variety of aircraft, detached for days or weeks at a time on propaganda visits to factories, doing flying exercises with Combined Operations, trying out night-fighter schemes over Norfolk airfields, and carrying out searchlight tests with the army AA Command.

The factory visits started in September. Pilots from all three RAF Commands, Bomber, Fighter and Coastal, were called on to make these visits to factories that produced munitions or equipment used in action, the purpose being to boost the workers' morale. I was probably a happy choice for these stunts as I could always concoct some story that showed how vitally important their valve, or fuse, or whatever it was they made, had been to us on some fictitious occasion.

We would start off in the management office, usually with a drink or two, then I'd be taken around the factory where the loudspeakers would be blaring out 'Workers Playtime' with songs like 'Give a Little Whistle', 'Amapola', and 'Over the Rainbow'. The women were particularly friendly, mostly in overalls, hair tied in scarves, young and old alike so cheerfully sociable you soon ceased to feel embarrassed and could relax and enjoy their banter. The men were mostly pleasant, but occasionally you came across one who seemed to resent your presence, jealous perhaps of the attention you were being given. After the factory tour we always finished up at the canteen with the work force gathered, and there I would stand on a stage and talked about flying operations.

Then came the long session of questions. They asked if I had been hit by gunfire, how many crews survived an operational tour, and always – not once in eight visits did I miss the query – they asked if I had bombed Berlin. When I confessed I had not, I frequently got from the floor the stories they had heard from a Bomber Command pilot last week who *had* done so. It was to counter this invidious distinction I so often resorted to fiction.

Once was at a factory in the Midlands where they were making parts for our ASV (Air to Surface Vessel) sets, a sort of radar with a little screen which you observed through a view finder; it was supposed to show up any surfaced submarine within range, but in practice no one in the squadron had ever found a submarine through the set. However, that day, in response to the aspersion about Berlin, I talked about a pilot who found one by the company's ASV, bombed it successfully, and discovered later from survivors that the U-boat commander had been none other than the famous Kurt von Platz who had sunk seventeen ships in attacks on Atlantic convoys. So my failure to bomb Berlin was overlooked in the glow of pleasure at the role their product had played in saving the lives of our seamen.

The parting could be tender at times; in the London tube stations they used to cheer you as a vengeful ally ('Give them hell from us'), but the words you most often heard from the factory workers when leaving to return to duty were 'Good luck, love', usually with a handshake, sometimes with a kiss.

At this time there were occasional intrusions by German fighters over our airfields during the night – later, many bombers were lost to such intruders over home base on return from operations. After the satellite field of Bircham Newton had suffered three such attacks that October, it was decided to try Blenheim patrols to discourage the intruders, and I was sent back to Norfolk to try out the scheme. This was Coastal Command doing its own thing; they should have worked with Fighter Command, which had experienced night-fighter pilots and specialized machines for the task, whereas the Blenheim had no special equipment to track aircraft, its radio was the primitive set used on bombing operations, and it was much slower than any intruding Me 110. I said it struck me as a crackpot scheme. The briefing officer said no one had asked for my opinion.

We tried it out for ten days over a full-moon period. There was broken cloud every night, the moon would be beaming through the gaps in great spotlights on the flat fields of Norfolk, but no German aircraft would oblige by emerging from the shadows to join us in the great lit-up stage areas. One night I tried above the cloud, it was strangely angular like stiffly beaten egg whites and not the usual woolly bulges, and our shadow showed up so sharply as it wriggled across the pack-ice of cloud that I returned below before we became the hunted instead of the hunter. At the end of the trial I gave a damning report on the scheme which was received rather sourly by the officer from group headquarters who came to discuss it. I discovered afterwards that he had been the originator.

In early November I was detached again to carry out army co-operation exercises with a special service battalion. Later these groups were unified in Combined Operations Command and carried out major raids such as the massive landing at Dieppe, but at this time they were mostly in the development stage. My group was working out how to utilize aircraft on guerrilla operations; for the exercises we had three Blenheims, of which I was the leader, and we carried out simulated landings of parachutists on Salisbury Plain and boat parties on the north-east coast, supporting them with mock bomb and gun attacks, and the dropping of supplies. I was involved in the planning and post-action assessment of all the exercises, but spent most of the time trying, without success, to make the army officers accept that no pilot could guarantee to wipe out gun positions or enemy troops in a trench. Those army officers who had been in the retreat to Dunkirk, when the Luftwaffe had been so predominant, were particularly obstinate in this belief.

I returned by train so as to steal a night in London with Timmie. The next evening the sirens went as I was waiting at the station. I noted:

Sky kept flitting with light from gun flashes, searchlights waving about aimlessly, deep-throated rumble of Heinkel stooging around overhead (sounded very low, surely not crazy enough to come in below balloon height?). Air loaded with dust, and smoke too, thick enough to make breathing a business. Then suddenly the all-clear – just a miniature raid really. Glad to get on the train and escape not from blitzes but from dust and smoke and stink. Out of town the train stops for some reason, all is silent in the countryside, then it gives a melancholy three-note whistle that echoes like the call of a kurrawong across an inlet of Sydney harbour. And suddenly I am homesick almost to tears.

* * *

Back at St Eval the initiation night strikes with new crews were against the submarine pens at Lorient and the docks at St Nazaire, and I had an eerie experience coming back from one of them. It was a moonless night, no cloud at all but the star-show somewhat subdued, and we had been about an hour on the steady return course when I suddenly found myself convinced that we were upside down, out in space and flying down towards the stars. I could not dispel the feeling by looking down through the window because the sea was not visible, what my mind saw down there was the blackness beyond the stars, a blackness from which I was coming down to a starry universe. We were on automatic pilot but I am sure I would not have reacted to the illusion even had I been in control, strong though the impulse was, for the instruments plainly showed we were in normal horizontal flight. However, I had to concentrate on them for a few seconds, particularly the artificial horizon, to dispel the illusion, and then I found I could bring it back by a sort of passive acquiescence, like those ambiguous drawings such as the Necker cube where the front and back of the cube keep changing perceptually without you doing anything.

A long time afterwards Stanley Mayhew told me he had experienced the same illusion, and thought he was dead. At the time I mentioned it only to the flight commander whose reaction was to wonder, seriously, if I had been too long on operations and should be completely rested. I had to convince him it had nothing to do with operational fatigue. Earlier I had had occasional nightmares about a stream of fiery tracer swinging towards me with increasingly loud explosions, that bok-bok-bok sound, the final one bursting me out of dream into cold sweaty wakefulness, but that had been back in the summer when we had been out on strike night after night. I am sure the illusion about attitude was not the result of stress; it was not a stressful period just then, indeed it was more like a flying holiday with all those odd jobs coming my way.

There was a period of ten days' searchlight liaison around the end of November. The navy's precious battleship, *King George V*, was due in to Plymouth for servicing; AA Command, anxious about its protection, asked the RAF for someone with experience against the Brest defences to assist them checking out some ideas. The request filtered through to St Eval and the station commander chose me; so presently, with two other pilots – Waters and Stanley Mayhew acting as crew – I flew down the coast one afternoon to Perranporth whence the exercises had to be done through the radio communications set-up of the fighters there.

We were met by a major-general, a naval commander, and six assorted staff, and in the briefing hut heard their proposal for an adjusted searchlight defence of the port. They had more than fifty searchlights at their disposal and had practised creating a near convergence of the beams at five thousand feet, the idea being to move the big cone as a unit in front of an advancing aircraft. They thought this would create a light barrier such that the aircraft would have to swing away from its attack line or drop blind when caught. I was certain the idea would not work – there would be gaps in their barrier and the cone easy to avoid anyway – and the others expressed doubts, too. The general, who had had little to say, then intervened to suggest we gave the scheme a trial, made a run over the target area, and if it did indeed prove what we claimed then we should return at once, 'no sense in wasting your and our time'. We could then discuss the matter further if it seemed worthwhile. So we set off with a staff major as passenger on the fifteen-minute flight to Plymouth.

It was a moonless night but the stars were coldly clear, the sky almost devoid of cloud, and we picked up the searchlights already in static position from about ten miles away. The crossed lines did form a vague cone about a thousand feet above balloon height, but we had no trouble picking out the docks – nor had the major, once given the line. The only effect of their concentrated area of light seemed to me to pinpoint the target. The Hudson weaved a leisurely path across between the lights, which did move as a unit in an attempt to block our passage but they were easy to avoid and the docks remained in sight the whole time. The major shook his head and when we banked to make a return run he waved his hand in dismissal, but as the line was more or less our track back to Perranporth I flew straight across, and again we were not touched by light nor was the target obscured. When we landed the general was waiting on the tarmac, and after just a few words of our negative report he cut in with a rare admission from a major-general to three very junior officers: 'You were right, we were wrong. It doesn't work. Well, you've been over Brest plenty of times between you – I want to hear what ideas *you* have.'

At last! Someone asking us for ideas. He led us smartly back to the hut where the others were waiting and where two soldiers served us tea and chocolate biscuits – it must have been nearly two years since I had seen a chocolate biscuit, I had a second one but Stanley and Waters held back. The general gave us the floor, discouraging his own staff from raising questions but instead asking us to comment on the opinions of one another. Stanley had very little experience of night bombing but he was academically knowledgeable on the subject; Waters had done some airfield raids over Holland, and our RAF consensus was that searchlights alone had no hope of hiding the target. It was the immense number of guns at full blast that was the major component in blotting out sight of Brest harbour, but the German searchlights did incidentally contribute towards the concealment, and the way this occurred could perhaps teach us a lesson.

Smoke was the important factor. The smoke produced by the guns and exploded shells, together with the emissions from the thousands of smoke pots about the area, produced an artificial haze which when lit by searchlights did certainly help obscure sight of the ground. We suggested that instead of having lights pointing almost static into the sky it might be worth trying them out from tall buildings or high ground around Plymouth, slanting them into artificial smoke created over the target area. Such an arrangement would, we felt sure, give a far wider area of obscurity than naked uprising lights.

The artificial smoke could, of course, be created by smoke pots, as at Brest, but we wondered if anyone had ever thought beyond such stationary emissions. Why not have aircraft trail smoke across the area at first threat of a raid? In pre-war days barnstorming aircraft flew stunts with trailing smoke, so the materials and technique were obviously available; half a dozen aircraft could smoke-over most of Plymouth within minutes, and searchlights slanting into such swirling smoke might well make an effective screen. The navy had slow biplanes which might possibly be used for this.

Whether he did ever try out any of our ideas – we had one or two other suggestions that night – I don't know, for very soon afterwards we were all thousands of miles away beyond recall for discussion. But he did give me that night a pointer about generalship: it was that if you encourage junior officers to express an opinion, they will not only be far more eager to help solve a problem but might even occasionally come up with some helpful ideas.

We made our last flight from St Eval on Tuesday, 9 December 1941. It was also the last operational flight I was ever to make in England. These are the comments about that particular sortie which I wrote in my notebook a few days later:

Had to take a reporter from the *News of the World* on an anti-sub patrol. They wanted to lay on a specially safe job, so the orders were to fly west for 200 miles from Land's End then do a zigzag patrol. It was safe all right, the nearest we were to France on the whole trip was on take-off at St Eval. And no story for him in sortie. Low mass of cloud-fog whole day, hundreds of miles of the stuff, so saw nothing except few holes in it. Low cloud over base on return, dark by then, so went to Chivenor and put down there for the night. Ju 88 now gone [a lost German raider had landed at night by mistake, thinking he was over Lanveoc].

The cloud-fog bank was not absolute. You look around, you are up in brilliant sunlight, cloudless blue sky, below is blinding white blanket covering sea out to horizon in all directions, it's a different planet, like Venus perhaps, cover of thick cloud and no idea if hills or sea or what lies below. No matter, it's lost anyway. Then suddenly you see a hole. They keep occurring every now and then, no pattern, and not much bigger than a tennis court. From your brilliant wide world you look down into a deep pit, about five hundred feet deep, with dark foamless water lurking at the bottom. Very mysterious. What causes these holes in the vast fog-mist prairies? Often see them, and never a clue to explain their existence, just ordinary sea below, not yellow or boiling or water-spouted, must be same temperature as all the rest, same wind, so why a hole? Like those mysterious little wind eddies you see on the absolutely flat surface sometimes way out in the Atlantic, as though someone or some *things* had fled away when you suddenly appeared on the horizon, weird and secretive things, not for us humans to know. What are they? And what were they up to, way out there in the empty sea, making those strange whirls on the surface?

My note gives the prosaic facts about this sortie. The reporter, however, produced this fanciful version in the *News of the World* on 14 December 1941.

DAY IN LIFE OF A HUDSON BOMBER

VIGIL BOTTLES UP NAZI WARSHIPS IN BREST

By Our Own Reporter

THIS is the story of a few hours in the life of a Hudson Bomber crew, belonging to a coastal squadron which has become " a pain in the neck " to Hitler and his henchman Goering.

It is the story of their patrols all along the coast of France; their sorties into mid-Atlantic, ceaselessly hunting U-boats; and their constant shuttlecock vigil which keeps the German warships Scharnhorst, Gneisenau, and Prinz Eugen bottled up at Brest.

The story is written by a " News of the World " reporter who was the guest of the coastal squadron's wing-commander—he is known as " Tubby " to all R.A.F. men from Singapore to Kingsway—on patrol in " X for X-ray," one of the latest and most heavily armed Hudsons.

After a hectic trip to see the Crystal Palace display of enemy searchlights and " flak " along the coast of occupied France. I walked into the Operations Room just before the dawn with " Tubby," writes our reporter.

There was a list of all the machines which had gone out during the night and the times of their safe arrival back.

" X for X-ray," the wing-commander ordered, " will take off on patrol. Examine the Biscay coast, go out into the Atlantic, and hunt submarines and enemy vessels."

A minute or two later, cluttered up with maps, " Mae West " flying harness, parachutes, and a container holding sandwiches, chocolate, raisins, a thermos flask and an orange, we scrambled aboard a tender driven by a blonde W.A.A.F., and drove straight across to where " X for X-ray " was drawn up on the grass.

We were a mixed lot. " Pat," the pilot and captain, who comes from Maitland, near Sydney, was in copra in the Solomon Islands, and on the way to making a fortune when he heard the call of war, sold everything, and came to Britain. To-day he holds the record for attacks on Brest.

" Peter," the navigator, comes from Cheam, Surrey. " Ginger " was our tail gunner. He is a young Scot from Melrose, near Edinburgh, and this was his first flight since he crashed into the Channel three months ago. He had to swim through a dirty sea, the surface of which was ablaze with burning petrol, and then continue swimming for another two hours until rescued.

" Crook," a typical Londoner, manned some other guns, and I, a Fleet-street reporter, and member of the Home Guard, was promoted to the seat of the second pilot.

On the same page, but further down and not so importantly headlined, were details about the loss of the battleships *Prince of Wales* and *Repulse*, which the Japanese planes had sunk a day earlier. Official comment at the time, in public at least, avoided direct criticism of the admiral's action, but nearly every report implied censure for sending the battleships without air cover. To us who had worked out of St Eval attacking enemy shipping, and trying to protect our own, it was an incredible action. Around England even single merchantmen had an air escort, convoys not only had a continuous patrol overhead but were also covered by fighter contacts. If the two battleships could not be provided with strong fighter protective cover, they should have been pulled out of the area altogether; they would have been a most valuable adjunct to the Australian navy in the Solomons presently. In the Singapore area, without any air cover, they were nothing more than sacrificial targets.

The intervention of the Japanese had suddenly made the war more personal to me, for it seemed they might actually attack Australia. It was maddening to be stuck in England doing these fiddling jobs, thousands of miles away from the scene of potential action in the Far East. For days I kept pestering Tubby to use what influence he had at the Air Ministry to get me a posting out there. I told him about the months I had spent working on a schooner in the coastal waters of Siam and Malaya, and my command of the language, experience which must be of value locally – all lies of course, but told convincingly enough to weaken his resistance. And when I was having a drink at his house on return from that *News of the World* sortie, he suddenly capitulated. He would, he promised, see what he could do to get me posted to the Far East.

Coincidence intervened. The very next day a signal arrived from the Air Ministry instructing him to select fifteen crews from the squadron to fly out to Singapore immediately. New Hudsons with extra fuel tanks were being prepared at once, and the selected crews were to be given seven days' leave before reporting to fly them out to Singapore.

Tubby must have agonized over some of those names – the recently-married, the couple with a new baby, the untested crews, the pilots under strain – but he did have one he could put down not merely without a qualm but as a positive favour. I was the first on his list. And when he heard I was going Stanley Mayhew, I discovered later, asked to be included and he had his wish.

It was on 29 December 1939 that I arrived in England to join the RAF. I left on 29 December 1941 to lead a flight of Hudsons back along the trail over which I had come, now far far older than the mere two years that had passed since the time of that civilian journey.

Chapter 14

——o——

It was a different war outside England. It had been *our* war in England, particularly that year after Dunkirk when we were alone in the stockade under threat of invasion; you would fly over the green fields with their mesh of shadow-mounted hedges, over villages with waving children and towns with beetling vehicles, and you knew that the millions down below claimed you as one of them, that you were together in a battle for survival. But in the Middle East, India, the Far East, you had nothing to do with the lives of the inhabitants; you and your enemy were aliens using their land as a battleground, all they could do was suffer in silence, perhaps earn a crust by serving whichever of you happened to be in occupation at any time. Their indifference to the fight took some of the sparkle out of the champagne.

I was nominally in charge of that first batch of five Hudsons to leave England, but the charge bore little responsibility; the route through to Egypt was well organized for ferry aircraft and the others were all experienced operational pilots, friends with whom you agreed a plan, not juniors to be given orders. Except for Stanley Mayhew, who had asked to accompany my group, the others were simply those who happened to be ready: Waters who thought it would be a 'wizard show' out in Singapore, and two comparative newcomers, Johnson and Matson.

We took off a few hours before dawn on 29 December, flying separately, carrying two wireless-operator'gunners and a fitter in addition to navigators. For both political and topographical reasons Gibraltar had to be approached carefully. The airstrip was across the narrow isthmus joining the great cliff to the continent of Europe; this, the only piece of flat ground about the rock, had been the racecourse and the airstrip ran along the old finishing straight within a stone's throw of the Spanish border. A normal left-hand circuit would take you over this border and that was Fascist country. So with forbidden land north of the strip, and forbidding rock 1500 feet to the south, it was impossible to make even an unbalanced circuit; you had instead to approach from the south, and, dependent upon the wind, fly either to the right or left of the rock, then turn in immediately when past it to land across the isthmus. That was the principle. In practice the inexperienced needed many attempts.

For the airstrip was perilously short. In 1942 they extended it out over the water (even then a take-off crash killed the Polish leader General Sikorski), but at this time it covered only the width of the isthmus – eight hundred yards, less than half what was considered a short runway for bombers in England. I put down first that day, having told the others I would do a dummy check run, but our approach happened to be so good I grabbed the opportunity to touch down within the first fifty yards of the strip, so pulled up without difficulty. The whole area up to the frontier fence was packed with parked aircraft, we had to taxi carefully after the airman guiding us through the motley collection to a space near the fence. The others squeezed in by us, all landing safely, though Waters came in too fast and finished with smoking brakes – 'in bags of panic', as he put it.

The racecourse grandstand had been taken over by the RAF, and the Officers' Mess was in the space underneath, where I joined the others presently when the sergeants were settled. They were chatting with crews of a Hudson squadron that had been at St Eval in the summer and were now on anti-submarine patrols of the supply route to the North African front. Auchinleck had launched a successful attack recently, advancing over eight hundred miles, and in an attempt to halt this advance the Axis powers were concentrating their air and sea forces on our supply lines through the Mediterranean, so the Gibraltar RAF units were being driven hard. It was not all work, however. While we were swopping information and sharing drinks with the locals – I was squeezing lemon rind to get the tiny spray on my cheeks and about my nose – someone put his head through the door and yelled, 'The Blenheims are coming.'

He disappeared at once, and the others began to gulp down drinks as if a curtain were about to rise. We learned that reinforcement Blenheims for the desert squadrons came through almost every day, flown by crews direct from training units, so the landings on the critically short strip were full of interest. We were urged towards the door, drinks still in hand, thence up into the grandstand itself where you could sit and watch the spectacle, betting odds already being called on the chances of all four landing without mishap.

It was an extraordinary view from the grandstand. The strip, blackened about the midway mark by scars from a thousand frantic brakings, ran across in front of you on the line of the old finishing straight, and on both sides of it the dusty ground was covered with parked aircraft. Among them I identified Hudsons, Beaufighters, Bostons, Swordfish, Blenheims, Wellingtons, Beauforts, and with American markings two Mitchell B25s and a Martin 26. It took me a puzzling moment to realize what was peculiar about the mix. They were all twin-engined. On a busy operational station in England you would see some four-engined heavies, a fighter or two, some light communication aircraft. There were none of these at Gibraltar; the big ones could never land on the strip, the fighters and little ones could never reach it from England and would serve no purpose anyway. So it had only these sixty or seventy medium-sized aircraft.

Beyond the frontier fence on the far side of the field was the town of La Linea – white walls, terracotta roof tiles, khaki dust-haze – but nearer just outside the fence was a tree I recognized at once . . . gaunt trunk, mottled brown and white, strips flaking from it, drooping leaves so scanty the branches were clear in definition. It was a eucalyptus, the first I had seen for two years. I wanted to go over and give it a friendly slap as a fellow expatriate, but it lay out of reach in an alien, and somewhat hostile, land.

The four Blenheims had already done a low check run in line astern over the strip, one of them having to bank steeply at the last moment to get direction right. The noisy betting talk in the grandstand would have bewildered any ghost left lingering there from horse-racing days. The punters were back but where were the horses? And what had they done to the track? A bookmaker pilot offered us two to one against them all landing without damage and Waters joined Johnson in a pound bet. I refused because I reckoned the locals would know the form, Stanley refused because he thought it immoral to bet on such a matter.

It was quickly clear the locals did indeed know the Blenheim form. They said the first one would stop in time even though he touched down about a quarter way along the runway and he did – with a hard-braked swerve just by the beach. The second one did two heavy bounces as they shouted he would go round again, and sure enough, with a sudden roar of engines, he staggered into the air again and was away for another circuit around the great rock. The third one lost Johnson and Waters their bet. He came in too fast, ballooned on touchdown, dropped with a thud I thought would break the undercarriage, and the grandstand crowd shouted, 'He's had it! He's had it!'

He surely had. Despite smoking brakes he toppled off the end of the strip, one wheel collapsed, and the nose of the aircraft slowly dipped into the shallow water. The aircraft looked like a huge beetle that had crawled to the edge for a drink. The crew were all right, and the remaining two Blenheims managed to get down in an exciting display but without breaking anything. The bets were settled and we left the grandstand as the crash crew started retrieving the wreck.

The flight to Malta was the longest leg on the whole journey to Singapore, and because enemy fighters controlled the surrounding skies we had to arrive there just on dawn – the Blenheim pilots, unpractised night fliers, went off in daylight formation, to be met and shepherded in to the island by fighters based on Malta. We night runners had to rely on navigation to avoid Algeria where the Germans had numerous AA batteries, and the island of Pantellaria where the Italians had a heavily defended fighter station, diversions which put us at the extreme limit of endurance, so navigation was critical.

We took off first at midnight, discovered that the predicted head-wind was at least useful for lift-off, and passed the message back to the others waiting on the ground – Matson in particular had been worried about taking off with the overload of full fuselage tanks. Minutes later we were in such a deluge Peter Gibb had to shout his course changes against the roar of water crashing on to the fuselage, and in the streaming cockpit window the quivery reflection of my face showed sickly green from the receiver light – I finally covered it with my cap. We never saw a star again for the rest of that night, flying through blackness sometimes wet, sometimes dry, but always impenetrable. In the core of the weather front we plunged through a series of thunderstorms, but all the lightning showed outside was that we were embedded in tumultuous cloud.

After nearly six hours without a checkpoint or radio bearing in such unknown winds our switch to the new course had to be made on dead reckoning and a prayer. Our reckoning was out, our prayer ignored. The moment after the course change we roused a nest of searchlights and a battery of guns. I swung away and after some minutes of fuel and distance calculations decided we needed help, so asked the radio operator to put out a priority call to Malta for a QDM (radio bearing). His pip-pip-pipping Morse penetrated through the cabin as we continued on an easterly course that was, at least, taking us closer to Malta.

By this time there was no longer any turbulence in the cloudy night, just a solid blackness all about, and we were flying so evenly on automatic pilot we could have been doing an engine test on the ground. In the Blenheim you flew as an intrinsic part of the machine, an embedded working component, but in the Hudson on automatic pilot you sometimes felt bereft of power; that night I had a curious feeling of detachment as we went on throbbing in the darkness, the radio bleeping, all instruments locked into position, no feeling of movement within the void. I could see and hear what was going on, but had no part in it, no influence, no concern. I could have been anywhere. Or nowhere. Or no one.

I was back to sharp reality when Malta finally responded to our call. They gave us a bearing, then we were able to ease around the dangerous Pantellaria in the grey dawn and finally sight Malta black on the horizon against the rising sun. They called us to wait south, there was an air raid, but by then fuel was too low so I ignored the order; we saw black cloudlets of AA over the harbour but no enemy aircraft as we headed in to land on the grass field at Luqa. It was pockmarked with pallid scars marking filled-in craters, and a truck whisked us away into trenches the moment we stopped the engines. It was a cloudless morning and the light had a limpid clarity that reminded me of Australia, the few buildings about the airfield were so brilliantly white I found my eyes narrowing once more back into the grooved wrinkles established in childhood.

The others landed presently, having waited for the all-clear. On the drive to our billet we passed a large clump of prickly-pear sprawled over a narrow terrace on which was a line of small glossy green orange trees decorated with tiny lamps of fruit. Progress was slow along the narrow road between low rock walls; a herd of goats brought us to a halt as they padded and bleated past us, followed by an old man wearing a violet blanket over his shoulders in the warm sunny morning. There was another air-raid warning as we approached the green-shuttered villa that was our billet, but the driver gave it no attention.

I did, however. The insistent evidence of continuous enemy air attacks had me worrying about the safety of our aircraft, despite their bomb shelters. I phoned the station commander to see if we could be refuelled and take off for the security of Egypt at once, despite our sleepless night. We could not.

He explained that tankers were kept off the field in daylight, five of them with their precious petrol load had been destroyed by bombers, so we had no alternative but to leave our aircraft at risk till next morning. And as fuel had to be brought in at such cost – of five ships in a convoy that tried to get through that month not one survived – we could have only enough to reach our nearest occupied airfield in the desert, which was Mersa Matruh.

We went in to have a look at Valetta. The bomb damage was unusual in that there was scarcely any evidence of fire; most of the bombed structures were reduced to piles of honey-coloured limestone, the common building material on the island. Only around the Grand Harbour area were there more familiar bomb scenes such as blackened and twisted girders, and hollow sockets of warehouse skulls. In the town damage was severe – white walls collapsed to show a room like a stage set, wooden shutters dangling by a single hinge, delicate railings of a balcony tilted precariously across the cluttered street, huge doors of a coachway carrying white scars from shrapnel. Twice during our tour the sirens sounded and people did seem to take note of them, going off unhurriedly to shelters. The caves and tunnels under Valetta built by the Knights of St John three hundred years ago had been developed and widened, they were like narrow streets, even had street names painted at the junctions, and let into the sides were cubicles that could take whole families. It was like an underground city, and safe from bombs; but for this refuge the loss of life above ground in the raids would probably have forced capitulation.

Luqa airfield was bombed twice that day – 'the usual dose', they said. None of our aircraft was touched, but such luck could not last (three were lost in the subsequent transit flights), and I felt an immense relief next morning when we had all escaped intact from the island. It was a five-hour flight. Near the coast of Africa the sky separated into two segments – from about ten thousand feet upwards it remained azure blue, but below that it became a uniform tawny yellow; the lower band blurred all detail in the desert and when we descended into it you could feel your skin tingle at the impact of grains through the open window. It was not a severe sandstorm, Peter did manage to map-read us to Mersa Matruh, but once on the hard bare ground we could see no sign of life in the sandy gloom. We were presently found by a man riding a motorcycle with side-car. He flashed his headlights to lead us to the refuelling tanker and we stepped out into a gusty airstream that was hot and dry and gritty.

We took shelter in the mess tent during refuelling, and discovered that two fighter squadrons were stationed there. The pilots were all in khaki battledress, white silk scarves, suede shoes, many of them flailing fly swats; the whole picture was such a copy of those seen in *Life* or *Picture Post* captioned 'Fighter Pilots in the Desert', you felt it was a set-up, that they were not real pilots in a genuine squadron but a posed group assembled for visitors and then dispersed in their normal varied clothing once you were gone.

En route to Cairo an hour later, still in the tawny haze of the dust storm, our port engine suddenly began to streak oil about the cowlings and the pressure dropped sharply. I had visions of sand in the cylinders, and a friction fire about to burst out of the engine, so I shut it down and feathered the propeller; unlike the Blenheim with unfeatherable propellers, the Hudson was quite happy on one engine, but all the same I diverted to the Fleet Air Arm station at Alexandria where I handed our problem over to an elderly chief petty officer.

He had been a farrier in the cavalry during the First World War, switched to the Flying Corps, and had chosen to go with the navy when they broke away into a separate air force. Next morning I found him and several ratings gathered in the cockpit, bemused at the luxurious layout of the Hudson. This was to happen constantly on that flight to Singapore. To the old hands, those who had served in the first war, a cockpit was merely a sort of working bench from which you could reach all the rods and wires that kept the machine moving and fighting; the plush seating in a Hudson cockpit, green carpet, throttle casing, enamelled switches, rheostat lighting – all these struck them as ridiculous extravagances, like dressing up the horses of the cavalry in tutus. Talking about the engine, however, the CPO was soberly professional:

173

'It's your rocker boxes that's the trouble,' he said gravely.

He made it sound like some sort of intestinal complaint. I had no idea what a rocker box was, but happily our fitter was in on the consultation and confident the treatment given would get us to Iraq where we were due for an inspection. Cairo Command tried to hold us for their own use but a peremptory signal from London changed their mind and the following day we escaped to fly on over the pipeline where the car had passed us in the Hannibal battling against a headwind, and we finished the day landing for our inspection stop at RAF Habbaniyah in Iraq, close by the turquoise lake where I had caught the flying boat after the pilot had refused to take off in the arthritic old biplane.

Across India the transit route was rigidly established. We had to follow the stages, but we did manage to circuit the copper-red Akbar fort at Allahabad where a whorl of vultures were ascending with sailing splendour in a thermal south of the town; and we followed the Ganges down to Benares to see the river bank pebble-dashed with pilgrims, then climbed up to twelve thousand feet, where in the cool clear air above the haze we could see the white jagged line of the Himalayas etched brilliantly clear against a pale blue northern horizon. Again the local command tried to hold us, again the Air Ministry slapped their wrists.

We flew out of India Command the next afternoon, slanting down across the Bay of Bengal to Akyab on the coast of Burma, a cluster of white houses, coconut palms and lush green paddy fields around a little bay with a lighthouse in the centre. There was no RAF station, just a grass landing field with a refuelling party, however the local Europeans arranged accommodation with an Indian contractor, and at their club plied us with drinks and food, including large luscious prawns which they cooked on a hotplate and served in the shell – messy to eat and delicious to taste. Luckily I had picked up an imprest in India so could pay the Indian contractor, who put us up in a basha hut with new charpoys and nets for the bed and breakfast stopover for the twenty of us.

Next morning we climbed away from the little harbour with its decorative lighthouse, then crossed over jade-green mountains to the Burmese plain where, on the dusty airfield at Toungoo, we parked by a line of Kittyhawks with nose cowlings painted as gaping shark-jaws, the mark of Chenault's Flying Tigers. We lacked the range to reach Singapore itself, so for a refuelling stop I had to discover how far down the Malay peninsula the Japanese had then advanced, but when I spoke about this to the squadron leader in command at Toungoo he said he had instructions from his Rangoon HQ to hold us, as we were urgently needed in Burma.

'Not again, for Christ's sake!' I cried.

He stiffened into rank at this, then relaxed when I explained the reason; but he was unwilling to argue our case, so early next morning I left the other four aircraft as pledge and flew south over valleys clogged with cotton-wool mist and down the Irrawaddy where quivery stalks of pale blue smoke were rising from the clusters of bamboo dwellings and little white pagodas that marked the villages. By Rangoon the sun had climbed high enough to dissipate the mist, and from twenty miles away we could see the dome of the Shwe Dagon pagoda flashing golden clear in the clutter along the river that slides through the capital.

The RAF Command headquarters was located in the botanical gardens. The path from the gate was lined with hibiscus, in canary yellow, coral pink and crimson flower, and varieties of plantain one of which had a cluster of tiny scarlet fruit that was dripping mauve juice on to the gravelled path. Inside the gauze-screened building was a vine with huge dark purple flowers growing up a bamboo screen, there were weird orchids jutting out from moss-filled containers at its base, and by the windows water was dripping from baskets of staghorn and other tropical ferns. It was like going into a luxury florist shop. And Wing Commander Percy, with whom I discussed our delay, was like an amiable manageress trying to soothe an angry customer.

Of course the hold-up must be upsetting for us! How well he understood our distress! But Air Ministry would reply presently. Why not pop down to the Silver Grill meanwhile? They did a jolly good lunch; he could recommend the oysters.

I told him about the previous failures to hold us, and how cross they had been in London about it. He did become thoughtful at this, said he would discuss it with the air commodore, so we went into town to await their post-siesta discussion. I had spent a night in the capital on the flying boat stopover two years earlier; with its shady walks in the white-pillared arcades, old-fashioned shop signs ornately printed in black and gold, and avenues of flamboyant and jacaranda, it reminded me of Brisbane when I had first tried to enlist in the Australian Air Force. But despite the pleasant nostalgic street scenes, and Percy's jolly good lunch, I was anxious not to become entrapped in this Burmese pitcher plant, so was glad to hear on return that we were released. The air commodore, it seemed, had decided not to risk a reprimand.

The next day, flying at a cool height over the Andaman Sea where patches of reef seemed to be bleeding colour into the blue surface, we met the ITF (Inter-Tropical Front); it solidified on the horizon like a mighty mountain range, rising up to forty thousand feet directly across our track. We plunged into the great wall of whiteness without concern, emerging now and then into majestic canyons and vast cavernous chambers; only later did I discover how violent the tropical cumulus can be, how lucky we happened to meet the ITF in a particularly benign mood. Our luck lasted to the end, for at arrival time the sky suddenly cleared and there in front of us were the dark jungle-clad slopes of Sumatra.

We had been briefed by Percy to land on an islet off the north coast and this briefing turned out to be as untrustworthy as I suspected. The grass strip was perilously short, so we took off presently with our near-empty tanks and put down on a new big field on the mainland. Sumatra has a mountainous spine which even at that northern extremity has ridges up to four thousand feet within a few miles of the airstrip; on the mountain slopes from a distance the jungle looked smooth and consistent as a carpet of Irish moss, but the foothills and lowlands were checkered in cultivation, with rice paddies and rubber predominant, and along the black-sanded sea front was a strip of coconut palms with frond-edges flashing silver in the sunlight.

The nearby town was called Kotaradja, and there we spent the next day with the wife and family of a Dutch naval officer whom we had met on the islet. She and her three young children took us on a tour of the town, the most attractive we saw in the whole of the Far East, with its shady shopping arcades, gleaming white domed and pillared public buildings, colonial-style houses set in spacious gardens with colourful tropical shrubs, and many palms such as coconut, areca, ivory-nut and the tall carioca that I had known back in the Solomon Islands.

Later they took us up the mountain to a spectacular swimming pool, cut out of rock and fed from a stream which tumbled down from the high cloud-concealed peaks above. On the downward side you looked over the ribbing of rice fields to a patchwork of coloured vegetable plots between the larger plantations of sago, coconut and rubber. After its long drop the crystal-clear stream gushed into the pool effervescent as soda water, icy cold, shocking, invigorating. The children screamed as they repeatedly ran under the entry stream, you had to thrash around to stop going numb, and long after you were out of the water your skin still went on shivering and tingling in reaction from the shock. And how delicious the Bols tasted as it thawed your chilled body!

Eight of us out of the twenty who set off in that first flight survived the Far East campaign, and each has his own special pictures of places visited, of times and experiences shared. But if you were to start running the reels of each individual memory, there would, I am sure, be one clear frame common to us all – a picture of a rock pool cut high in the mountain side, tingling water, play with delightful children, and carefree laughter amongst friends.

That was the end of our holiday journey from England. We took off early next morning and, to avoid Japanese-occupied Malaya, flew along the foam-flecked western coast of Sumatra to our turning point near the equator. There we changed course to cross the densely wooded spinal ridge and down to the flat swampy area on the far side, then for the next hour flew over the most fearsome terrain I have ever seen from the air. It was like a vast inland mangrove swamp, a semi-submerged tropical forest where the water glinted with an oily sheen through dark green mangled growth, and never a sign of human or animal life in the whole two hundred miles of brooding menace. In some of the earth's most inhospitable terrain, such as icy mountains or raging seas or burning deserts, you can imagine means of survival, but nothing on earth I have ever seen offered less hope than that dark steamy jungle swamp, and no death more frightening than the lingering horrors it threatened. It gave way at last to mangrove foreshore, wide clean sea inlets, and the welcome signs of humanity manifested by the black spidery lines of fish traps stretching out into the still blue waters of the Malacca Straits.

So finally the first flight of Hudsons to Singapore had arrived. It was not the land we saw first, it was a huge column of black smoke rising like some monstrous genie thousands of feet above the bombed oil tanks on the east of the island. They never stopped burning all the time we were to remain in Singapore.

Chapter 15

—◦—

It was easy to imagine RAF Station Tengah before the rot set in – a month before we arrived say, – back at the beginning of December 1941 and still in local peace. The Officers's Mess stood proud on a grassy slope to the south of the field, from the terrace you looked over the lush green grass, then a smooth-topped expanse of rubber plantation stretched away to misty blue hills on the mainland of Johore. You could picture officers and guests out there on mess nights chatting under the Southern Cross, resplendent bearers in blue and gold livery carrying silver trays of drinks, behind them the strains of a waltz coming from the dance band in the spacious lounge brilliantly lit and aswirl in colour.

Now, a month later and into war, all that was gone forever. Many of the windows were now empty of glass, so the rain came misting through in the frequent tropical showers, one of the louvred doors was hanging askew on a single hinge, the electricity had failed, most of the mess servants had left, water supply was erratic, sewage drains blocked.

In the living quarters we found the same desolate abandonment. There was no longer any door at all on the room allotted to Peter and me, the wall mirror was smashed, but there were six clean folded sheets on the foot of the bed waiting to be put away somewhere – they had been there so long they had dented the damp mattress. And on the floor was an upturned chair. It all brought to mind the poem by W. W. Gibson about the lighthouse on Flannan Isle with its mute evidence of disaster:

> Of the three men's fate we found no trace
> Of any kind in any place,
> But an open door and an untouched meal,
> And an overtoppled chair.

We dumped our bags there on arrival and went back up to the mess where the green exterior wall was white-scarred from shrapnel. On the door to the bar was a notice saying we should sign for any drinks taken but even that rule had now lapsed, for there was no book to sign. We collected a couple of bottles of 'Tiger' beer from the refrigerator, which was out of action because of an electricity cut, and went on through the billiard room where a half-empty glass stood on the end of the table and a big leather settee had a sheen of bluish damp-mould that must have been growing for a week or more. Outside on the terrace, relaxing in long-armed cane chairs, we questioned a station officer about what had gone wrong with their war.

The rest of our squadron aircraft arrived in the next day or two, the final total being thirteen; our sister squadron in England had also sent aircraft and five of them reached Singapore before the end. The local command had decided we should be split between the two Australian Hudson squadrons, but Air Commodore Staton who had come as passenger on one of our aircraft supported the argument of our senior officer Peter Lilly that squadron unity was important for morale, so we from St Eval went instead to 62 Squadron. They were without aircraft, all their Blenheims having been destroyed – nearly all on the ground – in the first few days after Japan declared war.

The squadron commander, Wing Commander McKern, had an impossible task. How on earth can you efficiently command a squadron equipped with a type of aircraft you yourself cannot fly? How can a man brief crews when he has no knowledge of the aircraft's capability, and has far less operational experience than any of his pilots? How can he possibly measure his crews when he is not only incapable of assessing their present performance, but knows nothing of their previous experience? McKern did his best, none of us blamed him for our problems, but he had been given an impossible task by a purblind staff. Lilly should have taken command; however, to a local staff besotted with service protocol, seniority was more important than experience, so Lilly became deputy commander – but in the event he controlled all flying activities.

The next morning after breakfast we hurried outside on to the terrace at the sound of gunfire. There had been no warning and we saw that just a single gun was firing at one aircraft, flying so high it was barely discernible in the cloud-strewn sky. It was the weather plane, the adjutant said. The Japanese had an established routine.

The weather plane flew over the island at about the same time every morning, studied the wind and cloud conditions, then intercepted the bombers coming down the Gulf of Siam and passed them the information.

The bombers usually started out in a formation of eighty-one aircraft and nearing Singapore would split into three groups, twenty-seven aircraft for each target, bombing in salvo on the leader's signal. Their targets were the four airfields, the naval base, and the docks, but they also did an occasional terrorizing attack on the town itself. It seemed sensible therefore that we should fly away somewhere during the bombing hours, but when Lilly tried to arrange this he was refused permission; regulations stated that our fuselage tanks, installed for the journey, had to be removed before we could fly locally.

It was ridiculous to preserve such a peacetime order. Far better the slight risk of meeting an enemy fighter in the air than the certainty of losing planes on the ground to the bombers. I wondered about disobeying the order that morning, taking off illicitly, but the field was too open to view. Lilly decided to bypass the group captain, go into Air Command to argue the case, and asked me meanwhile to check the dispersal of our aircraft. There were both earthen and brick blast-shelters on the field and I went down to ensure all were being utilized, and that aircraft without shelters were at least dispersed.

We were walking back up to the mess when the sirens began to wail and presently, guided by the AA puffs, we were able to sight the Japanese aircraft. There were twenty-seven of them evenly spaced in V-groups of three, the whole formation shaped like a Gothic arch, sliding across the sky as a perfect unit. They must have been above twenty thousand feet, and the sensible reason for this was that the vast majority of the guns on the island were three-inch, which could only reach up to seventeen thousand feet – the Japanese knew this, of course, as they knew everything else about the prepared defences of the island. The bombers moved across in a steady throbbing formation towards the naval depot and presently we heard a sound like distant thunder.

Two more similar formations followed, one crossing towards the docks, the other passing north of us to Sembawang airfield seven miles away. Again all the gunfire seemed to be two or three thousand feet below the bombers and we saw no RAF fighters. We saw no

Japanese fighters either, but they were on escort duty out of sight above the formations; through the throbbing drone of the bombers you could hear their faint buzzing sound, intermittent and surging in strength, like a theme being assembled to emerge from a Beethoven storm. Two bluish smoke columns rose from Sembawang airfield, a single dark cloud from the town area. It was infuriating to see how easy it had been for the bombers. You longed to rush down to your plane, take off after them, and blast their own aerodrome just as they were landing and laughing at our defences. This was the paramount feeling among us newcomers, fury at the impunity of the Japanese attacks.

There was, however, also great anxiety about our aircraft and I spent the next hour or so down on the field trying to speed up the removal of our fuselage tanks. By lunchtime I was confident we would be ready to fly next morning, and when Wing Commander McKern arrived at the mess I told him we would be ready to do an air test next day, suggesting a two-hour one south of Singapore during the Japanese raiding period might be a suitable time. He said he had orders that under no circumstances were our aircraft to take off until headquarters had given permission.

Stay on the ground to be bombed? It was madness. Most of the resident bomber force in the Far East had been lost on the ground in the first few weeks of hostilities and you would have thought that Air Command might have learned something from that; in England when an airfield was at risk we used dispersal fields some distance away, sensibly having the planes somewhere else when the enemy bombed the field. I hunted down Lilly to ask him to intervene, but discovered he was himself already simmering about the order, having spent all morning in a vain attempt to get permission for at least those aircraft already detanked to fly off. No! We were to stay on the ground next day – and await the bombers.

That afternoon I went into Singapore with Richard Johnson; his family owned a toy company in England, and their Singapore agent sent a car to collect us. There was little evidence of bombing along the road, and people seemed to be living normal lives. We saw a group of Chinese squatting outside a hut and flashing chopsticks as they ate a late midday meal, were held up by a Malay boy shepherding a flock of noisy ducks along in front of us, and passed a turbanned Indian haranguing some labourers by the railway line. In the city outskirts, below a huge billboard with a gaudy advertisement for the film *Mata Hari* starring Garbo and Navarro, a Chinese calligraphist was sitting at a table fitted with an umbrella and drawing characters with sinuous gestures, while another man, presumably his client, squatted in front of him.

There was a strong smell of burning rubber in the smoky haze over the city and in one street littered with rubble the rescue workers in tin helmets were still digging. Nearby a Chinese woman was squatting by a rickshaw half buried in broken cases of what looked like tinned fruit, beating her head and crying. The street was closed off by an Indian policeman wearing what looked like outstretched wings on his back – he controlled traffic at the junction by turning his whole body. There was still plenty of traffic weaving about the bomb-damaged streets, including swarms of little yellow Ford taxis, and the place did not give the impression that an enemy invasion was imminent. We finished at Raffles Hotel, on the terrace of the palm court where doves and swallow-tailed butterflies were flitting through the inky shadows of the palms. We had just sat down at one of the white cane tables, under a ceiling fan wobbling on its long stalk, when a man crossed to join us.

'You didn't shoot many down today, did you?' he said.

It was not meant unpleasantly, just a sad statement of fact. He was 'in shipping', a friend of the agent and much more outspoken. He was bitter about the ineptitude of the establishment, of the government and its officers, and even of the senior staff in the services; the whole bungling crowd of them were telling people a pack of lies about the state of the war, creating a situation 'in which thousands will be trapped and killed'. He himself had followed the advance of the Japanese down the peninsula not from rosy bulletins issued by the government or the heavily censored newspapers but from commercial facts; when one of his agency offices was no longer answering the phone, or the bank sent him a circular saying a branch was 'temporarily closed', he knew the place had fallen, despite what the government communiqués were saying.

'There's precious little left the other side of the Causeway now,' he said. 'No more than ten miles or so, I'd say.'

The cretins of the establishment, he said, were still not telling the truth when it was now actually in their interests to do so. Civil servants were as insistent as ever about the formalities of emigration;

passports had to be stamped with necessary visas, accompanied by medical certificate where required, passage money had, of course, to be paid. As a result of this, and the lies about the disastrous military situation, boats were leaving Singapore with plenty of berths to spare; one had gone that week with thirty-six empty cabins. This was happening whilst families fleeing down from the peninsula had to be billeted in schools on the island; such refugees were a drain on resources now, and would only be a worrying burden on the defence when the siege began.

It is curious that although we accepted his assessment of the situation we were not concerned about ourselves. On the way back that day, when we talked about the imminent fall of the island we took it unmentioned that we would fly off in due course to continue the fight from Sumatra or Java or beyond. The safety of our aircraft was therefore of concern. When I discovered that evening that our fuselage tank had in fact been removed, I told Lilly that a flight test to check the fuel lines would be advisable next morning – once in the air I intended to stay there well beyond the raid period, regardless of orders.

It was not possible, however. He had made a further appeal that afternoon but Command had been adamant. It was stupefying; even on simple mathematical chances, Tengah, as one of the targets not attacked that day, was likely to be hit next morning, but our presence would by now be on photograph so that made the likelihood a certainty. It was hard to contain the anger and frustration felt at the stupidity of such a decision. You longed to trace it back, track it carefully through the corridors of command until at last you found the fool who originated it, then kick him literally out of his office. We were not far from revolt that night. A group of us had a mutinous session in the mess, apart from the station officers, drinking a lot, purposely raising voices in criticism of the calamitous order, and damning those responsible. None of the staff group, which included the station commander, made any attempt to quell the protest.

The near mutiny that night is another example of the importance of treating those who do the actual fighting not as disposable units but as intelligent human beings. If someone had come to us that evening and put the case for staying on the ground next day – assuming such a case existed – then whether we accepted the logic of his argument or not we would at least have respected his integrity.

Without such an approach we naturally assumed there was in fact no rational argument for the decision; all common sense cried out against it, therefore it had to be a blunder by the idiots who commanded us. That the staff at air headquarters were ignorant of, or indifferent to, such widespread sentiment is an indication of the quality of command in the Far East. It also explains why in that first week the feeling among the aircrews in the squadron varied between mutinous fury and black despair.

The following day there occurred an extraordinary event which no staff officer could possibly have foreseen. The Japanese bombed Tengah airfield.

Their reconnaissance plane came over as usual shortly before eight o'clock and from then until raid time we waited sullenly for the attack. When the sirens sounded we moved across to the slit trenches cut into the red laterite topsoil behind the mess, and from there watched the first twenty-seven formation come straight for us, visible intermittently through the scattered cloud. We heard nothing as the bombs fell through the air, just the explosions on contact, like a thunderous tattoo on the drums, and a shuddering of the earth. The sound seemed to come from beyond the far perimeter but this was an aural illusion as we discovered later, caused by the hill and buildings perhaps, for the complete bomb pattern fell within the airfield. Just as we were congratulating ourselves that our aircraft had probably survived the raid, and were beginning to emerge from the trenches to check the actual result, another formation appeared just south of us heading towards the town area.

This time something exciting happened. They had just passed us, in perfect formation as usual and safely above the puffs of gunfire, when a lonely Hurricane made an attack, diving straight through the throng. We actually heard his guns, a sound like the ringing clangour of those iron-legged forms on the concrete floor at Uxbridge, then saw the flash of an explosion within the bomber group. I heard nothing unusual, perhaps the explosion was absorbed into the AA gunfire, but we could see the flaring debris falling down and a hole in the middle of the formation. It seemed to me that two aircraft had been destroyed and I was standing above the slit trench trying to count the formation as they continued on towards the town when Tom Waters shouted at me. I looked up, saw another formation almost overhead, and dived back into the trench.

Again they were at about twenty thousand feet and the patchy cloud made it difficult to count the number correctly; I had to imagine the shape of the whole, then reach the count of twenty-seven again from the pattern. As they came directly overhead and the throbbing intensified, I lowered my head into my shoulders again to await the downfall, exchanging a quizzical look with Peter Gibb beside me. Then there came a strange fluttering noise – the closest equivalent I can think of is the noise made by a bird trapped in a confined space, of its wings brushing rapidly against wood. The fluttery sound grew rapidly louder and had me wondering for a fearful instant. What on earth was it?

Then the salvo of more than a hundred bombs exploded all about us. There was no rising scream like the German bombs, no whistling or whining sound at all, just that wing-fluttering noise abruptly cut off by a tremendous blast of shattering violence. The ground shook, thudding our bodies away from the side of the trench; the explosion seemed to continue, like a monstrous engine revving up, the sound waves vibrating so that you went on feeling and hearing the noise. When we finally clambered out, chattering almost hysterically about God knows what, we discovered our trenches had been straddled by the formation salvo, but no one in our immediate vicinity had been hurt. Further down the slope towards the field one trench had, however, been hit and eleven airmen killed.

The effect on the Hudsons was not as bad as I feared. One was a complete loss, an almost direct hit had blasted it over on its back; another was badly damaged by a near miss, and two more had shrapnel damage presently discovered under the red clay splattered over the fuselages by the blast. Our own aircraft was untouched. Having assumed the loss would be far worse, I was at first grateful that we still had eight unscarred aircraft, but the longer I stayed around the scene with the others the more angry I became with the staff who had kept us so vulnerable on the ground. Even Peter Gibb, normally so tolerant of mistakes by others, was moved to cry: 'Four aircraft, flown two-thirds of the way round the world – now wrecked because of sheer bloody inefficiency.'

In the end we lost only two completely, but that was still two more than we should have lost in such a manner. And because of the spares used to repair the damaged ones, we had to write off two aircraft later for lack of spare parts.

When we gathered at the mess for lunch afterwards we made our resentment clear to McKern, the charge becoming personal when I argued, 'If *you* had let us take off . . .' I apologized for this later; he had, so Lilly told me, gone into Command HQ with him in an attempt to have the injunction lifted. We did tend at first to treat the wing commander as another stultified local to whom an established practice was a sacred ritual, but the very fact that he would listen to harsh criticism from a junior officer, never try to silence you with rank, did gradually create sympathy for his position. Even that day in the mess when we expressed our feelings so recklessly his reaction was not imperious, just regret at failure to prevent the loss. That afternoon he and Lilly did finally get Air Command to allow us freedom to move, and the following day we were over the coast of Sumatra when Tengah airfield was bombed again.

The afternoon after that second raid I went with Peter Gibb and Richard Johnson on a little local tour. We had been moved from the stricken airfield barracks to huts in the rubber, and at the turn-off into the plantation I asked the driver instead to continue on towards Johore Straits, to see if any Australian units were among the defence force. We drove on, and within a couple of miles came to an abrupt stop in a little clearing where the road ran literally into the sea. There was no village there, just three bamboo houses under the paltry shade of casuarinas by the shore, and beyond them an angular fish trap of black wooden stakes stretching out into the flat mirrored surface of the Straits. It looked to be a mile or so across to the peninsula mainland, we could see a white-clad figure over there chopping something on the ground and hear each blow of the axe as he was half-way up for the next one.

There were no soldiers about, nor any signs of their presence. The only person in sight was a Chinese or Malay woman, ankle-length ruby skirt, grubby white blouse and coolie hat, making a slanting cut in a rubber tree on the far side of the road. I called to ask if there were any soldiers nearby. She turned and looked at us, knife poised in one hand, the other wiping down a small canvas apron suspended from her waist, then shook her head and patted her mouth with her hand. I have no idea what the pantomime meant but my echoing shout had raised no heads anywhere about the foreshore. She alone, with just a knife, and not even a slit trench for protection, was all that stood between us on the airfield and the Japanese army now driving down the peninsula.

Just twelve days later when the Japanese landed on Singapore island the route they took was the one we saw that afternoon, across that narrow stretch of water and then down the road to Tengah airfield. Happily we were in Sumatra.

We left two days after that inspection of the island defences, all away by seven o'clock in the morning, flying separately and clear of the island before the reconnaissance plane arrived. It was a clear morning and as we climbed towards the causeway a train was puffing southwards across it, moving slowly with regular thrusts of power that left separate puffs of smoke poised like Indian signals in the still air. To the south on the racecourse I could see a horse doing an exercise gallop, and nearby on the golf course two figures were walking along a lush green palm-lined fairway. We flew across the Malacca Straits at a comfortably cool height, carelessly brushing through the tops of gathering cumulus which at that early stage of development were harmless as mist, and passing over dark mangrove-green islets set on a solid block of blue. The sea in that land-locked area was nearly always flat, but in the afternoons when the clouds became dark and heavy with moisture the calm surface would be roughly brushed by torrential rain, grey columns of it which seemed to be supporting the cloud canopy from which they sprang.

Palembang, the largest town in Sumatra, is about fifty miles upstream of a wide navigable river – we saw a ship of about ten thousand tons moving upstream that morning. Three miles short of the town was the great oilfield and depot, the storage tanks spread out like silver coins arranged in careful display on a green baize cloth, four or five groups of them in separate blocks. It was an enormous site, yet there was not a sign of a single bomb having fallen; clearly the Japanese wanted to take over the facility in perfect condition.

Upstream where the town straddled the river there was much activity, a large ferry sending up dense black smoke and dozens of smaller craft making slow-changing patterns of ant-like movement as they swirled between the red-roofed buildings on both sides of the river. The airfield was close by the town and easy to find, as was evidenced by the aligned red-earth circles of repaired bomb craters left by Japanese raids. But this was not our destination, we continued on south-west for the secret aerodrome called P2, some fifty miles away.

Here it did require some attention the first time to discover the field, even though we had an exact bearing from the town. What made P2 so successful a concealment was that it looked just the same as it had before the war, merely a jungle clearing that was either natural savannah or one of those patches that many tropical peoples clear and work for a few years then abandon when the soil is exhausted. It was shaped like the silhouette of a woman in a full-length flared skirt, over two miles long and narrowed at the waist by a grove of trees the Dutch had shrewdly left untouched. Around that area of Sumatra was a scattering of such clearings, so the field was an unremarkable feature in the topography; there was no proper road anywhere about it, only the typical webbing of jungle tracks which had been discreetly widened just enough to take service traffic. The Japanese never found P2 until their landing force stumbled across it.

The place was not only almost invisible but also almost inaccessible. Apart from the lack of road communications, there was no nearby town or market to supply a thousand or so men with a variety of fresh food, so we had to subsist largely on tough zebu meat, rice, and pineapples from a nearby plantation. We lived in wooden huts fitted with double-decker bunks, four of us to a tiny room, about a mile away from the field where our aircraft were secreted in jungle alcoves. The station commander was an Australian, Group Captain McCauley, with whom I happened to have a personal contact through his wife; her youngest brother had been a close friend in my pre-Solomon days and I had often stayed at the family home on the lake shore at Belmont just off the Sydney road.

In his determination to preserve the secrecy of the airfield, McCauley had created some interesting problems for the pilots. Apart from having to tuck our aircraft into jungle alcoves and cover them with branches, we were forbidden to circle the site, which meant we had to land down-wind if we happened to arrive from that quarter, so the extreme length of the field was sometimes useful. Night flying had special complications. Once you started the engines you had to send a runner to the control hut to check there were no enemy aircraft in the vicinity, and when he returned with the go-ahead you then taxied lightless to the take-off point. There you switched off your engines, so enabling the night-flying officer to listen for presence of any enemy aircraft. If sonically satisfied that all was clear he then gave you a green to restart the engines.

In principle this should have resulted in the flare path appearing; there were ten airmen stationed down the length of the field and when you were given the green light the first man lit his hurricane lamp. He held this aloft for a moment so the next man down the line could see it, light his lamp and follow the same procedure, and so it continued down the line. Once all these matches had been struck and lamps lit you had a line which, although it could not be seen in totality, you could pick up piecemeal as you headed down the field, so enabling you to keep the aircraft more or less aligned till airborne.

There were two snags. The field was not flat but convex, so if one lamp-lighter happened not to see the waving signal then he could break the chain, for some lamps when lowered to the ground were not visible to a man standing a hundred and fifty yards away. Secondly, the frequent squalls of rain that swept across the field would often prevent the visual signal being passed. The consequences of such broken chains could be stimulating. We roared over the central hump one cloudy night to be faced with complete blackness, the last five lamps were unlit. I had instantly to switch vision from outside to inside, no jabbing of rudder in search for the remaining lights but eyes straight down to the gyro compass with a prayer that it had settled. Fortunately it had, it got us safely through the trees in the waist of the field, then up into the cloud-filled sky when I let out a whistling breath of relief.

The following day I spoke to McCauley about the danger and he said he would introduce a change; each airman would in future have to ensure the next lantern was lit, if necessary running down within shouting distance to pass the message. Unfortunately that same night, before the modification was put into practice, three Blenheims taking off in line astern missed the centre gap and flew into the trees. All nine crew were killed, all three aircraft destroyed. They were not the only aircraft lost on take-offs and landings at P2. We paid a price for the security of that airfield.

Then came 26 January. About midday I was leaning against the outer wall of our hut, scraping the glutinous brown mud from my shoes, when Tom Waters came plodding heavy-footed as a diver up the track from the field.

'There's a flap in ops,' he said. 'You've got to lead a strike. Six of us – against a Jap landing force at a place called Endau.'

So I went down to the operations hut to be briefed about 'a place called Endau'. Tom Waters, who then had about five hours to live, came with me. And already waiting there was Francis Matson, he too about to die.

Chapter 16

———o———

They tried to be dismissive in briefing. Their story was that three Japanese ships, each about ten thousand tons, were landing troops on the beach at Endau, a hundred miles north of Singapore. There was no naval or air escort, just three merchant ships. I was to lead the attack, to take off immediately.

Had Lilly been available this would have been just the start of briefing, but the three officers in the hut were all old long-serving seniors in Far East Command and I think they expected that a junior officer, having been given this information and order, would leave at once. They grew tetchy when I began to ask questions. No escort of any kind? How were the ships situated? What airfields had the Japs occupied up the peninsula? Any map? Return flight beyond our range, so which airfield in Singapore for refuelling? It was typical of Far East Command that they had few answers to these and other questions; despite all the years they had been talking about the Japanese threat they still had no detailed geography of the threatened coastal area, and no maps for us – Peter Gibb had later to use a page from a school atlas for a flight to Java, and a Hurricane pilot had to take a tracing of it for himself and friends.

It is worth mentioning what had already happened that day, just to show what information could have been assembled for us by an efficient staff. The ships had been seen, with what was *reported* to be a strong escort of cruisers and destroyers, by an Australian Hudson on reconnaissance that morning, and it was decided to attack with the maximum strike force available. This did not amount to much. At that time the total effective bomber force of RAF Far East was less than fifty aircraft – our twelve Hudsons, about the same number of Blenheims, and two squadrons of ancient Vildebeest-Albacore biplanes. In total that day the RAF managed to send thirty-five aircraft to attack the landing, some two-thirds of their total force, but not all reached the target; twenty-four Vildebeests and our six

Hudsons did so, the Blenheims of 84 Squadron, however, which took off shortly after us, stopped at Singapore because, in the startling words of their own commanding officer, 'It was growing dark.'

The Australian Air Force also attacked; they sent nine Hudsons from their base on Singapore just before midday, bombed from fifteen thousand feet and all their planes returned. At about the same time twelve RAF Vildebeests made a low-level attack and five were shot down, including the squadron's commanding officer.

The survivors of the morning attacks had all landed back at Singapore with their stories, and the particulars of the naval escort and fighter aircraft protecting the transports, well before we were being briefed with such scanty details in that dark hut on Sumatra. We knew nothing about the morning attack, worse than nothing about fighter and naval escorts. We were told there were three Japanese ships all by themselves landing troops on the beach at Endau – but nonetheless we would have Hurricanes protecting us in our attack.

Lacking information about occupied airfields I decided we would approach from the sea, split into three groups for the attack, two aircraft going to each ship. The attack would be at sea level, skipping the bombs into the hulls if the ships came up broadside, alternatively along the deck – we would not manoeuvre into position, just hit the ships as we happened upon them. Bombs would be fused at eleven-second delay, so ensuring the second aircraft was not caught by blast; we would resume formation once inland of the target, the easier for the Hurricanes to cover us in case enemy fighters appeared.

For a change we did not have to walk down through the mud to our aircraft. A truck took us slithering down the track then on to the alcoves where our aircraft were sheltered. It was secondary jungle surrounding the field, dense undergrowth with spindly trees up to about fifty feet, so the fuselage with its camouflage layer of branches became a baking oven during the day. Three of our aircraft had to be refuelled and I thought that during the delay all I did was to lie down under the wing and chat with the crew. However Stanley Mayhew had a note that I walked along to his alcove to have a final discussion with him – he was to lead the second vic – and that my first words were, 'I don't trust those blimps in briefing. This won't be an easy one.'

It appears I said that if we in the lead were knocked out before reaching the target, then my remaining two would drop back to tail behind him. According to his note, I told him to pass this on to the others parked beyond him. I do not remember this. All I can recall of that waiting time was lying stretched out under our Hudson wing with Peter Gibb and the others, then starting up at a sudden loud sound like the sails of a ship hit by a gust of wind. I recognized the sound at once, from the Solomons days, as the flapping of a hornbill's wings – it can be heard several hundred yards away on a still day.

We were airborne at two-thirty and then, so as not to endanger security, flew separately to the coast where we joined formation. There was no point in travelling low from the outset, it would have meant three hours of attentive flying, so we climbed to a cool height and there spaced widely enough to allow automatic pilots to be engaged, and crews to relax. We tested guns, shut down on R'T conversation, then either dwelt with our thoughts or shut them up by fussing about with flying details. But pilots and gunners particularly kept keen watch outside, towards the lowering sun in the west, at the few small puffs of cumulus scattered about, and at the dark blue expanse of the sea below. North of Singapore we ran out of islands and thereafter the only marks on the flat blue surface were blemishes of reefs and black flecks of native fishing craft.

When the green hump of Tioman island came into view I waggled our wings as a signal for the others to close up, and we slanted down in a gentle dive to flatten out on the far side of the palm-piled shore. Then, ten feet or so above the smooth ultramarine surface, we headed in for the mainland, and Endau.

It was about five-thirty by this time, and the sun was low enough for a small humpy islet to our left to show up black, like a crouching cat, against the great orange circle low on the western horizon. I looked to the other Hudsons buoyant by our wing tips, exchanged waves with Tom Waters and Richard Johnson. The sea was heaving slightly, oily smooth and blotched with huge jellyfish, and I leaned forward to wind the little wheel of the elevator trim so as to create upward pressure on the stick. I always did this in low-level attacks, right from early Blenheim days; it was a safety measure to ensure we climbed rather than dived if I lost control. The trimming tab is a narrow inch-wide strip on the edge of the elevator, when moved up or down the airstream against it exerts pressure on the elevator to dive or climb. That habit to trim back before going into low-level attack was to save our lives presently.

The first hint of action was the sight of a large ship coming up on the horizon to the right of our track, when we were still several miles from the coast. While we were studying it, almost certain it was a cruiser, other shapes appeared and then suddenly in the sky ahead of us there was a series of flashes which left black puffs of cloud poised above the water.

The escort that did not exist! But I was not surprised. As Stanley was to remind me later, I was convinced they had lied to us in briefing.

The flak intensified as we continued low towards the land. There was no tracer, the shells were time-fused, all you saw were small black clouds starting suddenly out of the clear sky a little ahead of us and slightly above our level. I might have continued on course straight through to the coast, but then they suddenly threw something else at us. Four flaring waterspouts exploded out of the surface across in front of us, so close we heard the thudding explosions and the windscreen was obscured when we flew through spray from the nearest one. They must have been heavy naval guns, impact-fused. Flying so low and suddenly blinded, I relaxed the forward pressure on the stick so as to give us a safety margin above the sea surface. The screen cleared at the same time but I went on up for a moment, to about three hundred feet, to check the opposition and if necessary to adjust our course. What I saw in the first quick glance made me decide to change our line of approach.

It is hard to be accurate here. I only had a few seconds of observation after that upward zoom, and about a minute later I was to see the Japanese force from an entirely different angle, so there is a composite picture in mind. I think, however, that the first sighting was of four naval vessels, possibly a cruiser and three destroyers, aligned shorewards on our right. All were hazed in the smoke of their gunfire. I could see the coast ahead but not the transports, we must have been four or five miles out, and the impression I had was that we were heading along the line of a shooting butt, setting ourselves up so that the guns could have maximum swing at us as we flew towards the shore.

All this was in a few darting glances, then I swung away to port and, once beyond range of the naval firing party, back towards the coast again; a small escort vessel which had been alone on the southern side of our track continued firing time-fused shells in line alongside us for a few moments, then we were in the clear. From the moment the big guns had exploded the waterspouts until we were beyond range had taken less than half a minute, and by then we had lost sight of all but Johnson. I discovered later from Stanley that when he saw our aircraft centred in those explosions he thought we had been hit, particularly when we shot up out of the spray and then curved away to the left as if out of control. Deciding we had been knocked out, he dropped back down to sea level and continued on course; Tom Waters on our right swerved away towards him, perhaps thinking it was the time to break into pairs, and indeed the four of them did so once he joined them. Johnson followed me closely throughout.

By the time I realized what had happened it was pointless to try and reform; we had intended to split into pairs anyway, we had our appointed number two, so we continued as originally planned. We were skimming across the variegated shallows towards the dark green barrier of the shore, and nearing the swampy tangle of mangrove I hand-signalled Johnson to fall back into position behind, then I banked to starboard and flew northwards below mangrove height along the foreshore towards the landing beach at Endau.

Locating it was no problem. Close by the shore ahead was a little rocky islet about which a number of aircraft were swirling at low level, RAF biplanes and Japanese Zeros engaged in conflict. There was no sign of any Hurricane fighter escort, but then I had put no trust in that promise either. The ships were behind the offshore islet, and it was only when we came curving over the top of it that we saw them in line half a mile away – three transports, the nearest about six thousand tons, the others slightly smaller, one listing badly with something like a corvette alongside it. Scattered about them were a number of landing barges and small craft, and immediately below us on the crown of the little hill was a clearing with a group of Japanese clustered about a mounted machine gun that was swivelling in fire at us.

The transports were a few hundred yards off the shore which curved back into a little beach of white sand, the centre of the landing activity. The nearest ship was pointing away from us, a landing barge alongside the starboard gangway with a derrick lowering a filled sling towards it. Just above our height were two Vildebeests moving so slowly they seemed suspended in the sky; we were so close I could see the helmeted gunner standing in the rear cockpit firing at one of the many Japanese Zeros darting about the whole area. All this was caught in those few seconds as we curved over the gun party on top of the islet and down to sea level. Then we were heading for the huge curving stern of the big ship.

I had to ease back on the stick to climb up at the dark red mass of the hull. I started firing the wing guns, and our midship gun was also firing, but I had to stop when we soared up to miss the stern mast which seemed to stretch to the sky. Then, just before starting to curve down over the front mast, where an unarmed man in the crow's-nest was gaping up at us, we dropped the bombs.

Then we were over the bow, banking towards the beach, no time to think about bomb result as we thundered down towards the landing barges, the piles of equipment, active machine-gunners, slanting grey trunks of coconut palms. It was just as I was about to open fire on them that we were hit so vitally.

The stick gave a slight jerk in my hand, just a tremor, then all tension snapped and it flopped back limp and useless as a gear lever in the neutral position. Something catastrophic had happened. The effect of losing elevator control was that we began to climb, just as I had trimmed us to do, but far from being grateful for this at the moment I was in a fury. I had been concentrating on getting into position to fire at the troops on the beach and slammed the stick forward in frustration, but then came abruptly to my senses when I saw the palm top looming ahead. I banked sharply to miss it, we smeared over a lower one beside it and continued on our climb, up and up and up, until I managed to reach down and give a few frantic turns to the little trimming wheel by my knee. This took us over in a big heaving curve to finish in wallowing flight, a porpoise-like motion as I kept turning the little trim wheel clockwise and anticlockwise in an effort to get some measure of horizontal control.

All this time the gunners in turret and midships had been blazing away at the beach and Japanese fighters. I glimpsed one Vildebeest going down with actual flame streaming from the engine, another under attack by two fighters, then the gunner shouted a warning about a Zero coming in at us on the quarter. I started to turn towards that one – the ailerons were still working – but the banked turn steepened at once, threatening to spin us down into the trees, so I suddenly had too much on mind to worry about fighters. I was trying to control ailerons with my left hand on the spectacles of the stick, and leaning almost over it to get my right hand down to the little trim wheel, so shouts from the fuselage and confusion in the air outside had to be ignored for a moment.

We were still heading vaguely away from the turmoil, straight on inland towards the west, and finally when I had the aircraft more or less stable at a reasonably safe height, and was able to take an interest in the surroundings, I discovered we were alone in the sky. Our guns were silent, there were no shouts over the intercom, and down below were just little mirrors of rice paddies over which we were undulating gently like a small boat in a long ocean swell. We had got away with it – so far.

I found the aircraft did respond to hard forward pressure against the stop but it tended to go on plunging after the pressure was released, and the same uncontrollable dive followed when I tested the automatic pilot. I deduced, correctly as it turned out, that the climb cable had been completely severed, and the dive cable snagged in the damage, so I had to rely on the little trim wheel to keep us horizontal, but keep my left hand on the spectacles for lateral control. There is a pleasing memory of Peter Gibb, just after I had this organized, when he came back from his forward compartment: he puffed out his cheeks and waved his head about in a show of vast relief at our narrow escape. I had the stick in central position, both hands on it and pretending to be flying normally, as he sat down beside me.

'Look what I can do,' I said.

With that I pushed the stick forward, lifting my hands clear. It fell forwards to the stop, a position which would have put us in a vertical dive, then rebounded and wobbled about centrally before falling back to rest uselessly at full climb position. The aircraft kept on steadily in gentle undulating flight. He gaped, absolutely still for a moment, then turned to me and his blue eyes were big circles of astonishment. The shock must have been like that of a front seat passenger who when speeding along a highway sees his driver suddenly flick the steering wheel to set it spinning like a roulette wheel, the car continuing down the centre of the road. The surprise I had prepared was such a stunning success, his bewilderment so complete,

I burst out laughing. Reassured perhaps by such carefree indifference, he did make a strained effort to join in the fun, but once he learned the elevator cable had been cut the vital question came out quickly enough: 'What can you do?'

I asked him to give me time, I was working on it. Almost reverentially he gave me a course for Singapore and then, mentally on tiptoe, went back to tell the others we had a problem; however, he so altered the trim by his walkabout, sending us up in a sudden climb, that I had to discourage further movement while I conducted some experiments with the trimming tabs.

The situation was not merely outside my experience but may even have been unique in the history of flight, so I had to be my own instructor. We could stay in the air all right, I had got the hang of that by this time, but there was no future in that. I was like someone riding a bicycle without using his hands, he can keep going all right, even turn corners by leaning his body, but once he tries to slow to a stop the front wheel starts to wobble and down he crashes – unless he grabs the handlebars at the last moment. We had no handlebars to grab at the last moment. And there was not a lot of time to learn the characteristics of this type of flight. Singapore was barely forty minutes away, the sun was on the horizon, we had to get there quickly for daylight in the landing attempt.

For I never considered baling out. Some months later I discovered by accident that Lilly recommended me for a decoration for the Endau action – it was turned down by Command – but there was nothing courageous about my decision to stay with the aircraft, no heroic determination to save a valuable fighting unit for our glorious war effort. It was selfishly inspired. The challenge of trying to land safely without elevator control was exciting (an aviation first?), but more importantly it would save the aircraft. I had taken over V9129 from new, flown it half-way round the world to the scene of action, got it away without bomb damage from Malta and from Tengah; it was my very own aeroplane, no one else had ever flown it and if I lost it there would be no other aircraft for me to fly – already we had far more pilots than we had machines. It was unthinkable to abandon it. The crew might take that option, not feeling so personally involved with the plane perhaps. But I was going to stay with her.

That left me simply with the technical problem of how to get us both down safely together. I began experimenting. I twiddled the little trim wheel to get us up to five thousand feet, then adjusted it back to its version of level flight, still keeping on course for Singapore, as a night landing would be a fearsome complication. First of all I throttled back to see what happened when the speed dropped, and discovered that below 100 m.p.h. the trim wheel ceased to have any useful effect, so that meant the landing attempt would have to be well above our normal 80 m.p.h. levelling-out speed. That was no problem.

The next test involved the flaps. I always tested these after having been under fire, because if the flaps have been damaged and only one goes down in your landing circuit, then you are almost certain to spin into death. This time I tested them very gingerly, but even the first few degrees caused such a sharp dip of the port wing and jerk of the spectacles that I instantly slapped back the lever; the reason for the wing-drop may simply have been an air eddy, but I dared not touch flaps again after that chilling reaction. We would land without them. It was no great sacrifice anyway; they would be of little use at the high landing speed we would be adopting.

The wheels, however, were essential, for there was no chance the aircraft would ever be repaired after a belly landing. So I stopped breathing for the fifteen seconds or so that they were going down, and had to keep winding the trim wheel all the time to keep our attitude more or less steady. To my immense relief they did finally lock in position, and the trim wheel still gave the same vague control of our attitude. I did a few more practices with the wheels, lowering and retracting them so as to get the pattern of the trimming drill settled in mind, then was ready to try out some dummy landings.

It would have been helpful to practise on some clouds but none were on offer. We were still heading south over the peninsula in the apricot-coloured evening light, the land was shadow-scarred by the setting sun with only a single huge anvil-topped cumulo-nimbus far off in the east, so I had to use the horizon haze as a practice landing field. Keeping on course all the time, I carried out the trials for about a quarter of an hour, lowering the wheels, easing back the throttles, adjusting the pitch, then trimming us down in a more or less steady descent on the haze line until the ASI dropped to just above 100 m.p.h., all set for touchdown. To end the practice I would trim into a dive to pick up speed, retract the wheels, trim for a climb, then do another one. By the time we had done six or seven dummy landings I felt confident about the procedure.

Peter had watched only the start of all these practice landings, then had relaxed into his normal flight behaviour, sitting beside me for a bit of map reading, going forward for plotting. Once satisfied about the landing procedure, I told him what I intended to do – and that he could bale out over the airfield if he preferred. He was taken aback. He had always had confidence in me as a pilot; on this occasion had been disturbed for a few minutes by our plight but had seen me subsequently make a few practice landings and been reassured I had perfect control of the aircraft. Now I was talking to him about baling out. Why on earth should he bale out? He was even reluctant to tell the gunner and wireless operator that they could jump if they wished.

I insisted he ask them, however, so he went back, with slow care, to do so. When he returned he told me rather brusquely that there was no question of them jumping. It was not only pleasant to feel such confidence, but also something of a relief, for there was a valuable bonus I had not mentioned to him. The three of them and their equipment weighed over five hundred pounds. That weight back in the tail at the last moment – the safest place for them if we crashed – would give an enormous boost to the limited effect of the trimming wheel. I felt a bit tipsy, as if at about the three- or four-bottle stage, when I heard the decision; Peter too was like a convivial drinking partner as we chatted about how and when they would go into their huddle-party in the back of the fuselage.

When we crossed the Straits and came over Singapore island it was after six-thirty, already dark enough to pick out a cooking fire outside a hut near our designated stop of Sembawang airfield. We had tried to rouse them on R'T but they had closed down, so we fired off a red Very light as we crossed the field – it was now growing dark too rapidly to waste time in a full circuit of inspection. There was no concrete runway, just a grassy area with bomb craters scattered about, but with a wide clear landing strip about the same length as Tengah, and a good unobstructed approach over market-garden plots. I let down the wheels and set the pitch into fine at once, so as to get these matters out of mind, then made a wide turn that took us almost over Tengah. There was no temptation to land there, Sembawang still had the Australian Hudsons on the station so there would be experienced ground crews and spares available.

We must have been about five miles away as we started a long gradual descent to the field. During the approach Peter and the gunners stayed amidships; the plan was at signal from me in the final few seconds they would hurl themselves back with their parachutes to the extreme rear of the fuselage, so helping get the tail down. Once committed to landing we had no alternative, it would be impossible to climb away for another try, so to forestall any hindrance from ground control I let off another red Very light as we neared the field.

The air was absolutely still, and at a speed of 120 m.p.h. she moved sweetly down the incline, with me bent over the stick adjusting the little trim wheel for the angle of descent, head craned forward in concentrated visual check on the approaching ground, left hand on the spectacles for aileron control. A hundred yards or so short of the perimeter cane fence I began to flatten out, the trim wheel still exerting enough control to keep the nose up as I eased back the throttles, but as the perimeter fence flashed past underneath, with the ASI showing just over 100 m.p.h., the trim wheel was fading rapidly in effect.

Then it was all action. I yelled for the crew to move, slammed back the throttles, and wound the little wheel furiously to its stop. We were still slanting into the ground at a perilous angle, but when they hurled themselves back towards the tail the effect was dramatic, just as if they had jerked back the actual elevator. We levelled out above the ground instead of thumping into it at ballooning speed, she floated sweetly along for a little before touching down as lightly as a gull against a gentle breeze. We ran on a good bit before the tail dropped, as was to be expected in such a high-speed landing, but we stopped in good time without panic braking, and still with nearly a hundred yards of airfield left. There was a cheer from the fuselage behind me.

We taxied back up the field, cut the engines near the control block, and stepped out on to the solid grassy ground. Immediately, however, an officer came running out to say all aircraft had to be in shelter even at night, so we started the engines again and taxied back to the end where we had just finished our landing run. There we settled V9129 in the rubber trees, collected our equipment, and got a lift from a passing truck up to the operations room.

There was only one officer there, he stopped talking on the phone just long enough to say there would be no debriefing, that he thought all our planes had landed, and to excuse him because he was busy as they were leaving the station next day. Just as we emerged from this brush-off Stanley Mayhew arrived in a van, having been down in the gloom to search for us, and it was from him we learned that two of our aircraft had crashed. Tom Waters and Francis Matson had both been hit in the attack, either by fighters or flak. They had managed to get back to the island, but then both of them had crashed in the circuit and all eight crew members were killed.

Later we heard something of their part in the attack. Tom Waters had been seen just after the attack, apparently unhurt himself because he waved to the formating pilot, but his aircraft was damaged in the port wing. He had spun in on the circuit at Sembawang, and I wondered whether he might have suffered flap damage in that port wing. The other aircraft had been Stanley's pair in the bombing run, and he said Matson had stayed beside him afterwards for a minute or so when the Japanese fighters were attacking them. He thought Matson was already badly hit by the time he dropped away behind, it looked as if the navigator was bending over him at the controls; somehow the plane had got back to Singapore but there it crashed and burnt out, no one having seen exactly how it came to dive into the ground. The other three all had a bullet hole or two but none were seriously damaged apart from ours, and they would be able to get away to safe Sumatra in the morning before the inevitable raid.

Sembawang was the home of two Australian Hudson squadrons which were due to move to Sumatra the following day. All the help I could get from the few station officers in the mess was the suggestion that I should 'talk to someone' in the morning, but I could not wait that long, so I left Peter to arrange accommodation and went back alone to the field. There I had luck. An Australian sergeant fitter in the bombed hangar was sympathetic, and he took me back down in his van to have a look at the aircraft.

It was dark by this time but there was a brilliant near-full moon, so we could see almost as well as in daylight. I had examined the aircraft when we first got out, noted a few small holes in the wings and fuselage, nothing of any importance, but had not been able to find the elevator damage. The sergeant discovered it almost at once. After checking externally that the elevator itself was untouched and free to move, he went into the fuselage, flicked on the gunner's light, and before I had come up beside him he had found the damage.

We had been hit by a chunk of shrapnel low down in the starboard side. It had cut obliquely through the cable channel, severing the climb cable completely and snagging the other on jagged metal. There was no structural damage but the cut cable would have to be extracted and replaced; just an hour or two to get it out, he said, but a fiddly six- or seven-hour job to install the new one. First, however, he had to discover if they had a cable in stock, and that might take some time as the station was in such a turmoil about the evacuation next day. I had to be content with that, recognizing my luck in having found such a willing helper in those final moments of the station's life. His attitude was a friendly change from that of the station staff officers, and he drove me all the way back to the mess before setting off on the cable hunt.

The others were waiting for me in the mess with a bottle of ice-cold lager – trust the Australians to have their beer supply organized. I learned that in the attack their pairs had bombed the two ships north of ours and were sure they had made hits. They had had a token debriefing on landing, no notes being taken on their reports, nor record of their names. During our meal a message came from the sergeant to say there was no spare elevator cable on the station, that he would discuss the position with me next day. After that gloomy news we went off to bed in a hut out in the rubber – and up in the sky a moon so bright we could have been bombing the Japanese ships and shore party all night, and probably not losing a single aircraft. What a waste of all that night-bombing experience against harbours and ships in the heavily defended ports of Europe!

Let me then summarize the action at Endau, which rates a mention in all the histories of the Far East campaign. Apart from that high-level attack by the Australian Hudsons, there were three RAF bombing units involved – 36 Squadron, 100 Squadron, and 62 Squadron. The first two put in twenty-four aircraft, all Vildebeest and Albacore biplanes. They lost five Vildebeests in the morning, and in the afternoon five more Vildebeests and two Albacores, and amongst those killed were the commanding officers of both squadrons. We in 62 Squadron, going in coincidentally with their afternoon attack, lost two aircraft out of the six involved. The ships I personally saw, apart from the three transports and the numerous auxiliary craft, included one cruiser or very large destroyer, three other destroyers and a smaller escort vessel – Stanley declared there were six naval vessels, including a 'large cruiser' in the offshore escort that opened fire on us. As for damage inflicted on the transports, we were the last on target and I saw three still above water, one of which was barely afloat it was listing so badly, another emitting so much smoke it was probably on fire. The third one, our target, must surely have been hit by at least one of our bombs.

There is later evidence about the damage to these ships. The Royal Navy record states that during that bright moonlight night two of our destroyers, the *Thanet* and the *Vampire*, made an attempt to attack them, but that they were repulsed by 'the powerful Japanese naval force' and the *Thanet* was sunk. A gunner from the sunken ship reached Singapore two days later and a summary of his report is included in the naval record. It contains this statement: 'He observed two transports sunk with their masts above water, and one immobilized.'

As the British destroyers had not been able to open fire on the merchant ships, the damage he reported must have been effected by aircraft. The Japanese official account does not list the shipping losses but confines itself to the air action. It states: 'There were attacks by enemy aircraft throughout the day, in the afternoon by thirty enemy fighters and bombers. We shot down twenty-four. The battle lasted thirty minutes and we lost two aircraft.'

The British official record of the action omits reference to our Hudsons and even the RAF casualty record implies that our aircrews were killed in some sort of flying accident, for there is no mention of them being in action. So let us at least make this clear: Pilot Officer William Thomas de Rouffignac Waters, DFC, and Pilot Officer Francis Cedric Richmond Matson, and the six members of their crews – I regret not knowing their names – were killed in an attack on the Japanese landing force at Endau on 26 January 1942. Future writers dealing with this incident should remember those names when they read the curtly dismissive, and incorrect, official report.

The incident is also a good example of the parochial nature of much of the debriefing in those days – and true not only of Far East Command. All stations had a lively interest in the sorties of their resident squadrons, but a diverted aircraft was never given anything like the same attention. The other units involved that day, the Vildebeests and Albacores, were operating from their own bases, the stories of those who took part in that heroic effort in their old biplanes were extracted in full, their action is set down in the record, their dead honoured. But we, landing at a stranger's place, brought no news that anyone wished to hear, our dead were ignored, and in the archive is only a tainted record of their passage.

There is one final comment, not directly about Endau though springing usefully from it. It concerns the Blenheims of 84 Squadron which took off shortly after us from Sumatra. Instead of following us to the target, as they were briefed to do, they abandoned the operation near Singapore because, in the squadron commander's own astonishing words, 'It was growing dark.' The squadron commander was Wing Commander Jeudwine, and the unit had just come out from the Middle East. Jeudwine did keep a record of his squadron's activities and wrote a full report about it subsequently; he was the only squadron commander to do so, and this is unfortunate because Air Vice-Marshal Maltby relied on it exclusively in his official report on the Far East campaign published two years later in *The London Gazette*. That official report singles out for exclusive commendation both Jeudwine and his squadron, and the tenor of Jeudwine's own report suggests that this is only proper – here are some of his invidious distinctions:

> The morale of 84 Squadron was perfect, and this squadron and 211, also from the Middle East, were the only bomber squadrons which showed any interest in fighting.

> The RAAF personnel were discourteous, dishonest, undisciplined and lacking in morale.

> The order to evacuate to Java was given, and the Hudsons and the Hurricanes left in a flash [while Jeudwine and the good old Fighting 84 waited bravely alone for the dawn].

Jeudwine filed his report in the Middle East in July 1942 and its influence has seeped through into numerous subsequent records, either directly or through Maltby's official report which relies upon its biased details and comments. There is certainly room for criticism of some of the units and personalities involved in the Far East campaign, but I would have rated the pilots and aircrews of all but Jeudwine's paragons as being very low on any such list. The reason we on our squadron did not inflict more damage on the enemy was that we were not utilized to our capabilities, and the fault for that lies not with, but above, us. The crews of the two aircraft we lost that day could have bombed those ships just as effectively some three hours later, and almost certainly lived to fight again – even that very same moonlight night had we been asked.

There was nothing wrong with their morale, Jeudwine. They, like you and the rest of us out there, were badly led.

Chapter 17

When you spend five or six hours in a cockpit in the tropics your shorts and shirt are crumpled and wet with perspiration, your underpants are clammy, your socks stink. To have to put on all the same clothes next day after Endau was particularly depressing. Pulling on my shirt, still damp and musty-smelling in the heavy tropical atmosphere, was like reassuming yesterday's gloom; eight of our group dead, two aircraft lost, and it seemed likely we might lose our own for lack of elevator cable just when we thought we had saved it.

In the tumult of the evacuation that next day there was little interest in our situation. Shortly after Stanley's group had left, one of the Australian squadron commanders came to offer us a lift out in his Hudsons. With his ground crews working frantically to save three unserviceable aircraft, they would have cannibalized ours the moment we turned our backs on it, and I refused his offer, as did my crew; all opted to stay in the hope we could get ours repaired, my friendly sergeant having said that if no cable could be found he would try to effect 'a splice job' on our ruptured one. I put my trust in his promise.

The airfield was not bombed that morning. Outside the landing line many of the previous craters were untouched, the cavities still surrounded by blasted clods of red earth. The reason for this neglect was the shortage of labour, and the reason for the shortage of labour was a piece of bumbledom typical of the Singapore disaster. The Chinese and Malay labourers wanted a few pence more a week for the special risks on airfield and dock repairs, the armed services had agreed this was a reasonable request but the civil administration worried that it would create a precedent, that 'others such as street cleaners' would then want the rise. The local legislative council was still arguing this supremely important issue while we were there at the end of January, with the Japanese about to land within the next few days.

In the early afternoon the adjutant called upon me to identify the bodies from our two crashes. I refused this at first and the disagreement resulted in a wing commander intervening. To him I reiterated that the order was not merely unreasonable but also unnecessary. They were insisting I make a positive identification of two bodies, the captains of the aircraft; but I had seen them in their aircraft at Palembang, and they had been seen by several of us in the air both before and after the attack, so their bodies had to be among the eight extracted from the two crashed aircraft. But the wing commander stood there in smart khaki, puffed up in angry dignity, and declared he would have me court-martialled for gross insubordination unless his orders were obeyed. I finally agreed, not because of his silly threat but because once under close arrest I would lose control of our aircraft.

The task was as horrible as I feared. They had the bodies on the concrete floor of the ambulance garage, and the medical orderly who led me in just waved a hand at a pile of seven separate dark things against the wall, and said, 'You'll find there's really eight.' And he pointed at one somewhat larger than the rest as he added, 'That's two together.'

What he was talking about were the bodies of men, of friends I had known back from squadron days in England. He stood by with professional unconcern as I faced the dreadful sight. They were nothing like the usual human shape of a rectangle with limbs at the corners and head on top, these were just irregular black-charred lumps. In some it was not possible to discover heads, let alone identify faces. I did identify the first as Tom Waters – he was the only one on the squadron who ever wore the metal VR clip (Volunteer Reserve) and this was partly visible in a burnt surface – but then the orderly did something to the next one that stopped any further genuine effort I might have forced myself to make.

In a misguided attempt to be helpful he knelt on the floor beside it and tried to show me a face, doing unspeakable things to the black shape. I saw a glint of unburnt blood in the opening he prised, and that was the end. I lied, giving him the Matson name that was wanted, then turned away quickly and went outside, and tried not to think of those things against the wall. But I can still see the picture clearly today.

*   *   *

My RAAF sergeant had gone over to the machine shop at the naval dockyard to manufacture some part for one of his Hudsons, and it was after sunset when he returned with the news that the naval base was being abandoned next day, so he would have to return there early to finish his machining job. He repeated his promise to start work on our cable as soon as he had completed the job for his own aircraft. I had by then thought of another possibility, however: this was to go over to Tengah and extract a cable from the Hudson that had been destroyed in that first bombing attack. The sergeant agreed this was the ideal solution, and promised to send a fitter with me, not only to extract the cable but also perhaps to scavenge some parts for the three crocks of his own squadron he was still trying to get away.

Next morning I set off for Tengah in a small van driven by the fitter, an RAF corporal from Manchester who was suffering from a hangover. The day was suited to his gloom, heavy dark cloud covered all our corner of the island, and the vegetation along the road was dripping from the morning rain. In one lush tangle of greenery I saw a hoarding that showed a huge brightly coloured tiger, an advertisement for the well-known local beer; it looked like a Douanier Rousseau painting of the tiger bright skulking in the jungle.

The only aircraft now left at Tengah were five Hurricanes, and some of the pilots were sprawled in deck chairs on the terrace outside the mess when we arrived. We drove past them down to the bombed Hudson and my heart sank when I saw the tumbled mass of red clay and metal where the aircraft had been sheltered. A second bomb had struck, this time it had not just damaged the aircraft further, but had reduced it to a blackened skeleton. We clambered about the pile for a few minutes in the absurd hope of being able to find, let alone extract, a good cable but the wreck was a dead loss. The sergeant's splicing expertise was now the only hope of saving our own aircraft.

I spoke to the Hurricane pilots for a few minutes before leaving. They had the electricity working again and their beer was now cold as well as free. They did not seem unduly concerned about their future; one of them, an American, said that if the Japanese started to shell the place then he guessed it would be 'distressful'. Four days later they avoided such a distressful experience when the remnants of the squadron flew off to join us in Sumatra.

Instead of driving straight back to Sembawang, we went first up the road to the Straits where Richard Johnson and I had previously discovered our only defence against a Japanese landing to be that elderly woman rubber-tapper. Things had improved. This time we found impressive evidence of military occupation, only four soldiers but what they lacked in number they made up in rank. Beside an army staff car parked under the casuarina trees were a major, a colonel and a major-general. The latter, as the driver informed me, was Gordon Bennett, commander of the Australian forces. Like the rest of the group Bennett was smartly dressed, neatly ironed creases in his shirt and shorts, leather belt and shoulder strap brightly polished. He looked to be in prickly mood.

The colonel discovered I had brought a Hudson out from England and then Bennett intervened to ask brusquely how many of us had come. I told him there were about fifteen altogether and he gave a dissatisfied grunt; when he questioned me about our experience I stressed night bombing, not only of ships but of precise docks and buildings, in the hope he might bring some pressure on Air Command to utilize that nocturnal experience, but he was inattentive until I brought up the Endau raid as an example where we should have been used at night. He was eager then for observed facts about the landing. How had the troops been moved from ship to shore? Had they fanned out from the beach? What heavy equipment had I noticed? Finally he asked a few questions about methods of attack on landing barges, obviously with the Straits in mind, then he muttered something to the colonel and abruptly started towards his car. After a couple of paces he stopped and turned back towards me.

'Thank you for our talk,' he said, and then he left.

The sirens began to wail as we passed Tengah on return, and we had only gone a couple of miles beyond when we were stopped by an army captain standing with arm raised by an open-topped camouflaged car. He came up to my side and asked if we had a can of petrol. There was no partition in the van, and I looked behind but could see only a parachute complete with harness and two red fire extinguishers. The captain, an Englishman in some Indian regiment, would not take my word for this, went around himself to look in the back, then returned outside my door and told me he had to get to some place down on the west coast, about six miles away. This was in the opposite direction back past Tengah and I said we would take him there and he could collect petrol. He made no reply but began to fiddle around with the pistol holster on his right hip and I thought he was looking for some document or note. He was a plump figure, khaki shirt darkly patched with pungent sweat, jittery in his movements. Next thing I knew, he had dragged out a Smith and Wesson .38 and was pointing the thing at me, so close I could see almost nothing but the black hole of the barrel.

'You take me where I say or I'll blow your head off,' he said. 'I will. I will, I tell you. I will.'

I thought to argue, but only for an instant. The gun was quivering in his hand, so close it was difficult for me to focus on the wobbly black hole, and I was terrified his shivery grip might cock the thing. I told him to put it away, that we would take him to his post. But he made me get out first and stand at the edge of the road, then he moved along the side of the van still waving his revolver and scrambled into the back before calling to me to return. He knelt on the parachute harness and when I turned to ask him exactly how far his post was he told me to keep my eyes to the front, then ordered the corporal to turn around and go back along the road we had just come.

I tried to get him talking, to find out why the desperate rush, but he not only refused to tell me but said we were both to keep silent, again threatening to blow my head off, or put a bullet in my brain. So then we drove in silence for about a couple of miles until somewhere beyond the turn-off into Tengah aerodrome, he told the driver to slow down. There was a gateless opening into a rubber plantation on our left, and there we had to turn in and follow a track through the grey tree trunks. Just afterwards there came a thunderous reverberating explosion from a formation bombing which seemed to have been intended for Tengah, and when I merely said it was just as well we had not gone there for his petrol he seemed to lose his head completely, shouting, 'Shut up! Shut up! Shut up!'

He went on repeating it at the same time as he kept jabbing me in the back of my cap with some part of the gun which I took to be the barrel, and I bunched up my shoulders and crouched forward trying to protect my head. There was one final thump with the gun high up where the cap touched my skull, so hard it dazed me, and for one wild moment I thought he had actually shot me.

About five minutes later we came to a little tin hut where an estuary cut into the plantation and he ordered the corporal to stop. There was no other human being in sight, nor any evidence of army presence except for a slit trench just beyond the hut. He ordered the corporal to turn the van around, then got out and shouted at us to drive away immediately. We did. It took us nearly an hour to get back to Sembawang, partly because we lost our way at first when I was so busy raging about the hold-up that I missed our inward track, then when we finally did get back on the road we discovered it had been included in the bomb pattern we had heard fall. We had to weave a way through the rubber to get around the damaged section.

Back at Sembawang I learned to my dismay that through a misunderstanding an airman had ripped out our severed cable in preparation for the one expected from Tengah. Now there would be the installation task as well as the splicing. My friendly RAAF sergeant dismissed the mistake as unimportant, however; he said he expected to have all his aircraft cleared by next morning, when he would be able to devote himself completely to our problem.

I stayed with him as he worked on the carburettor at the bench and he told me about his visit to the naval base that morning. The navy, it appeared, were just walking away from the mountain of equipment and stores in the base. In one shed he had seen 'thousands' of cases of tinned meat, and other foodstuffs, another damaged shed was filled to the roof with marine engine spares, another with boots and shirts and other clothing in crates and baled blocks, all free for the taking. All that morning the navy had been streaming away from the place as if fleeing from a plague, and he was told that by nightfall there would not be a single RN man, or even civilian employee for that matter, on the base. He could have the whole sixty million pounds' worth of the base if he wanted, the cranes and docks and houses and cinemas and churches and football fields, as well as enough ammunition to blow the island apart like another Krakatoa.

All bomber aircraft were supposed to be away by the end of next day, leaving just six Hurricanes on the island, but at nightfall there were still four left. The ground crews had to spend a lot of time in the slit trenches, for there were three alerts in the morning; one twenty-seven formation dropped its bombs north of the field near our sleeping quarters just after I had gone back there to shave, and that awful fluttering sound of a formation load descending nearby had me crouching against the trunk of a rubber tree in sullen fury

213

at our impotence in these attacks. It would have been sensible to go miles away from the field, but to leave our aircraft unsupported was too risky. Either Peter or I had stayed within watchful distance of it all the daylight hours on the airfield, fearful of the scavengers waiting for a chance to move in on it.

It was not until about eight o'clock that night that the sergeant was able to start on splicing our cable. He and another man worked on it in the damaged hangar and when I went down there a few hours later with some cold beer the place was in complete darkness. I wondered if, having completed the splicing job, they had packed up for the night, but rejected that thought at once and instead went across the brightly moonlit field to check a livelier suspicion. Sure enough they were inside the fuselage, had a torch hanging from the gun turret as they stripped out the side panels. They stopped for a moment to drink the beer and the sergeant said they would just install the easy fuselage section that night, about another hour's work, and as there was nothing I could do I should get back to my billet while transport was available. So I left them to it, walking along the perimeter through the black tree-shadows cast by the full moon, and pausing for a few moments to listen to the loud mellow call of a koel echoing across the field – just three ringing peals, then velvety silence.

Feeling confident that our aircraft would be safe from the vultures that next day, now that the sergeant was about to install the spliced cable, we had breakfast before going down to the alcove in the rubber to watch progress on the work. To our surprise there was no sound from within the fuselage, no sign of life at all about the aircraft except for a red-cheeked bulbul that was stealing insects from the numerous spiders' webs spread over a pile of dead branches that had been used for camouflage. I opened the door of the fuselage and just inside was one of the Tiger beer bottles, with a piece of cardboard box jutting out of the top. On the grease-smudged surface was printed a pencilled message:

GONE TO BREAKFAST. SHOULD FINISH THIS ARVO.

Arvo. It was a word that took me back to a land of dry heat, thin grey tree-shadows, parched spears of grass and the ear-ringing sound of cicadas, far far different to the lush green hot-house of Singapore. I had to explain it to the mystified Peter Gibb from Cheam in Surrey,

England . . . our cable should be finished by that afternoon. They must have worked on it most of the night.

The sergeant's estimate was correct but in a day broken into working pieces by air raids it was very late in his arvo by the time the cable with its thickly-spliced joint – a mixture of cord and wire finally – was located to his satisfaction. Then the sections of flooring and all the panels had to be replaced and screwed down, and controls tested at each stage, so there was no chance of getting away from the field in daylight. We would have been happy to take off that night, for the moon was brilliantly full, but to the local command taking off at night without airfield lights was as inconceivable as the idea of turning them on for us. So we had to stay another night. Twice the sirens went; I heard no sound of bombs nor of planes but that did not stop me worrying about an enemy low-level attack which might be blasting our aircraft.

It was hard to escape that thought into sleep – particularly when a frog close outside kept on interminably making a sound like the clipping of a barber's scissors . . . cut-cut-cut . . . pause . . . cut-cut-cut.

We were on the field before eight o'clock next morning and were just about to board the aircraft when we heard the thunderous explosion of the demolished causeway. This was about three miles away. A moment later we saw the grey cloud rising slowly against the dark green hills of Johore, up and up into the clear morning sky. The island was now cut off, the brief siege was about to begin.

We started the engines, warmed them up quickly, then taxied down to the far end for take-off, jerking the stick frequently to test the elevator wire and, to save time, doing the cockpit check as we rolled along. There was no airfield control, they had already left for Sumatra, we were free to go when we chose. We stopped at the far end, checked each engine on full throttle as usual, closed them down, and at that very moment the sirens started to wail.

It would have taken a direct hit to stop us by that time. I pushed forward the throttles to set us moving, turned her into line, then opened them fully on the run and we went roaring down the cleared gap of the cratered field. I first kept rocking the stick gently to feel the cable strength, then finally jerked it hard as a real test to get our tail off the ground. She responded perfectly, the same after lifting off when I see-sawed in a gentle climb, so then I relaxed and thought no more about the spliced cable.

We banked away to the left, with the corpse of the naval base almost below us, then continued around to pass over the causeway with the exploded gap in its white line conspicuous like a missing front tooth. Still turning we passed Tengah airfield where a Hurricane was threading a path through the bomb craters, then we straightened out on a southerly course over the merging line of translucent green rubber and sombre green mangrove where the fat army captain had held the gun to my head.

He was going to need that gun very soon now.

Chapter 18

—◦—

A bomber or fighter aircraft, like a battleship or a tank, is a weapon to be used against the enemy, so you take some pains to prevent its destruction when idle; you keep it in harbour, camouflage it out of sight, protect it with AA guns. It is disastrous, however, both for the outcome of the conflict and the discipline of fighting men, if preservation becomes such an obsession as to inhibit risking the weapon in actual battle. Those who wish to fight become frustrated and angry, rebellious against an authority that denies them use of a fighting machine when its need is clearly desperate.

Throughout the vital thirty days up to mid-February 1942 the allied bomber force in the Far East never operated up to anything like its full strength, and never utilized the full capability of its crews. The largest number of actual bombing strikes done by any one of the pilots in 62 Squadron during this time was five; other squadrons were equally deprived of fighting opportunity – this, over a period of four weeks when a whole campaign was teetering in the balance. We in the 62 Squadron Hudsons at that time had more experience in bombing heavily defended naval targets at night than any other unit in the world, but if the local command knew that – as they should have – they never showed it.

We could have been out night after night on strikes or searches, but instead we spent most of that critical period hiding our planes and selves in the jungle. There cannot have been a dearth of targets, we could have hunted for naval ones and it would have been better to attack even imprecise ones on land rather than insist aircraft and crews stay hidden in the jungle. Not once did we send out a night strike against occupied airfields up the peninsula. Worse still, not a single sortie, day or night, was flown against the Japanese forces assembling on the mainland for the attack on Singapore. Even if we did not know their precise assembly point we could have bombed the most likely ones.

Had our troops waiting on the island to repel the onslaught heard and seen us streaming overhead during those moonlit nights of early February, heard and seen continuous bomb explosions among enemy positions on the far bank, it might well have made a vital difference to their morale. When the Japanese forces did make their night crossing the position was lost within thirty-six hours, but had our troops been supported at least in spirit by sight and sound of hundreds of bombs crashing down on the enemy positions and assault craft in their night crossing, they might well have fought with more hopeful determination, and the bomb-harassed enemy with less confident assurance, than shown in the event. The first Japanese assault might well have been held in consequence, and although in the end the island would have fallen anyway – that was inevitable – the resistance shown there would have made a difference to morale and confidence among those who faced the Japanese elsewhere in those early days.

In the battle for Sumatra, too, our air force could have made a crucial difference had we discovered by twenty-four hour patrols the advance of the enemy transports, then utilized our bombing force in night attacks. Our air resources, limited as they might have been, were never used to anything near their full capability. Almost half were lost on the ground – one of which did at least provide me with a new elevator cable to replace my spliced makeshift. So the old-established RAF command out there also has its share of blame for the sorry tale of the fall of Singapore, and the collapse of the Far East campaign.

During the first two weeks of February the remaining bombers, about forty in all, and a dozen or so of the Hurricanes, were located on the two Palembang fields (P1 and P2) in Sumatra. The fate of Singapore had ceased to be a cause of anxiety by this time, clearly it was lost, but we did make temporary landings there for another week or so after the Endau raid, one being a night stopover preparatory to a daylight raid on the airfield of Kluang up the peninsula. This operation was marked by a blunder not at all untypical of the Far East campaign.

The plan was that our strike force of eight Hudsons would be escorted by the Hurricanes still in Singapore, but these never left the ground. Because of a blunder their guns were inoperable. It was a justifiable security measure to remove the gun panels at night, but such was the concern about security that the staff lost sight of the prime objective, and no proper arrangement was made to restore the panels for actually fighting the enemy. The Hurricane pilots arrived that morning eager for battle, only to discover their aircraft were sterile. Our strike force had to leave without escort, but luckily no Japanese fighters intervened and all our aircraft returned to Sumatra. That afternoon the station commander put a pistol to his head and pulled the trigger.

I made my last call at Singapore a day or two after this. The whole squadron was stood down that afternoon, most had gone in to Palembang forty miles away, when the wing commander caught me writing on the hut veranda. An aircraft had to go to Singapore at once to pick up a colonel on Wavell's staff. I took off with a scratch crew and on arrival over the island saw three large ships in harbour, one of them a passenger liner of about fifteen thousand tons. The dock area was writhing with people but otherwise the town looked much the same – further north we saw a herd of Jersey cows in a scene of pastoral serenity, grazing on lush green pasture near the reservoirs. Smoke from the oil tanks in the naval dock area towered to an immense height in the still afternoon. It was so compact it gave the background scene of Johore the aspect of a torn picture, the jagged edges pulled apart and showing this dark grey mounting behind it.

The airfield at Sembawang still had the wide cleared strip between the bomb craters, and one Australian Hudson slotted into a hideout in the rubber, but there was no sign of life about the field. I kept the engines running when we pulled up by the deserted control building, then a car appeared driven by a man I took to be our colonel. He hurried over to the door and presently the gunner came up to say his message was that our colonel had instead gone out by boat. Meanwhile a truck arrived with some men carrying haversacks and an RAF flight lieutenant. He came up to the cockpit to say his signals unit had been ordered to report to Palembang and were just leaving for the docks. Could they go with us?

I told him to bring them aboard and when they moved towards the door I noticed the army major tag along behind them. He saw me looking and mouthed something, and I called to the gunner to check. He came up presently to say that the major claimed he was also due to leave that night by boat and would be grateful for an air lift instead. I doubted the story but let him stay. He came with us to the operations room when we landed in Sumatra; I never heard what he told the Controller but it must have been a good story because they sent him back down to the field to catch an Australian Hudson about to leave for Java. I feel sure he would have got away from there, too, before the end.

During the first week of February I took General Sir John Laverack on a special reconnaissance. He was commander of the 1st Australian Corps which had been pulled out of North Africa for service in the Far East. The Corps left Egypt in separated ships, the first being the *Orcades* with 3500 men due at Palembang in mid-February. There was argument between Churchill and Curtin, the Australian Prime Minister, about deploying this precious Australian army corps in the campaign. Curtin felt strongly it should return home, as Australia itself was now under threat, but the empire-minded Churchill wanted it to fight in the East Indies, and if not there, then in Burma. Laverack, through the advice he tendered to Curtin, had an important if not decisive part in the argument; he arrived at the end of January in advance of his troops to assess the situation and discuss the matter with Wavell, the overall commander in the Indies.

Wavell's intention was that this first detachment of the Corps, the 3500 men from the Australian 7th Division, should be landed at Sumatra and it was in preparation for their disposition that Laverack made the reconnaissance flight with us. I have no idea why we were chosen for such a job when the Australian squadrons still had about a dozen Hudsons left, but anyway I was sent off early one morning to Palembang town airfield to pick him up for the sortie.

Laverack was waiting by the terminal building with a surround of senior army and air force officers. After a word with the commander of our Hurricane escort I brought Laverack up to the cockpit beside me, settled two of his staff officers in the fuselage, and we took off with two Hurricanes formating each side of us in the air. Laverack was already asking questions about distances and speed and height before we set course; a much friendlier character than Bennett, he had that attractive characteristic of leaning forward keenly after asking a question, as if intensely interested in what you had to say.

Heading towards the coast I climbed to seven thousand feet, where our shadow was flickering distinctively against the larger clouds, and we had just reached the sea and were flying across a webbing of fish traps and marbled swatches of reef when the nearer Hurricane on our port side suddenly waggled his wings then heeled over and away out of sight. I called the gunner who reported all four had turned away and were fast disappearing back towards Palembang. Laverack, an interested observer of this activity, raised his eyebrows when I told him what had happened. I asked if he wanted to continue without escort.

'What do *you* think?' he asked.

I said that if on a discretionary patrol subject to cloud cover I would continue; cloud was only about five-tenths but some of the cumulus were great white mountains already up to ten thousand feet, you could plunge into them in escape and spend hours inside if necessary, waiting for the daily cloud build-up when you would have complete protection to roam where you wished. But this was not a discretionary anti-shipping patrol, we had a VIP on a reconnaissance sortie, and I reckoned the choice was up to him. He decided to continue.

Once he had given the word I turned slightly off course to fly across to the nearest big chunk of cumulus, climbing steeply to ten thousand feet which took us above the churning white bulges on top of the cloud. Laverack noticed this change in tactics and looked towards me quizzically as we slanted down at speed towards the next convenient cloud bulk. I explained that we would be cloud jumping for the rest of the sortie, deviating from the direct line planned but covering the same area even more widely in our weaving track. He questioned me at some length about my experience in these tactics off the French coast, kept nodding as I mentioned each point, then commented, 'Pity we in the army can't use cloud cover like that for an advance.'

On his knees he had an aeronautical map which Peter Gibb eyed jealously, but Laverack gave it scant attention; down below us were dark green islets with haloes of reef scattered about the flat blue sea, he made no apparent effort to identify any of them, just studied the seascape. He answered freely to questions about the activities of the 1st Australian Army Corps in the desert, and for his own part probed about my experiences in England – I had to go into detail about why I was in the RAF and not the Australian Air Force. And he was receptive to my arguments that our expertise in night bombing should be utilized.

We spent about three hours on the reconnaissance, and he did ask for a good look at Banka Island which is just off the estuary leading up to Palembang. I went down low over the island, the centre of which was jungle dense like broccoli, and flew along the foreshore so that he could examine the open beaches, the inlets with dark tangles of mangrove, and the fences of fish traps many of which were associated with huts on spindly legs. When I asked why he was so interested in Banka he said that if he himself were planning an attack on Palembang, he would launch it from the island. Peter Gibb joined in the conversation at this stage and asked if the Australian forces would therefore be involved in a battle for Sumatra. Laverack answered obliquely: 'Our nearest base is Perth – that's over two thousand miles away.'

His tone indicated that was too far, and in the event the *Orcade* never did disembark its 3500 men at Sumatra; much against his will however, Laverack had to land them on Java, where they were presently included in the surrender and became prisoners of war without ever firing a shot. Churchill wanted to divert the other troopships to Burma, and the argument between him and the Australian Prime Minister led to cable blows; Curtin refused to give way, Laverack's corps returned to Australia and presently inflicted the first reverse on the Japanese army when they halted their advance in New Guinea. Both generals, Bennett and Laverack, escaped from Java before the fall – Laverack was returning to his command, Bennett was abandoning his.

During that second week in February, there were almost daily attacks on the airfield of Palembang town, but still, despite all their air activity, the Japanese had not discovered our P2 airfield which was less than ten minutes' flight time from the town. During the cloudy days that week we frequently heard their aircraft throbbing away overhead but we kept our heads and our voices low, and they never noticed us hidden away in our jungle clearing.

By this time it was becoming difficult to differentiate between many of the officers and the airmen, because few of us aircrew carried badges of rank. On the flight from England we had brought only a single change of tropical kit, all that had been allowed; most of us now bought local shirts and as these had no shoulder-tabs for epaulettes we went about the place rank naked. Conditions in Sumatra were basic, anyway. In the mess we sat on wooden benches at bare wooden tables, tropical downpours misting through the slatted walls; there were scorpions as big as hammer-claws clattering on the slats of the toilets, your writing blurred on the damp paper, your watchband rotted, mildew formed on your shoes. In this limbo we waited that second week in February for inspired leadership; instead we had a complaining and insulting address from our chief.

This was Air Vice-Marshal Maltby, head of the Allied Air Force. He flew in to P2 one afternoon and all officers had to assemble in the shadowy mess to listen to his talk. He accentuated all the appropriate words of inspiration ... 'never surrender' ... 'fight and fight again' ... 'win through to the end' ... that sort of thing, but his high-pitched voice was unsuited to Churchillian grandiloquence and the only positive feeling he aroused in most of us was a deep and bitter anger at the criticisms he levelled at us lowly aircrew, whilst he and his headquarters staff remained immune from blame.

He instanced among the craven the RAF crews who had been stationed up the peninsula at Butterworth for their 'panic flight' at the start of the campaign, and was particularly vitriolic about an RAAF fighter squadron which he declared had 'abandoned their aircraft and equipment on mere rumour' of the approach of a Japanese force. The adjutant of the Australian squadron raised his voice to try and explain how and why the airfield had been evacuated so precipitately, but Maltby ordered him silent. My notes about the speech have his final words:

> The Air Force has put up a bad show by running away from aerodrome after aerodrome. This will now stop. We will not, I repeat not, run from this field. Here we will fight. We will use the aircraft gun turrets to repel the Japanese soldiers, we will fight with our revolvers, we will fight with our bare hands if necessary, but we will not abandon this field. The struggle here is to death.

He then took off for Java, and two days later we were ordered to abandon the field immediately and fly after him.

The hectic period started with a report that the Japanese had captured Palembang in an airborne assault and were heading at speed up the road towards us. Later that day this information was qualified. The Japanese had in fact landed parachutists about the town airfield area but failed to gain possession of it, being beaten back by the airfield defence units and RAF air and ground crews. The following

morning, however, a large seaborne assault force arrived off the
mouth of the river and this led to the disintegration of RAF Command
in Palembang town. From them there issued a stream of incoherent
and contradictory orders that were further confounded by our own
staff at P2 airfield. Here is a note of the events of those two days
which I wrote at that time:

13 Feb. About 11 a.m.
    Sheltering in cockpit from thunderous
    downpour. Open truck arrives. Wanted
    urgently in ops.

11.15 Still in ops. Told Jap surface force reported
    heading for mouth of river. Me to lead an
    attack, six of us.

11.30 Raid cancelled. Report that Japs landed at
    Medan, hundreds of miles up coast. Aircraft to be
    de-bombed. Me with Wimpy [Johnson] to do
    recce Medan area and discover situation.

11.45 Message not to take off. Medan report inaccurate.
    Stand-by.

15.00 Called to ops room. To lead a strike on Jap ships
    off Banka.

15.30 Cancelled. Meeting in mess of all officers.
    Instructions about denial measures to take
    when Jap army attacks. Burn all spares. Burn all
    unserviceable aircraft. Burn all documents. Wait
    in planes with engines running till told take off.
    If no such orders in 'reasonable time' take off for
    Java. (Reasonable time = ??)

14 Feb. 08.30 Ordered lead attack of three aircraft on Jap
    barges in river.

09.00 Wait. Three others detailed. We to do armed
    recce west of Banka.

09.30 Recce cancelled. Put on stand-by.

10.30 To lead attack of 3 aircraft on ships off mouth of
    river.

10.45 Wimpy takes my place. Trio of
      Johnson-Robinson-Anderson to attack ships. I to
      lead second trio at 12.30.

I went down to the field to see the first trio off, sharing a green-skinned tangerine with Johnson. Having done this I went to our aircraft, where the crew had been waiting all morning for take-off; it was now lashing with rain, great wallops of water thundering down from the black sky, and I brought the crew back for a coffee before our briefing. At about eleven-thirty, as Peter Gibb and I were about to set off through the mud to the operations hut, the duty officer came rushing in to say the airfield was being abandoned, and that I was to report to the wing commander immediately. On the veranda of the hut where McKern had his bed and office, he was burning papers. His first words were, 'I want you to get all the aircraft away to Java immediately.'

Our operation was cancelled. He and Lilly, with all the ground crews, would make the short sea crossing to Java at dawn. I was to take command of the flying unit, the six aircraft left on P2 and the three out on the sortie, and hold them in Java until they arrived. My log book entry shows we took off at 1250, and at 1450 landed at Batavia.

Thus it came about that we 'left in a flash'. Despite the precision of those orders, however, we had serious staff officer trouble on arrival at Batavia. The airport there was a civil as well as a military one, there was an imposing grey terminal building with spacious marble-floored hall and huge undamaged windows looking out on the field. When I came up the steps through the big glass doors, after arranging refuelling of our six aircraft, I saw an RAF group captain in crisp clean khaki haranguing our little dishevelled group in the middle of the hall; there were a number of civilians scattered about the hall, many looking embarrassed by this loud public rebuke. Peter Gibb said something to the group captain and pointed in my direction as I approached; he turned and his first well-remembered words were: 'Are you in charge of this rabble?'

He waved his hand at the assembled crews, two of whom had just landed from an attack on the Japanese ships when they were ordered off from Sumatra. I told him I was. He asked my rank, wanted to know why I was not showing it on my shirt, and where I thought I was taking my little group. These were not questions for information just loud rebukes. By this time everyone in the hall seeemed to be looking in our direction. I started to explain that we had left Palembang under orders, hurriedly because of the Japanese landing, but he interrupted me to declare that there had been no landing in Sumatra and that I was to take the unit back there at once.

'I'm not going to do that,' I said.

Nothing more – I had given up 'sirring' him by this time. I expected him to explode, threaten me with court martial, but I was beyond care by this time. I had had enough of being ordered, re-ordered, un-ordered, and dis-ordered that day, I wanted contact with someone who knew what was going on in the war and whose orders made sense, not blind dictates from another of these old blimps of Far Eastern Command. He just stared at me for a second or two of snuffling tension after that refusal, then demanded to know my name and rank. I told him. He said nothing more, just turned sharply and strode off in a manner suggesting he would return shortly with an armed guard.

I decided to take our unit up to Bandung, about a hundred miles away in the hills. That was where Maltby had his air headquarters and I reckoned he was the one who would have to decide what we were to do. But it was after six o'clock by the time all the aircraft had been refuelled, and no one knew if they had a flare path at Bandung, and the Johnson-Anderson-Robinson trio who had gone out on the shipping attack had still not arrived to join us, so I decided to wait till next morning. As no accommodation was available we settled down for the night on the floor of the terminal.

The missing trio had still not arrived by seven o'clock next morning, so I left a message for them and we all set off on the forty-minute flight up to the air marshal's headquarters. Bandung is on a plateau fringed with pinnacles of volcanoes, some of which are still smoking actively, and when we landed there we saw about a dozen of the Australian Hudsons which had left Sumatra before us the previous day, but there was no sign of the crews. After some difficulty I tracked down a staff officer of Maltby's headquarters and although he gave no definite order he said he considered it advisable that we stay on the ground in Bandung until they had definite news about the position in Sumatra.

Back on the airfield, however, I met a Dutch pilot who had taken off from P2 that morning. He told me that they had sick and wounded to be evacuated from the airfield and needed aircraft urgently for this. I discussed the matter with the other pilots and the RAF consensus was that we should return, but the flight-lieutenant leader of the Australian Hudsons disagreed. His view was that we had been ordered out of Palembang by Group Captain McCauley, and should stay in Java until a more senior officer countermanded that order. Should P2 be in Japanese hands, he argued, the Far East would lose all its remaining Hudsons, the bulk of our bombing force. My feeling was that we should go and check the situation from the air, landing only if the field was clearly still in our hands. The flight lieutenant maintained his static position.

He had no command over my group, nor I over his, and so we each followed our separate decisions. I give a résumé of our discussion on the field that morning – it was amicable throughout – because the RAAF came in for severe criticism subsequently, and I consider this without justification. The balance oscillated finely between staying and going, and had we lost aircraft in the return I would have at least been castigated as a fool and more likely court-martialled for disobeying an explicit order. As it was we were lucky and did the commended thing; they were unlucky and found themselves censured for obedience.

It was after midday by the time the six of us were away and at Sumatra we were guided in by the huge fires at the oil depot below Palembang – it had been fired by the Dutch as part of their scorched-earth policy. The immense pillar of smoke was visible from a hundred miles away and after we crossed the coast the main column was lost to view in the pall that covered hundreds of square miles to windward of the conflagration. From the activity on the airfield at P2, which included a Hurricane taking off and a Blenheim taxiing, it was clear we were still in possession, so we all put down without delay. The Blenheim pilot waved to me and it took a moment to realize it was Stanley Mayhew; he had found a fitter to patch up a Blenheim abandoned by 84 Squadron, and he flew it to Java.

His own aircraft was missing. It had been flown by one of the trio that had gone out on that sortie the previous day and had not joined us in Java as planned. We never did discover what happened to them but Japanese post-war reports tell of several Hudsons shot down that day by fighters protecting the naval force off Palembang, and our three must have been among them – had it been a night attack they would almost certainly have survived. I was saddened by the loss of Johnson particularly, I used to enjoy his laughter.

It was left to each pilot to decide how many people he could take, for the serviceability of our aircraft varied, but one aircraft took off with twenty passengers aboard; considering that the normal payload of a Hudson is 1000 pounds, and that twenty people with their kit must weigh about 3000 pounds, you get an idea of the overload. We ourselves were last off because we were carrying all the tool boxes in addition to nine passengers; we took most of the enormous length of P2 to clamber into the air, and the Hudson lolled about in the flight to Java, but there we did a fast tail-up landing in the dusk at Batavia to deliver our load safely. Unfortunately the aircraft with the twenty passengers made its landing approach too slowly for the excessive load and sank down short of the perimeter to hit a ditch which destroyed the undercarriage and therefore effectively the aircraft. Luckily the fuselage was so tightly packed with human beings that none was hurled about or injured in the crash.

We took off from Batavia immediately after unloading, and in the gathering darkness weaved a passage through vast piles of cumulus up to the plateau and the blacked-out airfield of Bandung, where there was enough moonlight to effect a landing. Stanley Mayhew met us with a car and took us into a luxury hotel where he had arranged rooms, but on arrival a pilot officer intercepted us in the foyer to say I was wanted urgently at the headquarters of Far East Command, so I had to forgo the bath that had been such a delicious promise and go straight to supreme authority.

At the headquarters building Air Commodore Williams was waiting for me on the moonlit veranda outside his office. Of all senior staff officers we met in the Far East, Air Commodores Williams and Staton were the only ones who inspired confidence in any of us on the squadrons – the fact that they had both only recently come out from England might have had something to do with it. I daresay there were other efficient seniors whom we did not meet – working pilots do not usually have much contact with senior staff officers – but we did associate quite closely with the mighty in the contracting battleground during the final days in Java so the valuation of those two is not without comparative validity.

That night Williams was frank. He did not know if the enemy had

228

taken possession of Medan airfield in Sumatra and he wanted me to obtain this information. And to overfly P2 to check if now occupied. He had wished to send one of the Australian Hudsons which had remained on the ground all day at Bandung, but had been unable to find any of the crews. When I said I would do the sortie myself, he said that as commander of the little unit I had better stay with them, that I should brief someone else. I told him that I was probably the only pilot who could now be guaranteed to be completely sober for the dawn take-off he wanted, so he agreed I should take the sortie. He said that if I were 'delayed' in return – a euphemism to cover all eventualities – he would arrange control of my little group; then he sent me back to the hotel in his staff car.

I have a complete memory-blank about an incident on return to the hotel. I can recall going into our bedroom – scent of gardenias, polished wooden floor, lemon-yellow curtains, rose-pink cover on a double bed, bathroom the size of a ballroom – but before that I was apparently met by Peter Gibb and Stanley Mayhew in the foyer. There, they told me years later, the group captain who had assailed us at Batavia airport the previous night came across specifically to tender his apologies for his ill-informed rebuke and the manner in which he had delivered it. His apology left no mark on me.

One reason for the memory-blank may have been the good news that followed shortly afterwards, when the night suddenly became open to unlicensed freedom, and apologies a trivia drowned in festivity. I was at last having my bath when Stanley came in with the news that Air Commodore Williams had sent his driver to tell me he had made contact with the Australian group and had ordered one of them off on the sortie, and that we should all have a drink on him; the driver had handed over to Stanley two hundred-guilder notes which had been sent for that specific purpose. So we all drank a toast to Williams and had a magnificent rijstaffel that had twenty-six dishes, among which was one that so seared the palate we were gasping for water-ices midway through the meal.

Next day we were back to war down on the plains.

Chapter 19

—◦—

I had bomb trouble the night we flew into Buitenzorg. After our five Hudsons had landed I went on to Batavia to collect some of the men from the overloaded Hudson that had crashed in the ditch. The sun was setting as we took off for the return trip, sending daytime searchlights flaring out behind the dark cloud mass to the west, and when I finally checked in at the Buitenzorg house where the Australians had set up an operations room the squadron leader on duty told me rather testily he had been trying to find me for hours. He wanted two crews for dawn take-off on an armed reconnaissance.

One of the men we had brought back was an armourer, and I took him back to the airfield with me while Peter went on to the barracks to advise the selected crews. It was dark by the time the armourer and I set off in one of the little box taxis, but the Indonesian driver knew the airfield set-up and took us to the canteen where we found the Dutch armourer, who led us on his motorcycle to the bomb store. This was located behind a huge earthen mound in the remote southern corner of the field, not an underground concrete store as in England, just a low wooden building. Inside he switched on a shielded black-out bulb to disclose a line of crates stretching away into the darkness. Each bomb was in a separate crate. He prised open several before we found some 100-kilo bombs, the nearest equivalent to our normal 250-pounders. We collected eight of these, four for each aircraft, then had to go to a separate group of boxes for tail fins which were covered in grease that smelled of urine.

It was now black night, and the rain was thundering on the tin roof of the bomb store so we had to shout to make ourselves heard.

Fitting the fins by the dim light of one blacked-out bulb took us little more than half an hour, as the Dutch armourer was impatient to get back to the canteen. When we finally had the bombs ready outside under the awning he said something unintelligible, locked the door, then spurted away into the slushy blackness on his motor-cycle. The box taxis with their two-stroke engines were just tiny vans with wooden forms each side on which two small local people could fit; there was no hope it could tow the trolley, and it could carry only two of the bombs at a time. We loaded the first four bombs, with me holding the tail fin and the armourer the nose, and the taxi wheezed downwards each time we let the weight thump on to the open rear entrance. The driver stayed in his seat throughout.

The rain had stopped by the time we squeezed ourselves in with the two bombs, but the field was now layered in soft mud and we went slithering about it for some time, the driver flicking on his headlights every now and then, before we found the first aircraft. Then our troubles really began. We had no pulley, the Dutchman had spoken little English and had simply gaped when the armourer tried to explain that need, so we now had to do the job by hand – and body. Once we had opened the bomb doors the armourer and I lifted one of the bombs over beside the fuselage, then I lay down on the muddy grass in position under the aircraft and he lift-rolled the 100-kilo bomb longitudinally on to my back. With him stabilizing the bomb I then raised myself on all fours as he tried to guide it into place. He fumbled, then took a hand off to grope for his torch, then fumbled again. My legs began to tremble with the strain and I cried out, 'For Christ's sake get on with it!'

'It won't go, sir. The lug's wrong,' he said, almost tearfully.

I flattened out, tilted off the bomb which sploshed into the ground, and stayed flat for a moment, waiting for recovery. Then he shone his torch from the cradle in the bomb bay, down to the lug on the bomb as he explained the problem. Its technicalities were beyond me, but he said the Dutch had an adaptor for the lug that overcame the difficulty, and they would certainly have them in the store, but by then I had had enough of bombs for the night. It would have to be an unarmed reconnaissance, which made much more sense anyway; instead of attacking any naval force sighted, it was better to come back with the news then send off a night strike. We dumped the bombs outside the store with the others.

This was not quite the end of field duties for the night. We took the taxi first up to the canteen to drop the armourer, then to the Dutch Air Force barracks to arrange for the two aircraft to be refuelled. By the time I reached the operations room I was tired, soaked with rain, mud and sweat, and stinking from the bomb-fin grease, so not in the mood to stand argument about altering their order for an armed reconnaissance. There would be no bombs, I declared.

'Don't worry,' the squadron leader said. 'The job's been cancelled.'

I could have hit him – then had to apologize for swearing when he explained he had tried to get the news to me but the driver had failed to find us. He then compounded the embarrassment by taking me to a bathroom to wash off the grease, and he gave me a shirt to replace my stained one. It was long after midnight when I reached our sleeping quarters, a concrete-floored store shed in an army depot; when I opened the creaking door an acrid warm blackness seemed to spill out, carrying with it the smell of sweat, the sound of someone snoring and of the aggressive whines of mosquitoes. I could discern a few shrouds of mosquito nets, and a dim line of bodies lying along the wall like those in Henry Moore's sketches of the London underground in the blitz.

Peter Gibb was waiting on a chair just inside. He whispered that there were no beds, only about a dozen mattresses for the twenty of us, and just six mosquito nets. Given the choice, he had opted, for himself and for me, a net rather than a bed, and for this I was grateful. We lay down on the concrete floor, the chair between us keeping the net more or less clear of our bodies, and fell into an exhausted sleep.

We carried out the reconnaissance next morning, a simple five-hour flight over the Java Sea that finished in late morning with nothing to report. It would have helped aircrew morale had we, as in England, been given reasons for such patrols, particularly because they often seemed obscure in scope, unnecessarily dangerous in timing, and arbitrary in location. To locate shipping, you do a coordinated sweep with several aircraft covering a wide area, not just a single line; and in those latitudes, and with so few aircraft now left to us, the morning was the worst time to fly such sorties. There is normally a build-up of cumulus during the day, so cloud cover is more reliable in the afternoon; moreover, a search in the afternoon had the additional advantage that if a night strike were to follow, as it should have done, the enemy force would still be relatively close to the reported position. But we were ordered out at dawn – the staff out there had their own peculiar way of running a war; right to the end they seemed convinced that night flying was far too dangerous to be risked, even in war.

Immediately after the debriefing Group Captain McCauley, who had now arrived from Palembang, took me back to the field to inspect my 62 Squadron unit. I had appropriated half of one of the hangars as our maintenance area and on arrival there found the ground crew impressively busy on our one unserviceable aircraft. He then drove down the strip to check our four exposed aircraft – the bomb bays had been bagged by the Australians – and in all of them, including mine, aircrews were in busy occupation. McCauley had nothing to criticize and I took advantage of his mood to point out that many of us had considerable experience of night strikes. Could we not carry out night offensive patrols towards Sumatra?

He was perfunctory in accord. Yes . . . that was a point . . . well, we'd see . . . he would talk to our wing commander when he turned up with the boat party. He was always somewhat wary with me, reluctant to talk about mutual friends among his wife's family, perhaps fearing I might presume on that personal contact. He dropped me by our last aircraft where the pilot was running an engine test.

There was a field of tobacco growing just behind the aircraft and all the plants were swirling and rippling about in the propeller blast, white flowers streaming in a blizzard towards the gun-site beyond. Looking at it I suddenly realized what was odd about all the gun-sites in the field: there was no activity around them, no men, no trucks, and no movement of the guns themselves. I threaded a path through the tobacco to check an explanation that occurred to me. Sure enough it was a wooden gun, an elaborate structure with a trailer and lorry wheels but with less offensive power than a toy water pistol. Presently I learned that all the guns about the field were wooden dummies. As were the four tanks. The airfield was utterly defenceless. Suddenly all those aircraft lined up along the edge of the strip, for here there was no jungle for sheltered alcoves, looked terribly vulnerable.

Late that afternoon I took time off to see the famous gardens. When I first went to the Solomon Islands with Levers Pacific Plantations, I used to see frequent reports from an entomologist who was doing research on *amblypelta*, a mosquito-like insect that caused premature nutfall. All these reports had included in their distribution list the exotic INSTITUUT VAN PLANTENZIEKTEN, BUIT-

ENZORG, JAVA. The whole title had captured my imagination, like those romantic names that had bewitched the boy Turner:

> When I was but thirteen or so
> I went into a golden land . . .
> Chimborazo, Cotopaxi,
> They had stolen my soul away!

Given the opportunity therefore, I had to go and see the gardens. On arrival I found the stark scientific isolation of tree types disappointing, it was all so clinically clean and labelled – the great liana-like roots and the soaring buttressed trunks of the many ficus types need close jungle to sustain their mystery. The governor's palace, however, a fairy-tale white Palladian building set on a slope of emerald green and fronted with a pond covered in pink water lilies over which dithered iridescent dragonflies, captured perfectly the spirit of my dreams. Suddenly proud of the gardens that had so obviously pleased me, the taxi driver decided to show me something more of his country's charms – 'No pay, captain. No pay.' He drove to a park ten minutes away, and there led me along a footpath bordered by a multicoloured hip-high croton hedge to a small open pavilion in which some Javanese girls were dancing. I think it must have been a lesson, a regular session perhaps, for it drew only casual notice from passers-by on the path. But the driver had good value from me. I was fascinated.

The girls were very young, about ten years old perhaps, wearing brightly coloured bodices and wrap-around skirts with batik geometrical designs in blacks and browns. They were dancing to the music of bells and a flute-like instrument. Their small hands arched stiffly back to gondola shape as they raised their arms slowly, moving them up sinuously to remind you of a snake rising from its basket to the pipe of an Indian charmer. They swayed their bodies from the hips, jerked their heads from side to side like mechanical figures, then sank down ever writhing to a crouched position, stretching out their arms in slow-motion bird-wing movements; they were dancing less with their feet than with their hips, and arms, and hands, and heads. Then, suddenly as if switched off, the music stopped in what seemed to me the middle of a phrase, the girls rose to their feet and flowed off to the end of the pavilion where they sat down in cross-legged ease listening to the elderly man who seemed to be their teacher. The driver drove me back to the barracks chattering in unintelligible friendliness.

The following morning, with dark rain clouds threatening overhead, we were driving up to the aerodrome entrance when we saw five twin-engined bombers in V formation approaching the field. The red disc on the fuselage of the leader was clearly visible, and we banged on the roof of the truck cabin and were out on the ground even before the driver stopped. As the formation passed over us they began to open fire at the strip, and a moment later we heard the explosion of their bombs. Then they were away. Not a mark on them, of course. We hurried fearfully on to the field.

It was a disaster. They had bombed in their echelon formation, and as they had passed on the only side of the field on which we could possibly park, and bombed with low-level accuracy, they had been deadly. Two of our Hudsons were completely destroyed, the Australians lost two and had another badly damaged even though theirs had been in bomb bays, and the Dutch lost the only three Sikorskis they had on the field. Several of the wrecks were burning, and ammunition was exploding. The allies had lost at least seven of their precious store of bombers, almost half of all our remaining force in the Far East. I began to feel the end was close at hand.

Our V9129 had escaped almost untouched, just a few holes in a wing. A minor gain was that we were now able to get from the wrecks the parts needed to put back into full service the plane that had been on the danger list. So by mid-afternoon on 20 February we had three aircraft serviceable and ready for action. When I reported this to the operations room they had no immediate tasks for us, but they had received a report from a Hurricane fighter pilot of a number of enemy ships south-east of Singapore, and I was ordered to have an aircraft ready for a dawn strike. I argued for an attack that night instead but McCauley brusquely refused it. I told him I would take the sortie.

Next morning, however, I was taken off the job. Our take-off had been delayed to await the report of a Hurricane sent to pinpoint location of the ships. It was not until about eleven o'clock that he returned, and by then McKern and Lilly had at last arrived with the Palembang boat party; they ordered another pilot off on the sortie so as to have from me a report on the events of the previous few days and the current situation of the squadron remnants. They had been wandering about Java for days trying to track us down and it was only more or less by chance that they had found us that morning at Buitenzorg. That we were now down to three aircraft saddened, but did not surprise, them. And before the sun set that day we had lost another. The pilot who had taken over our sortie was shot down by fighters over the countryside west of Batavia. Japanese fighters were patrolling the coastal area of Java in formations of eighteen during those days, and against such firepower a single Hudson was doomed on sight unless close to good cloud cover.

So now we were down to two aircraft, our V9129 and the one that had for so long been on the danger list. The Australians had six left out of the two squadrons that had left Sumatra with us. There was discussion that evening by senior officers at Buitenzorg and the staff remnants at Command about the organization of our tiny bomber force; all that was left in Far East Command now were the eight Hudsons at Buitenzorg, and five Blenheims on another field west of us. The decision of the staff was passed on to us next morning at a meeting of all the aircrews in the main hangar, which was just a large corrugated-iron shed set up on the bare earth. McCauley stood on a service gantry to address us. Our squadron would cease to exist as a flying unit; the surplus aircrew and all the ground crew would, as soon as transport could be arranged, go to a southern port to await instructions. The two Australian squadrons would merge into one, our two surviving aircraft together with the crews would join this amalgamated Number 1 RAAF squadron.

It was ironical that now I was being forcibly injected into the Australian Air Force some two years after I had been refused enlistment – most expensively for me in consequence. I was delighted all the same with this tardy success. Being a member of the Australian squadron also meant that we would be kept flying, saved from the fate of the others who were now grounded without any hope of further flying action. We still had a weapon.

Is a total of thirty minutes' service with the Royal Australian Air Force a record, I wonder?

About ten minutes after we left the hangar Peter and I were walking towards the gate when the sirens wailed and we ran to join a group in the nearest shelter close by the end of the strip. This was a so-called slit trench but a gouged ditch would have been a more fitting name, for it was scarcely four feet deep and disturbingly wide. You had to crouch low to keep below the rim and I prayed the bombs would land well clear of our area. With no thudding of anti-aircraft fire to disturb the sound of the approaching aircraft we could tell they were not bombers, and a cautious glance above the rim of the trench was enough to confirm it. They were Zero fighters, just about to break formation so as to attack in line astern, one group staying above as cover.

They manoeuvred into position at cruising speed, patiently careful as if in practice on the range – and probably smiling as they passed over the wooden guns, pointing up in ridiculous attempt at threat. I think there were nine machines in that first group but it was difficult to tell because each one made more than one steady gun-shattering run down the strip. Looking up from the trench near the end of the strip I could see them turn in slowly for each run as if coming in to land, they would straighten out at about fifty feet just in front of us, so low I could see a pilot clearly in helmet and goggles sitting upright in the cockpit, hood back to enjoy the breeze perhaps . . . down the length of the strip . . . thunder of gunfire . . . pull up into a gentle left-hand circuit . . . back down for another run. I saw one pilot turn his head on the run-in and he seemed to look straight down at us in that enormously wide shelter, which began to feel more and more like a gentle declivity in the surface rather than a manufactured trench.

Peter kept popping his head up to give a running commentary about aircraft that were being hit, but as our own aircraft was out of sight I had no interest in watching the destruction. I wished he would keep his head down, I could have cheerfully shot him myself he seemed so unconcerned. A column of black smoke spiralled up from the field and there were explosions as fire reached the aircraft fuel tanks. Then there was a lull for a minute, the first group had had enough, they climbed away to let the top lot down for their turn. Even Peter grew quiet then, staying low like the rest of us as the second group started on their orderly runs of destruction.

They went on and on and on, and the smoke from fires began to drift across the trenches. They could see us every time they turned, banking at the end of the strip to get into line, but still they concentrated on their prime target, the machines. Had we had just a single machine gun, even a repeater rifle, they must have suffered, but we were as defenceless as the aerodrome itself – even our revolvers had been handed in to be checked that morning. Suddenly the next one did not come, there was just the thrumming of many aircraft, and I looked up to see them circling into formation, and a moment later they set off northwards, their vibrating sound fading into the airfield clamour – the crackling of fire and the staccato chatter of exploding ammunition from burning aircraft.

It was the end. I could have wept at the sight of V9129; it had not burned like our other remaining Hudson but it would never fly again. It was riddled with cannon shell and bullets to such an extent that large chunks of fuselage and wings had ripped away. Cockpit and turret were smashed into a tangle of metal and perspex and cables. I cannot understand why it had not burned, both tanks had been hit repeatedly and petrol was pouring on to the ground. There was still a strong risk of fire, however, for the nearby aircraft was ejecting great woofs of flame through its twisting smoke coils. Suddenly realizing there were bombs aboard at least one of the burning aircraft, we all withdrew to the top hangar. No buildings had been touched. The Japanese had come to destroy aircraft and had done so with deadly effect.

With five of their aircraft sheltered in bomb bays the Australians had been comparatively lucky, and I think they actually managed to get four serviceable afterwards – helped by cannibalizing the wrecks; but after a further attack only three managed to fly off to Australia a few days later. It was beyond Hudson range but they overcame this by carrying twenty-five cans of petrol, then knocking out a side window through which a man reached out to take off the cap of the wing tank and empty the cans through rubber tube into the tank; it was a scheme Stanley and I had discussed with our engineer officer. The Blenheims lasted a day or two longer than us and in this they were unlucky; a delay of even a day at the end of February 1942 was critical for escape, and, because of subsequent prison conditions, possibly even for survival.

The decisive Battle of the Java Sea was fought two days later, and in that action five allied cruisers were eventually sunk, leaving the Japanese navy in unchallenged control of the seas about the Dutch East Indies. Whilst the battle was being fought off the northern coast of Java, we were on the southern coast at the port of Tjilitjap. Five merchant ships escaped that night of 27 February, escorted by four destroyers and the remaining auxiliary vessels of the allied fleet. The captain of our ship, the *Kota Gede*, made a personal decision that night to leave the convoy and strike out alone for Ceylon rather than continue with the convoy to Australia. We were lucky. The official report states:

> Some of the ships [that left Tjilitjap that night] escaped to Australia and Ceylon, but others were intercepted by the Japanese navy and sunk, including all four destroyers and the naval auxiliary vessels.

The 'including' does not offer much hope for those merchant ships that were with the naval escort.

When we broke away from the convoy the captain headed due south into the Indian Ocean for two days before setting our lonely course for Ceylon. The *Kota Gede* was a cargo ship of 9500 tons with seven cabins and lifeboat accommodation for eighty men; in that escape run it carried 2152 RAF officers and men, in addition to the crew. The officers slept all about the deck, some of us managing to rig up ragged shelters from the continual lashing squalls that came sweeping across the sea at all hours of the day and night. The men, more fortunate than us, slept down in the vast cargo holds of the ship, some of them so content with their situation they came up only to collect their scanty meals.

The heavy rain was welcome in one respect: it provided water. We grabbed what we could collect from the tarpaulin cover of the lifeboat nearest our deck position, for the shortage of water meant we were rationed to only half a pint a day during the eight days we spent on the trip. Food was short, the ration was doled out twice a day: two biscuits, a spoonful of jam and half a pint of tea for the first meal, then two biscuits and tinned meat later in the day. There were such long queues for each meal that it took up to three hours to get to the delivery point, so we spent most of the day queuing for food. And as there were only four toilets for the one hundred and fifty officers, we were probably queuing for them when not in that long straggling line for our food.

Considering the effort the Japanese made to prevent a Dunkirk-escape from the military collapse we were incredibly lucky. Had we been sighted by any of their numerous naval units, ships or submarines or planes, patrolling the area we would have been doomed. The ship was defenceless, she would have gone down with the loss of over two thousand lives. But the only sign of enemy action we saw was a floating mine on our second day out, lolling in a lazy sea during that still afternoon with plenty of time for the ship to miss it by a hundred yards or so.

The senior officer in command, an RAF group captain, Walkington, who came aboard complete with his tin trunk and other luggage, did not despair at the thought of being sighted by the Japanese navy. Each officer was put in charge of a section of the ship's hold where a dozen or so airmen were sleeping, and many spent some time down on station to escape the rain and chat with our charges. Walkington issued Daily Routine Orders which were typed and posted on a board we all had to pass in the food queue. One order dealt with the action we officers were to take if the ship were attacked. The words were unforgettable:

> Since lifeboat accommodation is inadequate, in the event of the ship being attacked by surface vessel or other means, officers will assemble the men on their various troop decks and supervise the construction of rafts from wreckage which will then be available.

Happily we reached Ceylon without having to put his survival plan to the practical test.

Chapter 20

——o——

We were an embarrassment to the RAF station at Karachi, a huge unplanned influx which clogged the depot. They sent us off for dispersal to the other side of India, by rail so as to give Calcutta time to decide our future.

The journey, covering almost two thousand miles, took more than four days. Reading my notebook of the time is like seeing a film, the carriage window a screen on which the recorded scenes run through in random display, an occasional one being stilled in sharper focus. There were big stations with their rows of restaurants for different classes and different religions, a people whose colour ranged from marble black to a light suntan, a land that began as barren yellow sandy desert near Karachi and finished as lush green rice-fields about the Ganges delta. At almost every station were beggars whose deformities were an asset – a legless man on a trolley scuttling across a platform like an enormous land-crab, a child with a spine so curved he scurried on flailing fours like a spider to the kill, a leper pointing to a hole in his face where once his nose had been. They came clamouring and clawing at the carriage window seeking benefit from your look of incredulous horror.

Many of the stations seemed like village communities. In the day the families cooked their meals on the platform, used the siding track as a toilet, finger-cleaned their teeth at the drinking fountain, suckled their children on the benches, and squatted in circular family councils in the shade of the awning. At night some inhabitants would be sleeping in the waiting rooms on low stretchers or mats on the floor, station employees in rope charpoys on the platform, the resident beggars against the wall at the end of the buildings.

Animals too kept appearing on the window screen. At one station the monkeys came tumbling down out of a huge dark banyan tree like monstrous insects shaken from the branches. There was a white brahmin bull on one platform with its head turned watching a woman patting together the pile of dung it had just dropped. Masterly aerobatic kite hawks swooped on scraps thrown from the restaurant car, bee-eaters clustered brilliantly on the curving telegraph wires, hoopoes undulated alongside the dawdling train, and one afternoon I saw a snow-white egret standing as still as a delicate marble statue on the back of a buffalo half-immersed in a muddy pool.

This was northern India in March when the country starts to heat up towards the monsoon. Across the desert east of Karachi the heat was drumming. Merely to look at the window from the darkened compartment was to make you squint not just against the aggressive glare but against the impact of the heat against your very eyeballs. Your lips cracked, eyes became gritty, nostrils caked dry. We passed through a sandstorm that drove the sand squeezing through the crevices about the doors and windows into the stifling carriage, covering everything with fine hard dust that crackled between your teeth every time you ate anything for the next twenty-four hours. Further east beyond Delhi the heat eased, and then at night with the great steam engine spraying fiery embers past the open window little eddies of cool air would come frisking through the carriage and soothing you to jolted sleep. And once in the early morning before the heat haze gathered I saw again the white ridge of the Himalayas far away to the north, set sharply clear against a daffodil dawning sky.

On arrival in Calcutta at the end of March our unit disintegrated. I became detached from the others when Wing Commander Percy, whom I had met down in that Rangoon greenhouse on our way through, decided that as someone who had actually flown an aeroplane in action I would be a useful assistant to him in group headquarters. It was not entirely a sedentary job; they had a communication flight which Percy encouraged me to use. In Burma the retreat was in full spate, the lower half of the country including the capital was now in Japanese hands, and the day before they cut off the escape route into China, and so effectively ended the campaign, I flew a Hudson into Myitkyina in northern Burma.

Percy had to report on evacuation facilities there, the last airfield left in our hands and the take-off point for the army and civilian escape route over the trackless mountains where thousands of them were shortly about to die in the attempt to reach India. Percy picked up a gunner through the armaments section and said he himself would act as navigator; he had no desire to touch the controls, had not flown any aircraft at all for two years, but assured me that as an old Burma hand he would have no trouble getting us to Myitkyina. I had some doubts about this when immediately after our early morning take-off from Dum-Dum, the old arsenal where soft-nosed bullets were first produced at the end of the last century, he gave me our course as 'about forty-five degrees, and we'll see how it goes'. It went a good bit awry, and I had to join in the subsequent map-reading and make my own course adjustments until the Chin Hills came into sight. Percy then folded the map and gave up the stressful effort altogether.

'After all we just have to follow the Irrawaddy,' he said.

I had come to the same comforting conclusion myself, so did not bother him further. There were just a few swathes of cirrus, like dissipating vapour trails, high above in the pale blue morning sky, and down below us the cotton-wool strips of mist had still not cleared from all the valleys; but at ten thousand feet we could see the ridges fifty miles away, so there was no need even for a map, let alone a competent navigator, to find the great Irrawaddy River and therefore Myitkyina on its banks.

The vegetation over the Chin Hills is a distinctive feature in the topography of the Far East. The ranges further over on the Chinese border, and the jungle slopes in Malaya and in Sumatra, all carry evidence of the slash-and-burn cultivation technique practised so widely in the tropics; there you see line-cut clearings scattered about the hills, the latest still charred black, others showing the verdant sheen of fresh rice shoots, or flaxen stubble after having been cropped, or youthful pea-green secondary growth on abandoned ones. In contrast the climax jungle of the Chin Hills gives a false impression of uniform dark green cover. On closer inspection, however, as when looking directly below that morning, you could see the canopy was many-coloured, leaf flushes of yellow and copper and translucent green, and a scattering of distinctive crowns in misty faint blossoming hues. Only the ridges stretching away ahead of us showed uniformity in colour, as if covered in smooth-topped fungi that varied from that deceptive dark green in the near distance to the typical mountain blue of the farthest ridge against the horizon.

By staying at height over the Burmese plain we were able to pick out from fifty miles away the flash of silver in the crank-bend of the

Irrawaddy just below Myitkyina. Then we slanted down over the grid of paddy fields west of the town, made our turn over the river now smooth as glass in its pre-monsoon low, and put down on the dry grassy field where a number of other aircraft were parked, including at least one other Hudson. I declined Percy's offer to join him in the discussion with the station commander, instead stayed to check refuelling and to contact any pilots who happened to be with their machines.

I found not one but about a dozen, gathered by a Dakota which had come in specially to fly them out to India. Unlike Singapore where there had been talk and plans about defending the island, there was no such reaction in the final days of the Burma campaign. The objective was clearly the same as at Dunkirk; to get the army out of an impossible situation so as to fight from a secure base. It is reasonable to ask, however, why they had delayed so long to come to that decision. There had been no point in continuing the fight in Burma once Rangoon had been lost; with the sea route in the hands of the enemy and no overland route to India – and certainly then no hope of sustaining an army by air supply – the position should have been abandoned at once. It is surprising that in the years that the local command were supposed to have been preparing for the Japanese invasion, and in the months that had actually passed since Pearl Harbor when they had been expecting it every day, no effort had been made to prepare a fall-back route for civilians to India. Thousands were now about to die because of that failure in planning.

The Chin Hills seemed far more sinister that afternoon on our return flight from the doomed airfield. We were flying into the setting sun, the ridges of the hills glowed like hot iron, and the indigo shadows of the valleys seemed without depth, great dark chasms set across the path of those thousands now about to set out towards India. Percy, however, was pleased with his day's work. They seemed to have everything under control in Myitkyina, he said. He sang 'Two Sleepy People', and then went to sleep himself. I found us our way back to Calcutta.

At group headquarters I had a desk in the operations room, so had frequent contact with the air commodore, and one day asked him if I could be posted to operations again. Either I handled him badly or chose the wrong moment because he told me coldly that if I had any request to make I should put it in writing and pass it through the proper channel – unless I were part of the old-boy network, he should have added for complete truth. I did tackle Percy but he was unwilling to back the application, saying my work was too important; what he meant was that if I left he himself would have to write the reports to which he was then merely giving his signature. He thought to do me a favour, however, and also perhaps to stop such efforts to sabotage his comfortable position, and arranged for me to visit the bombing squadrons to give a series of lectures on shipping attacks. It was this that led me to write up that full version of the Endau operation, helped by Stanley Mayhew who was then sitting idle at a holding depot.

Percy's attempt to retain me misfired. In mid-June 1942 I was plucked from his grasp and posted to Bombay. It happened that a senior staff officer from India Command was present in the audience one day when I was giving a talk to a group of about twenty aircrew. He questioned me afterwards about my background, then told me of a vacancy for which he thought I was eminently suited. It was as second in command, and chief instructor, at a school of General Reconnaissance about to open in Bombay. I was agreeable – at least it offered plenty of flying – and two days later a signal came through posting me to Bombay.

According to my posting notice the General Reconnaissance school was out at Juhu airfield, so on arrival at Victoria Terminus, the yellowstone Indo-Gothic railhead in Bombay, I took a taxi to Juhu beach about ten miles away. At my request the driver avoided the turmoil of the city and instead drove around the coast, past the palatial homes in Malabar Hill with their white walls smothered in purple and salmon bougainvillaea, then the Hanging Gardens and the sombre Towers of Silence behind grey bare walls with not a vulture in sight. Once beyond the racecourse it was squalor for miles, dirty factory walls and tin shanty housing and pavement dwellers and pi-dogs, and then vultures did appear on the scene, a row of them lined up like gargoyles on the ridge of the abattoir roof. At last, clear of the town proper, the houses became a little more substantial, white blocks with patches of green around them, then finally we came to the paddy fields and palms about Juhu.

The aerodrome was less than a mile in from the sea, a small grass field on low-lying ground behind a palm-fringed shore with luxury houses giving directly on to the beach, one of which was taken over as an officers' mess for the squadron aircrew operating from the station. This was a unit of the Indian Reserve equipped with the old biplane Dominees; their three aircraft, devoid of armament, were the sole air defence of Bombay. I discovered the General Reconnaissance school was not located there; the commander of the school, they said, was also their station commander, and also the head of the RAF-Naval Liaison Unit. Where could I find their multi-command chief? He spent most of his time in the Naval Liaison Office – that was in town, not far from the Taj Mahal Hotel, they said. Of course, I had dismissed the taxi by then. The Indian officer found me a van and driver to get me back to the city again where I met the Pooh Bah who was in command of all these diverse units.

I had a lot of luck with my RAF commanders during the war – a convivial companion in Tubby Grant, a considerate friend in Bob Hodges during the last phase, and before him the effervescent Squadron Leader Ronnie Knott in Bombay. I had more fun, and more carefree enjoyment, with him and his wife than at any other time in the war. He was fair-haired, slightly built, and active as a shrew. When I met him on that first day he stopped work at once to drive me to his home and meet his wife. We swerved a way through the Bombay traffic on squealing tyres as he told me a story about his service in the Khyber Pass area, shouted a friendly warning in Urdu to a bullock-cart driver, pointed out a landmark, sounded the horn in noisy greeting to an acquaintance in a passing car, and talked about Indian politics and shopping in the bazaar and the school we were to found.

He had been married less than twelve months to Hermione – gentle, softly spoken, and filled with secrets which could be sensed but were not defined in a booklet of imaginative verse she had published. They had a flat by the sea out at the end of the Causeway, and from that first evening when I dined there I spent nearly every weekend with them up to November when they left for England. During those five months when I spent so much time with them in Bombay, I cannot remember ever thinking about devising some scheme that might get me back on operations again. After they left, however, it was different.

Far from being a holiday, I probably worked much longer hours that autumn than at any other time in the war. The new unit was to be established in a private Indian school which had been built only a year or two earlier a few miles north of Juhu. We had to devise a syllabus and agree with Air Command the number of staff and qualifications required, arrange alterations to the building to house the staff and the sixteen officers planned for each course, decide upon furniture and get it made. Then when we had all this organized we were told to scrap the plan, and instead provide for an additional sixteen officer pupils on a navigation course we would also initiate. In addition we had to establish a flight headquarters at Juhu airfield for six Anson aircraft to be supplied for the practical sessions of the two courses, and organize all the ancillary services required in the new unit – cooks and clerks and drivers and medical services and so on.

After more than three years in India Ronnie Knott had the experience to handle such a commitment, could find and communicate with the civil suppliers, and knew how to carry out the complex routine of ordering and paying for goods from local merchants. All my time in the RAF, apart from that limited experience leading the flight out to Singapore, I had been accustomed to having facilities already in place, with meals and accommodation and service organized under specialist control, and it was a fascinating educational experience to help in the design and structure of a skeleton, then build on it the whole complex working body needed for our purpose. As well as commanding the new unit and Juhu airfield, Knott was also in command of the Santa Cruz airfield then being built near Juhu; this was to have a full-length concrete runway, and was subsequently handed over to the Indian government to become the present civil airport of Bombay.

Our first courses when finally we did get started in the summer of 1942 had to be prolonged because of the civil disturbances which followed the arrest of Gandhi. These prevented classes getting into the naval dockyard for certain of the planned lectures – we had a naval officer on the staff – as the mobs were flooding into the streets in protest, and lives were being lost in the conflict. It was clear some weeks prior to the arrest that there was going to be a clash between the government and the Congress Party. I did not understand then, and still do not, why Congress turned down the offer brought out by Stafford Cripps, for although it did not mean immediate independence, this was guaranteed at the end of hostilities, and as there was no realistic chance of attaining independence any earlier, the sensible course would have been to make the best of the offer and work meanwhile for unity when free.

Anyway, Gandhi, to his subsequent regret, turned down the offer as inadequate, and Congress had a big public meeting in Bombay on 8 August when they launched the QUIT INDIA movement. The Congress resolution authorizing Gandhi to lead the struggle was practically a declaration of war against the government and they reacted sharply. The following day Gandhi, Nehru and all the other main figures in the movement were arrested and then interned in the Aga Khan's palace in Poona. This gave Jinnah the field to himself for two years to develop the claim for an independent Muslim state. The consequence was the division of India, and the birth of Pakistan.

The government was prepared for violent reaction to the arrests. We had twelve hours' prior notice and issued an order confining everyone to barracks. In the event the assessment that the mobs would not attack military installations proved to be accurate. They gathered in the city itself, particularly in the mill area where they burned trucks, buses, tram cars and police stations, and looted shops and factories and godowns. The police reacted with lathi charges and, in a few cases, with gunfire.

Out at Juhu we had no trouble at all despite Gandhi's close association with the area – he would often go down to the beach for evening prayers, and it was at Juhu that he made his famous protest against the salt duty. I was glad we were not involved in suppressing the protest. Like many newcomers to the country – Stanley Mayhew was particularly vehement on the subject – I had some sympathy with the Indian cause; in some of us this sprang not merely in support of the principle of freedom but also in reaction to the arrogance of the English who controlled the civil service. You would have thought that by 1942 they would have learned that subject peoples consider efficiency in government a provocative irrelevance in any discussion about independence. The reaction is: Who are you to tell me what's good for me? Get out of my country! Or, as the Indians put it more succinctly on the walls, on the trees, on the bridges, and on the very surfaces of the tarred roads that summer: QUIT INDIA.

The resentment did not abate, but the actual violence petered out within a month or two, and we had no more difficulty after that short confinement during our first course. By the end of 1942 we were running four courses altogether, General Reconnaissance, Navigation, Ship Recognition and Air Tactics, with a total intake of forty officers. We now had eight aircraft in our flight, and were using both Juhu and Santa Cruz airfields, the latter only for bomb-loaded take-offs as it was not yet in full operation. The Naval Liaison Office and its staff of six still remained within our command, Knott spending most of his time there and leaving the other units largely to me. Then at the end of 1942 he became due for repatriation and, partly because of his recommendation and partly because I had become known to staff at Air Headquarters in Delhi through several meetings there, I was given command of all the diverse units. With the job came promotion to Squadron Leader.

Early in January 1943 I was able to arrange through contacts in Delhi for the vacant post of the Anson flight command to be given to Stanley Mayhew. He had been desk-bound in Bengal and was anxious to get back into the air even in such a placid role as training flights. We did actually manage occasional quasi-operational flights, having through our Naval Liaison Office applied enough pressure to be given a supply of anti-submarine bombs, and external carriers for them on two of the Ansons. The only aircraft stationed on the west coast of India were our Ansons, so there was a genuine need for us to be equipped to deal not only with any reported submarines but even with the threat of enemy surface craft off the busy port of Bombay – a Japanese naval unit had penetrated into the Bay of Bengal earlier in the year. We made about twenty armed sorties in all, but never had sight of an enemy vessel of any kind.

We were also involved in army cooperation exercises. The 36 Commando Division, under Major-General Festing, was stationed nearby and we jointly planned a wide variety of operations with them; we flew cover for beach landing exercises, made dummy bomb and strafing attacks, spotted for mortars and made aerial surveys of troop positions. One elaborate exercise I planned with them entailed the simulated drop of a unit behind the enemy lines and its subsequent supply from the air. A little later, early in 1943, I was fascinated to hear that 'a weird brigadier called Wingate' was actually engaged on such an operation. There was some resentment about this among Festing's staff who felt that units of their division should have been chosen for such a task; they argued that the Commandos, particularly the specialist groups in the Middle East, had a depth of experience in this type of operation, but it seems Wingate had personal contact with the Commander-in-Chief and against such an advantage the mere practical experience of Commando units was of little account.

By the spring of 1943 I had had enough of Bombay. It was not merely that I wanted to get back into the fighting war, but the job itself had become tainted. Visiting staff officers would carry on as if it were a prize to be sought, 'the cushiest job in India' was how one described it. They would speak with envy of the situation on the beach, the office in Bombay, attractive secretaries, direct and personal contact with Delhi headquarters, staff cars and aeroplanes at command, freedom to go wherever I wished – I had made one trip as far as Malta to collect navigation equipment. But I had not rushed into the war for that sort of life, and had never had much respect for those who arranged plush seats for themselves remote from the action. That such people should be envious of my command made it grubby. They could have it. I wanted to be back amongst those who were fighting the war.

In March 1943 there occurred what I thought was a good opportunity. An intelligence report from Delhi had made mention of heavy fighting on Guadalcanal, so I wrote an application along the lines of the one designed to get me out of England into the Malayan campaign. In this one I told about the number of years and experience I had had in the Solomon Islands, suggesting I had spent months in the bush on Guadalcanal and had sailed to nearly every island in the group – I claimed to have been a recruiter. Such experience, I argued, must surely be of interest to some American or Australian unit involved in that campaign. Air Headquarters passed the application on to the Air Ministry; it must have been in garbled form, or been dealt with in London by an idiot, because a week or two later the adjutant came into my office one morning with the signalled reply from London. It read:

CONSIDERATION HAS BEEN GIVEN TO THIS
OFFICER'S APPLICATION FOR TRANSFER TO
THE ROYAL AUSTRALIAN AIR FORCE BUT IT
IS POINTED OUT THAT NO FACILITIES
EXIST FOR SUCH TRANSFER WHILST HE IS IN
INDIA. ONLY ALTERNATIVE IS FOR
OFFICER TO RESIGN HIS COMMISSION IN RAF,
TRAVEL TO AUSTRALIA AT OWN EXPENSE,

AND ENLIST IN RAAF. THERE CAN BE NO
GUARANTEE HE WILL BE COMMISSIONED IN
THE RAAF. THERE IS NO OBJECTION TO HIS
RELEASE FROM RAF IF HE WISHES TO GO.
SIGNAL HIS DECISION.

His decision was to tell Air Ministry they could stick their miserable offer – the adjutant translated this into bland officialese.

Instead of sending that reply direct to Air Headquarters in Delhi I decided to pass it through our group command recently established in Bombay. I took it there personally because I had just received from them a letter which offered a possible escape route. The letter, marked 'To be opened only by the Commanding Officer', said that Air Headquarters were calling for eight officer volunteers for 'a dangerous mission'. They had to be aircrew, only officers up to the rank of flight lieutenant would be considered, and the commanding officer had to discover at once if there were any candidates on his unit. None of my staff wished to volunteer, and it was because I myself was too superior in rank for the offer that I decided a personal visit to group headquarters might get around that problem; my argument was that I was only an acting squadron leader, would go down automatically to flight lieutenant if posted to such a vacancy, so therefore I was qualified to volunteer.

Unfortunately the P staff officer at group, a wing commander, did not agree with the argument. He was in the administrative branch, to him the issue was simple: I did not at the moment conform to the signal requirement, so that was the end of the matter. He pointed out that if I were posted it would certainly be to a squadron leader vacancy, quite likely a wing commander one; only if I were packed off to a depot for some reprehensible reason, had health or personal problems, would I be likely to revert to flight lieutenant rank on posting.

I told the wing commander that by coincidence I did have a personal problem. The holding post was in Karachi, I had a cousin in the army who was stationed there and had been thinking for some time of requesting a compassionate posting to be near him. The two of us had been very close since childhood, his wife and all five children had recently been killed in an air raid on Bournemouth and I was anxious to help him in his time of anguish.

The wing commander believed this; he expressed his sympathy, and suggested I apply for interview with the air commodore about such a posting. So I wrote the letter then and there in his office, with some help from him, and a few days later appeared before the air commodore for the interview. He was one of the old hands from the first war, blunt and bellicose, had no time for compassionate postings. If I wished to see a cousin I should take some leave, he said. I was in command, so could arrange that surely without bothering him? Good afternoon.

I did take a couple of days' leave, not to Karachi of course, but to see a friend who ran the intelligence section at air headquarters in the plasticine-coloured Lutyens complex at New Delhi. His immediate reaction to my appeal was that if he could arrange postings to an operational squadron then he would have arranged one for himself long ago. He said that if my air commodore had decided I was to stay in command at Juhu, then even P staff in air headquarters would have difficulty overriding him. He advised patience; after a year or so in command at my 'miniature staff college', he said, I would probably be promoted to wing commander and might then take over an operational squadron. This, to me, was pie in the sky. And 'a year or so' was an interminable delay. I wanted to get back into action at once.

That very night a possible route appeared. We had dinner at Firpos with two friends of his, one of whom had been in command of a bomber squadron in England and he said something that gave me the idea: if I had been on operations, he said, it would be easy enough to get out of a group commander's clutches. All I had to do was to go LMF.

I seized upon the idea. There was a strict procedure for dealing with LMF (Lack of Moral Fibre) cases. When a man found himself unable to bear any longer the strain of operational flying, when terror finally overwhelmed all his defences and he refused to continue, he became classified as LMF. He was stripped of any acting rank and posted away in disgrace from the squadron. It was the perfect solution for me. When I told the others my idea that night they ridiculed it. My intelligence officer friend pointed out that you got posted *away from* operations for LMF, not on to them, but I argued that those occasional submarine searches we carried out were classified as operational flights, and I could have become frightened about doing those.

'Who's going to believe that!' he cried.

I thought my air commodore might do so. Back in Bombay I wrote him an official letter stating that for some time now I had been finding excuses to avoid taking a turn when we were called upon to check a submarine report, and I had finally faced up to the fact that I was an LMF case; whatever the consequences might be I had now to declare that I could no longer bring myself to fly on such operations in future. I typed the letter myself and took it to group headquarters that same night, delivering it to the duty officer.

Driving back to Juhu that moonlit night I had the same tingly feeling I used to get those nights when circling around a heavily defended target like Brest to decide upon the line of attack. Every now and then, alone in the car, I burst out laughing in the excitement of it. Stanley Mayhew was at the airfield and when I told him what I had done it added to the fun to see him so alarmed. What a crazy thing to do! The air commodore would see it was a pack of lies. He would be livid, court-martial me, have me washing dishes in the basement of his headquarters for the rest of the war. Stanley went on being gloomy for the first bottle of beer but then began to giggle as we speculated on the air commodore's reaction. Afterwards, driving on to my room at the School, I felt as if I were actually back on operations already, with the enemy guns swinging up into position to open fire on us.

And I got through. It was marvellous. The reason I was so lucky was, I think, that the mere sight of the initials LMF made the air commodore lose all common sense. He was incapable of examining the letter dispassionately once he saw the admission of cowardice – to him, and many other old hands in the RAF, the initials LMF were nothing more than a euphemism for craven fear. His reaction was that of the bull at the matador's cape; he had no sight for footwork and swaying body and all the background manipulation, he simply hurled himself at the provocation. His face quivered as he glared at me across the table in silence for a moment of furious contempt, then delivered his sentence. I would be relieved of command immediately, my deputy could take over temporarily, I would be stripped of my acting rank and posted out of his command. Then he ordered me, literally, out of his sight.

I went through the door suitably downcast, and once clear of the building rushed off to tell Stanley the wondrous news. Then I phoned

Delhi to tell my intelligence friend, who, when finally accepting the incredible truth, promised he would contact Personnel Staff about my interest in that call for volunteers. He did so, and with success. The very next day a signal arrived to say that Flight Lieutenant O'Brien was to report to air headquarters immediately.

Stanley flew me up there, and I found my luck still held. There had been no rush of volunteers in answer to the signal; in fact I was the first to arrive at headquarters. They told me the job was with a Wingate-inspired army unit called a Long Range Penetration Group which was to operate behind the enemy lines. It would comprise three battalions split into six columns. Each would require an RAF officer to march with them, to arrange air support, supply drops, and generally act as air adviser to the column commander. Did I still want the job?

Did I! And Stanley too, when he heard, asked me to try and effect his escape also from Bombay to join in the adventure – I had to do it for him, he was a hopeless liar, and anyway my stunt could never be repeated. I told him that once in the special unit I would devise some way to get him in on the operation. And subsequently I did.

In the meantime, however, I set off alone towards the middle of India, drawn irresistibly by the stirring sound of 'The Long Range Penetration Group', and the vision of a 'weird brigadier called Wingate'.

REFERENCES

There are some differences in dates, and even in targets, between the Operational Record Book (ORB) of 53 Squadron in the Public Record Office at Kew and my own log book. This, I have discovered from other wartime pilots, is not unusual. I have checked my entries against the log book of John Gilmore, and in some cases against notes made at the time, and have found that in every instance of discrepancy it is the 53 Squadron ORB which is in error. The ORB for 62 Squadron was not written up during all the time we were in the Far East, so I have been unable to check the timings of operations on which I was not involved personally; there are now available many Japanese records of the events in that campaign, but the claims by their fighter pilots are, to my knowledge in two incidents certainly, far from accurate so I have relied almost completely on my own sources for particulars of operations in the Far East.

Chapter 2

The commanding officer of the Whitley Squadron was Wing Commander Staton who travelled out with one of our group to Singapore two years later, by then an Air Commodore.

Chapter 3 and 4

By the following year the majority of aircrew were all being trained overseas, mainly in Canada.

Chapter 6

Page 66. When working in the Accident Prevention branch at Air Ministry in 1946 I saw a report which estimated that about thirty of our aircraft had been shot down by our own fighters, and 'probably more' than that by our guns.

Chapters 8 and 10

Postwar studies indicate that we were fully justified in the belief that our blind bombing of Brest was a waste of lives and aircraft.

Chapter 12

Page 154. Charles O'Brien was presently recruited by MI6, in which role he was to prove a renewed irritant four years later when contacted in the clandestine operations I have recounted in *The Moonlight War*.

Chapter 15

Page 180. Wing Commander McKern was conscious of the problems he faced. Just before he left India in 1942 to return to England he wrote to Peter Lilly saying that he had dreaded taking over the squadron in Singapore, for he knew nothing about us or our aircraft and was in awe at our battle experience. However, he counted himself lucky after the event, for never had he known a group so united in spirit and so dedicated in action.

Chapter 16

Page 205. Incorrect official records. The following either completely ignore the presence of our Hudsons in the Endau attack or are inaccurate in their account of losses suffered:

Gillison, D., *Royal Australian Air Force, 1939–42* (Australian War Memorial, Melbourne 1952)

Kirby, Major-General S. W., *War against Japan, Volume 1, The Loss of Singapore* (HMSO 1957)

Odgers, George, *Australia in the War 1939–45, War against Japan (Air)* (Australian War Memorial, Melbourne 1957)

Richards, Denis and Saunders, Hilary St George, *The Fight Avails* (HMSO 1952)

Tsuji, Masanobu, *Singapore, The Japanese Version* (Constable 1960)

Page 205. The official naval report is contained in Captain S. W. Roskill's *The War at Sea, Vol. II* (HMSO 1956), quoting ADM 199'1292.

Page 206. Maltby's official dispatch is in *London Gazette*, 26 February 1948. Jeudwine's report is to be found in the Public Record Office under the references AIR 27'696 and AIR 27'702.

Chapter 17

Details about the evacuation of Sembawang are to be found in McCauley's official report 37'501'107 of 18 March 1942.

Chapter 18

Pages 220–2. Lavarack's activities in Sumatra are recorded in the Australian Army Official History: *The Japanese Thrust, Vol. II* (Canberra 1957).

Page 222. Bennett arrived at Bandung in the final days and tried to get a lift out with the aircraft sent for Lavarack, but Lavarack told him there was no room for him on board. Bennett managed to get a lift on another aircraft.

Page 223. The Butterworth incident is mentioned in Maltby's dispatch, *Supplement to London Gazette*, 20 February 1948.

Page 225. The official histories quoted above, as well as McCauley's report, make it clear we were ordered to Java by Air Command.

Pages 225–7. The Australian official history by Douglas Gillison (*op. cit.*) states that Air Command ordered the return to Sumatra. No such order reached me. We returned after discussion with the Dutch pilot. It could be assumed from Gillison's account that it was the RAAF Hudsons which returned, but such an assumption would be incorrect.

Chapter 19

Page 238. Not all the Blenheim crews were captured. Wing Commander Jeudwine made a remarkable escape in an open boat to Australia. There were twelve of them on board and it took them over six weeks to sail the 1500 miles to north-western Australia, having somehow escaped a close scrutiny by a Japanese submarine which surfaced close by them on their first day out of Java.

Chapter 20

Page 249. The 36 Division did later take over the northern sector of Burma from the remnants of the Wingate force in which, as I have recounted in *Out of the Blue*, I was among the lucky survivors.

INDEX

Rank, titles and names are as at the time